W9-BNO-035

MAKING IMPORTANT NEWS INTERESTING

MAKING
IMPORTANT
NEWS
INTERESTING

REPORTING PUBLIC AFFAIRS

IN THE 21ST CENTURY

Perry Parks

Marion Street Press, Inc.
Oak Park, Illinois

Cover design by Gloria Chantell

Copyright © 2006 by Perry Parks

All Rights Reserved

ISBN 1-933338-03-2
Printed in U.S.A.
Printing 10 9 8 7 6 5 4 3 2

Marion Street Press, Inc.
PO Box 2249
Oak Park, IL 60303
866-443-7987
www.marionstreetpress.com

To Dad, who taught me to love newspapers, and Sophie, who's learning now.

Contents

PART 2: THE PRACTICE OF PUBLIC AFFAIRS REPORTING

PART 3: THE FUTURE OF PUBLIC AFFAIRS REPORTING

Preface

This book aims to develop reporters and editors who can produce the kind of public affairs journalism our democracy needs, instead of the kind we usually get. The public affairs journalism we need is lively, direct, honest, powerful, and transparently important. The public affairs journalism we get is dull, bureaucratic, insider-focused, and occasionally incomprehensible. Public demand for clear and aggressive government reporting is lukewarm at best, until we face a crisis on the scale of Sept. 11 or Hurricane Katrina. But the everyday accounting of what government is, says, and does remains American journalists' biggest job. From the president down to the drain commissioner, our system of representative government is the defining quality of our national character. Our leaders embody the people's will, and even though citizens too readily cede control of our institutions to moneyed interests and cynical power brokers, we remain the ultimate authority over our affairs.

Unfortunately, the needs of citizens have not been the driving force behind news decisions in recent years. Rather, news judgment is increasingly consumer-focused — based on a knee-jerk reaction to market research or, worse, a misguided perception that people invariably prefer the trivial to the significant. As a result, in the classic journalistic debate between emphasizing what's important or what's interesting, the superficially interesting is gaining ground. Even in major newspapers, which are most predisposed to public affairs reporting, a study by the Project for Excellence in Journalism found government and foreign affairs coverage steadily diminishing.[1]

These decisions hurt the public and, ultimately, news organizations themselves. Journalism won't survive as a frivolous diversion, and democracy can't thrive without attentive citizens. "The less that Americans care about public life, the less they will be interested in journalism in any form," James Fallows wrote in 1996.[2] "…The truth that today's media establishment has tried to avoid seeing is that it will *rise or fall with the political system*."[3]

So both duty and self-preservation require that journalists use the best tools to enliven democracy, engage citizens, intrigue readers and re-establish important journalism as an indispensable element of daily life. Those tools — at least the ones that have been invented — are the focus of this book.

The principles and practices outlined here aren't new or radical. The most fundamental principles are the consensus among hundreds of journalists represented in the landmark book *The Elements of Journalism: What Newspeople Should Know and the Public Should Expect*, which begins with the premise that "[t]he primary purpose of journalism is to provide citizens with the information they need to be free and self-governing."[4] As for the ideas and innovations, I encountered many during eight years as a reporter and editor at *The Virginian-Pilot*, one of the most prolific innovators in public affairs coverage. Because of the *Pilot's* record, and because it's the paper I know best, many of this book's examples arise from the work of my colleagues there. But this book has been informed by dozens of pioneering newspapers and by such proponents of journalistic innovation as Davis "Buzz" Merritt, Jay Rosen, and Roy Peter Clark. It includes vital arguments promulgated by both researchers and practicing journalists over the past two decades — arguments that have been underrepresented in public affairs reporting texts.

The book starts where most such texts leave off. It assumes you've been introduced to the basics of government reporting, like municipal budgets, how a bill becomes a law, the electoral process, and the judicial system. It assumes you've got a handle on the straight news lead and the inverted pyramid and the other fundamentals of solid journalism that everyone must know. And it assumes you're not satisfied that traditional public affairs reporting is sufficient to capture the imagination of today's citizens — including yourself and your peers.

There are journalists working to do better. But as *The Elements of Journalism* points out, techniques for making important news interesting "are usually self-taught, learned by trial and error or, secondarily, by borrowing ideas … from peers. The best ideas are not widely disseminated."[5]

What's been missing is a collection of the key principles of public affairs coverage, supported by examples of what compelling public affairs journalism looks like. That's what this book offers.

Introduction

[I]f democracy is going to be effective, one core value must permeate journalists' think-ing and guide their decisions: that democracy works best when people are broadly engaged in it. So helping people engage in democracy — through information, improved civic skills and discovered opportunities — becomes the goal and the overriding criterion for evalu-ating what journalists do.

— Maxwell McCombs and Davis "Buzz" Merritt, *The Two W's of Journalism*[1]

Journalism is storytelling with a purpose. That purpose is to provide people with infor-mation they need to understand the world. The first challenge is finding the information that people need to live their lives. The second is to make it meaningful, relevant, and engaging.

— Bill Kovach and Tom Rosenstiel, *The Elements of Journalism*[2]

American democracy experienced something of a revival in 2004, when a bigger slice of citizens turned out for the presidential election than in any race since Richard Nixon faced Hubert Humphrey in 1968.[3] Grappling with the aftermath of Sept. 11, a war in Iraq, a struggling economy, potentially crippling federal deficits, and a number of state initiatives to ban gay marriage, a record-setting electorate showed vigor and determination. Some voters waited hours in the cold and rain to exercise their rights; polling sites in sever-al states remained open for hours after they had been scheduled to shut down. The lesson for students of democracy was that when people see their stake in a public decision, they act. "'It's almost palpable, the attention, anticipation and the interest,'" a Cincinnati banker told *The Washington Post* on Election Day.[4] "'People you would never expect to talk about politics are paying attention.'" Journalists' biggest challenge in the coming years is to sustain the enthusiasm of people who discovered public affairs this decade, and to catch the attention of the many adults (roughly 40 percent) who sat out 2004. Winning them over requires stretching our imaginations to demonstrate how public decisions at every level play a daily role in our quality of life.

In recent years, the American press has failed to capture citizens' imaginations when it comes to democracy. Despite the relatively strong 2004 turnout, and the renewed interest in government's effectiveness after Hurricane Katrina devastated the Gulf Coast, millions of people are detached from politics. These disengaged citizens believe either that government has no effect on their lives — a dangerous miscalculation, as many Louisianans learned in 2005 — or that they have no power to influence public decisions — a self-fulfilling prophecy.

Instead, Americans focus their attentions on the likes of Martha Stewart, Michael Jackson, abducted young women, and other high-profile soap operas that offer compelling drama and water cooler fodder but do nothing to help people live better lives or solve common problems. The public's and news editors' preoccupation with the trivial over the monumental distracts our collective attention from historic threats and opportunities, a cultural sleight of hand with immense consequences.

On Jan. 31, 2001, a group of distinguished Americans commissioned by President Clinton and House Speaker Newt Gingrich issued a report warning of serious threats to American security — the most urgent being terrorism. A 1999 report from the same commission had predicted that "Americans will likely die on American soil, possibly in large numbers."[5] The response to these dire warnings was the sound of crickets chirping. A LexisNexis search turned up just two U.S. newspaper stories covering the commission's 2001 report.[6] Instead, the big national stories in the first two-thirds of that year were the disappearance of congressional intern Chandra Levy (a salacious reprise of the Washington intern stories that dominated the late 1990s) and a rash of shark attacks along the southeastern coast.

Coverage of the national security commission did take off — *after* 3,000 people were murdered by terrorists on Sept. 11, 2001.

Three days after those attacks, commission co-chairman Gary Hart was quoted saying: "What happened this week ought to call into question what is important in society and how the media cover it. ... There seems to be no self-reflection, no understanding by the media that they have a job under the direction of the Constitution to inform, not just entertain, the American people."[7]

By nearly all accounts, the nation's press responded admirably in the immediate aftermath of Sept. 11, treating victims with compassion, diligently reconstructing events, and helping Americans make sense of what had happened and why. But, almost incomprehensibly, even as the post-9/11 invasion of Afghanistan gave way to war in Iraq, the attention of the press and the nation began to stray once again. The trial of a guy named Scott Peterson, accused of killing his wife and unborn child, became a national obsession, though it bore no greater significance than any other murder trial in the country. When a CBS News producer broke into the end of crime drama *CSI: N.Y.* on Nov. 10, 2004, to report the death of Palestinian leader Yasser Arafat, whose passing would bear significantly on the Middle East peace process and therefore Americans' security, the network apologized to irate viewers for the "overly aggressive" effort to deliver the news. It was later reported that the producer had been fired over the incident.[8]

Editor & Publisher noted in September 2003 that most U.S. newspapers had pulled staffers from Afghanistan, the platform for Sept. 11 planning, based in part on "a perceived lack of reader interest."[9] Some reporters and photographers were shifted to covering Iraq — a story of obvious significance — but the retreat from Afghanistan demonstrated a dangerous short-sightedness. By mid-2005, with Americans' attentions diverted, there were signs of a Taliban resurgence and increasing violence in Afghanistan.

Meanwhile, the nation's most vital security stories remained chronically underreported. In fall 2004, some observers predicted that, in the face of another terrorist attack, Americans would once again scratch their heads, wondering how their eyes had lost track of the ball.

"[C]overage of the effort to prevent another 9/11 has been spotty, episodic, reactive and shallow," a *Columbia Journalism Review* article concluded. Despite evidence of government foot-dragging on security issues such as unexamined air cargo on passenger jets and poor protection of chemical plants, the story said, journalists had largely failed to fulfill their watchdog role.[10] And when, four years after being caught flat-footed by terrorists, emergency officials' clumsy response to Hurricane Katrina left thousands stranded for days without food or medical care, the nation was predictably shocked.

SO WHY, IN THE FACE OF war, disaster, economic uncertainty, and policy questions that affect millions of Americans and billions of earthlings, do we so routinely default to shallow reporting, surface-level analysis, sensational trials, and the politics of name-calling rather than thoughtful, meaningful, substantive reporting on matters of consequence? First, because the shallow stories are easier to report. Second, because they're easier to consume. Third, because news organizations are so frightened of losing their audiences that they've begun to reflexively emphasize news they think people "want" over news that people might need. (These decisions aren't making the news media any more popular. A Gallup poll in September 2004 found that fewer than half of Americans — 44 percent — trusted news organizations to present the news accurately and completely.[11] The measure improved to about 50 percent a year later, perhaps because of the news media's powerful coverage of Hurricane Katrina.[12]) And, finally, because the most important news is often, on the surface, boring.

The grinding machinations of government that, debate after debate, regulation after regulation, speech after mind-numbing speech, ultimately determine who goes to bright new schools and who attends dim, decaying ones, who goes to prison and who goes free, which forests are cut down and which stand, who gets health care, who gets invaded, and ultimately who lives and who dies — those processes are challenging to cover effectively because their scope is so big, and their developments so small. The city council meeting, the congressional subcommittee vote, the obscure executive order that could set in motion life-changing processes in a community or around the world, are often too incremental to carry their import along with them.

So these "dull but important" stories, if they are covered at all, surface as briefs or as dry, droning accounts, relegated to inside pages because just mentioning the subject — zoning regulations, budget negotiations — is enough to kill a conversation. The news is grudgingly presented with a taint of resignation that only political junkies and policy wonks could care.

It's this resignation, this lethargy, that we must confront and defeat if public affairs journalism is to survive this decade. The competition for people's attention is fierce, and we who cover government too often cede the important/interesting debate to weaker stories with glossier packaging.

To reverse this democracy-damaging trend, those who fulfill the First Amendment's charge in the purest sense must undertake something like a revenge of the nerds, rising up from the study halls of public discourse to take on the jocks, the preppies, the cool flashy kids who get all the attention. We have to make important news interesting.

It won't be easy. The celebrities and sports stars so prevalent in daily news and national conversations are there for a reason. They'll go to any lengths to be noticed, to grab headlines, because the attention sells their albums or movies or game tickets or whatever they're marketing that day.

The people we cover, on the other hand, tend to prefer shadows and anonymity. Governments are much easier to run in quiet, away from the glare of the public eye, where deals can be struck, favors granted, and self-enriching policies passed without the scrutiny of the governed.

Celebrities want to be interesting. Politicians and bureaucrats WANT to be boring.

Should there be any doubt, let's compare a couple of leads in the *Boston Herald* from February 2004. The first comes on the day after the Super Bowl, when Janet Jackson had some trouble with her costume:

> Nudity took center stage AND the sidelines at Super Bowl VIII, but the halftime shocker that was flashed across millions of TV screens ended with shamefaced apologies over Janet Jackson's bared breast. [...]
>
> Jaws dropped across the country in the last seconds of the halftime extravaganza, when Justin Timberlake pulled the top off Jackson's leather gladiatrix outfit, baring her bejeweled breast. The camera cut away, but not before stunned audiences glimpsed Jackson's aureole only partly obscured by a large, star-shaped nipple ring.[13]

Now, here's the beginning of a school budget story three days later:

> Boston schools chief Thomas W. Payzant submitted a $653 million budget recommendation yesterday, a 1 percent increase over last year that will still require cuts.
>
> "This is the third year of substantial challenges," Payzant said at last night's School Committee meeting. "My hope is that it will be the last in a tough three-year cycle."
>
> The $7 million increase is not enough to keep up with rising costs such as health insurance, leading Payzant to propose unspecified "substantial savings" from central office budget cuts.[14]

How can the 1 percent increase in the $653 million budget possibly compete with Janet Jackson's aureole? Who's going to get more attention? And who would rather have millions of people watching them: Jackson, or the head of Boston's school system? For an entertainer, public attention is a livelihood. For a school official, public attention can be the first step to the unemployment line.

Where does that leave public affairs journalists? It leaves us in a great position to change the way people think about their government, to overcome these infrastructural obstacles and show how that school budget shortfall could profoundly affect thousands of children. Janet Jackson's breast might have provided a moment of thrill or revulsion, but a bad school budget can lead to a lifetime of disappointment, squalor, rage, or violence for people in our own communities.

The thing public affairs has going for it is *impact*, the potential to change lives in complex and ultimately fascinating ways. Impact is the key to making the important, interesting.

IN JULY 2003, the City Council of East Lansing, Mich., considered an agenda item titled: "Draft ordinance to amend the Property Maintenance Regulations of the City Code prohibiting the placement of yard furniture out-of-doors."[15]

What that meant was that the council wanted to make it illegal for students in the city's rental housing to bring couches onto their porches for a relaxing afternoon in the sun.

A close reader of the agenda might have figured that out, but most people's eyes would just glaze over. So, because a "draft ordinance to amend the Property Maintenance Regulations of the City Code prohibiting the placement of yard furniture out-of-doors" is obscure and boring, the issue is easily overlooked. Could this be an accident?

What if the agenda, instead of being written for lawyers, was written for students? What if it said: "Let's keep those college kids from putting ratty couches out where we have to look at them." That item might get some attention. It's not a breast, but it is a policy that many Michigan State University students would consider a further imposition by a city government they find pushy and controlling. Maybe an agenda with that wording would draw some people to the meeting. Some might sign up to speak. Voices might be raised. The meeting would be longer. Students might threaten to vote in the next local election, knowing that if all 45,000 of them ever got together they could actually run the city. The whole process would get a lot messier.

That's why they don't do it that way.

Your job as a public affairs reporter is to translate the intentionally boring stuff that no one pays attention to into the interesting truths that policy embodies. The reporter covering the East Lansing City Council has a duty to slog through the agenda each week, sit through the boring meeting, and then turn around with something fascinating for the reader — without making anything up. The challenge is to use the language of readers, not government. We must report on officials' facts and their opinions. We have to accurately present what went on. We have to be fair. But we're under no obligation to represent the situation as boring. We have to pull the rabbit of interesting from the hat of bureaucracy, to write public affairs as though it's our hobby, just as music reviewers and feature writers do. There's no rule — only tradition — that says citizenship can't be fun and interesting.

So you can write a lead that says: "Some City Council members want to kick students off their outdoor couches," and go from there. You can give citizens the information they need to get involved *before* it's too late.

The rest of this book provides some of the tools you need to proceed. In Part I, we'll talk about the principles of citizen-focused public affairs journalism: People drive politics, public life is about identifying and solving problems, every problem affects a range of stakeholders, journalists need to work for citizens, news must teach as well as inform, effective reporting helps people act, and good journalism is never boring. In Part II, we'll look at how these values can be applied to elections, local government, state and national affairs, world news, business reporting, and the opinion pages. In Part III, we'll consider the evolving future of online and interactive journalism, and the need to reinvent news for the vital next generation of readers.

Making important news interesting — every day — is a daunting, but noble, challenge. If we succeed, freedom will prosper. If we fail, so will American democracy.

PART 1: THE PRINCIPLES OF PUBLIC AFFAIRS REPORTING

Chapter 1

Put People in Charge

[G]overnment of the people, by the people, for the people shall not perish from the earth.

— Abraham Lincoln, Gettysburg Address

The media establishment seems to talk at *people rather than with them or even to them.*

— James Fallows, *Breaking the News*[1]

Voters, come in please," a *Boston Globe* columnist invited in early 2004. "Take a seat. We need to have a little talk.

"Listen, you've done some great work over the years, you really have. The entire country owes you a huge debt of thanks. But on behalf of the news media, the Washington pundits, various powerbrokers, assorted columnists, and esteemed talking heads, I have some news that it doesn't give me any pleasure to give.

"You're fired."[2]

The column is satirical, but it conveys the message journalists and politicians have been sending citizens for years: Please stand back while we run your democracy.

Campaigns and governments are conducted and covered in apparent isolation from the individual citizen. Election reporting focuses on who's winning and why, not on who's got better plans for improving people's lives. Day-to-day government coverage emphasizes how officials use power to get their way, not how human beings are collaborating to solve problems. News audiences are encouraged not to help shape answers to public questions, but to follow the twists and turns of political life as they would the romantic intrigues of a Jane Austen novel.

Sidelined citizens are probably not what Abraham Lincoln had in mind when he visited the carnage-strewn hillsides of Gettysburg, Penn., to remind the world what made the American idea worth preserving at the highest cost: "government of the people, by the people, for the people."

The point and promise of American democracy couldn't be made much clearer. When Americans' future is at stake, citizens have the power to decide — by themselves, for themselves — how to face that future. Representative democracy is not a classical novel to passively experience, it's a national "Choose Your Own Adventure" story. But it doesn't always work that way. Much public affairs news descends from board rooms and legislative halls — proclamations rendered as foregone conclusions, oblivious to citizen concerns. Journalists, increasingly unwilling to cover the boring "process" stories of developing policy, often don't even raise important issues until they're decided, too late for citizens to get involved.

It's fine to focus public affairs coverage on our chosen leaders, in whom we vest decision-making power. But the other, equally important side of the equation is the continuing role citizens can play in shaping policy. When news coverage takes decisions out of citizens' hands, sidelining them while officials, lobbyists and special interest groups carve up public resources, the result is a feeling of powerlessness that leads to detachment both from public life and from news organizations that purport to cover civic affairs.[3]

News coverage that takes Lincoln at his word delights not in reinforcing this sense of powerlessness but in *empowering* ordinary citizens, first by showing how government affects their lives, and second by showing how they can help set the public agenda.

To do so, we need to change the assumptions that guide our work. Authors Buzz Merritt and Maxwell McCombs say most news reporting presupposes, unfortunately, that citizens eagerly await the latest pronouncement from a public hall, that governments always "act" while citizens are "acted on," and that all information therefore naturally flows from officials, through journalists, to people.[4]

But reality should quickly intervene. Average citizens have proven quite uninterested in day-to-day acts of the city council, school board, or state legislature. Sure, they *should* be interested, but most people weren't born reciting the preamble to the Constitution. We have to demonstrate the importance of government action for those who aren't rapt with attention.

Part of that work means repudiating the idea that citizens are passive receptacles for official action and news reports. The people are vital actors in a healthy democracy, and the newspaper is both a stage and a prop for public participation. For civic life to function, information must flow freely among the public, private, and journalistic spheres. That flow is fast becoming reality despite much institutional resistance, thanks to the Internet. As we'll see later, independent Web commentators called bloggers have elbowed their way into the conversation, taking both journalists and public officials to task for real and perceived failures to uphold democratic ideals. Many news organizations — some reluctantly and some zealously — have opened up Web space to reader commentary and even citizen newsgathering. Technology is overtaking the debate on the topic of empowering citizens; many are empowering themselves.

To stay relevant, journalism has to encourage and nurture this empowerment, to help connect citizens with the people and processes of government. The rest of this chapter looks at three aspects of public affairs journalism that can better serve the people both inside and outside the system: our selection of leaders, the process of governing, and our relationship with public servants. In later chapters, we'll develop a framework for covering public affairs that derives from this fundamental notion that in a democracy, the people control their destiny.

Choosing our leaders

USA Today took a common approach to campaign news coverage in fall 2004. Here's a selection of front-page, above-the-fold headlines from the waning months of the presidential race:

Sept. 7: "Bush has 7-point poll lead on Kerry"
Sept. 9: "Bush gains in 2 key states/Polls: Clear leads in Missouri and Ohio"
Sept. 17: "Bush clear leader in poll"
Oct. 4: "Bush, Kerry in a draw, poll says"
Oct. 12: "Bush's approval rating slipping"
Nov. 1: "On election eve, polls show photo finish"

This is the horse-race model of election coverage, emphasizing who's winning, who's losing, who's making a push at the final turn. If you're a political junkie, like many journalists, it can be very exciting reading. Observations about who's got the stronger staff, the more resonant message, the cleverest ads, and the biggest campaign chest are fun to follow — just as we follow professional sports teams drafting players, establishing game plans, and executing plays. There are twists and turns, daily surprises, heated words, and compelling dramas about success and failure. These are the aspects of political campaigns that many newspeople emphasize.

If you're mapping out campaign coverage, though, it's important to step back and ask a couple of questions. The first is: What is the point of our coverage? What do we want it to accomplish? Democratic philosophy and journalistic training lead to the inevitable conclusion that, first and foremost, election coverage should help people decide whom to vote for.

The next question is: Does focusing on the horse race really help people make good decisions on Election Day?

Now, the cynical answer could be: Sure. Polls tell us who's winning, and people like to pick a winner. Knowing one candidate's way ahead affirms some people's choices and signals others to switch horses. A lopsided poll shortly before an election can send a convenient signal to busy people that they don't need to vote at all, since the outcome is preordained. By these standards, horse-race coverage is a quick and effective way to help voters follow the crowd.

Most of us can agree, though, that this isn't the best way to shore up an eroding democracy. Style over substance might be an effective campaign strategy, but it's a bad way to govern. And it turns people off. "Is it any wonder that Americans say they feel disconnected from politics?" NewsLab President Deborah Potter, then of The Poynter Institute, said in a 1995 radio commentary. "When what they get from the press are up-and-down polls, soundbites and scandals, spin doctors and inside campaign strategy, how can they make informed decisions about who's best qualified to lead the nation?"[5]

If our interest is in helping people create an effective government, our energies must be directed toward substance. And yet, year in and year out, despite a general agreement that we can do better, journalists revert to the standard model.

Dante Chinni, senior associate with the Project for Excellence in Journalism, reported that a PEJ study had found roughly three-quarters of 2004 election stories around the debates "primarily focused on how candidates were affected by events — who was up, who was down. Only 8 percent focused on the effect on citizens, such as the implications of the candidates' policy proposals — less than in 2000."[6]

Not all horse-race coverage or polling is bad. Opinion polls provide valuable guidance on what people think and useful tips for pursuing coverage, and research suggests that some horse-race reporting helps attract readers' interest to political campaigns.[7] The question is where we should focus our attention — and readers'.

Journalism guru Jay Rosen has drawn a distinction in the electoral process between the *campaign* — the all-out effort political pros wage to get their candidates into office — and the *election* — the choice citizens must make about who will govern.[8] The campaign, which is about winning, is what journalists most aggressively cover. But if we expect our audience to be a part of democracy, and we should, then we have to start emphasizing the values of the election. Here's what that looks like:

On Nov. 1, 2004, the same day *USA Today* topped its page with a spread of poll results from seven states and a story headlined "Swing states lean to Kerry," the *Detroit Free Press* tried something else. While the front page included a one-column story discussing Michigan polls and candidates' last-minute visits to the state, it was dominated by a four-column-wide, top-to-bottom graphic (see next page).

The package summarized George Bush's and John Kerry's positions on issues like abortion, the minimum wage, and the war in Iraq. It referred readers inside to more details. And it teased to a "how to vote" guide, running down ballots and describing voting machines Detroit-area voters would encounter.

Bob Campbell, deputy metro editor of the *Free Press* and the point man on election coverage, said the paper's goal was to "answer the sorts of questions that we think our readers have and really make voting something they're engaged in, and something that they have as much information as we can give them to help make the decision."[9]

There could hardly be a starker difference between the priorities signaled by the *Free Press* and *USA Today* approaches. The cumulative effect of *USA Today*'s poll headlines in September and October (emphasizing choices already made by others) is a classic view of the campaign. *The Free Press*'s focus on issues (choices to be made by YOU) brings citizens into the election.

EFFECTIVE ELECTION COVERAGE involves a complex triangle of communication among citizens, politicians, and the journalists who cover both. Reporters need to find out what's on the minds of both voters and candidates and help each group understand the other. Candidates have to lead by promoting a vision, but they also have to follow the needs and desires of the communities they want to serve.

How does this look in practice? When the *Quad-City Times* learned that presidential candidates Bush and Kerry would both be visiting Davenport, Iowa, on the same day, they built an edition that greeted the candidates with this two-line banner headline: "PRESIDENT BUSH, MR. KERRY, WE WANT YOU TO KNOW…"[10] (see page 21).

The page was dominated by three stories: "Job loss worries region," "Voters equally divided," and the centerpiece, "Midwestern voices look to be heard." This last story was a wide-ranging conversation with nine readers — four Kerry supporters, four Bush supporters and one undecided — who had recently written letters to the editor. Inside the paper were two full pages of comments from readers, who had been asked what they would say to Bush

On the eve of the 2004 presidential election, this *Detroit Free Press* presentation put citizens in charge. (Reprinted with permission of the *Detroit Free Press*)

GATEWAY EDITION

Weather/ A16
HIGH 74
LOW 70

COPYRIGHT 2004 / QUAD-CITY TIMES

Quad-City Times

Wednesday, August 4, 2004

WWW.QCTIMES.COM / 50 CENTS

Can-tastic Give-away
INSIDE
FREE GAME PIECE/A2

QUAD-CITIANS SPEAK OUT

PRESIDENT BUSH, MR. KERRY, WE WANT YOU TO KNOW ...

The economy is the most important election issue for 27% of registered voters within the Quad-City region

If the 2004 election were held today, 49% of Quad-City voters would pick Bush with Kerry landing a close 47%

Job loss worries region

By Craig Cooper
QUAD-CITY TIMES

Only their campaigns will be close today when President Bush and challenger John Kerry make appearances in Davenport.

On the issues, particularly regarding the economy, they are likely to paint pictures to partisan crowds that are as far apart as Renoir and cave drawings.

Bush will point to a recovery in the economy post-Sept. 11, 2001. On economic issues he has been talking about the impact of tax cuts, his agenda to reduce regulations and the creation of jobs this year.

Conversely, there are reasons Kerry has selected Davenport and the Quad-Cities to talk about economic issues, which he is scheduled to do at 10 a.m. at the RiverCenter.

Since June 2001, the Quad-Cities MSA, or Metropolitan Statistical Area, has lost 5,624 non-farm jobs, according to the Illinois Department of Employment Security, or IDES, unemployment has risen, manufacturing wages have flattened and union-represented employees, a traditionally Democratic base, have experienced costly changes in their healthcare coverage.

Steve Ames, project manager of the Quad-City Development Group, noted the overall jobs losses in the past three years, but said there also have been growth areas.

Examples are the new local

ECONOMY | A16

"The thing I'd like Mr. Bush to know: It's NOO-klee-are. There's only one 'u' in nuclear."

— JULIE ABDEL-FATTAH, Rock Island

"I don't want to hear we have one set of values for America. Ideologies vary; they're not one-size fits all."

— JOE SOLIZ, Silvis, Ill.

Midwestern voices look to be heard

EDITOR'S NOTE: The Quad-City Times extended invitations to 15 readers who have had letters to the editor published within the last two years. Nine of the readers were able to attend the discussion. Four favored Bush; four favored Kerry. One was undecided.

By Mark Ridolfi
QUAD-CITY TIMES

Two presidential campaigns are scheduled to blow through the Quad-Cities today, dispensing slogans with strident rhetoric that one group of Quad-Citians says can bear little pertinence to the lives, struggles and sentiments of many who will listen.

This group hopes President George Bush and U.S. Sen. John Kerry listen at least as much as they talk today.

"It's good for candidates to listen to the Quad-Cities," says Rick E. Kislia. "They might get distracted by the volume of attention from the coasts. The kinds of things they hear from those areas aren't what matter to us in what they call flyover territory."

Here in flyover territory, this group of four Bush supporters, four Kerry supporters and one undecided voter finds partial agreement on what matters most: jobs, leadership ability, clarity of communication and a sensible, understandable solution in Iraq. What matters least are impossible promises of prosperity and a fixation on values, as if a common ideology is a requisite for being American.

Though all but one know who they would vote for if the election were today, none are in lockstep with his or her candidate. In a free-flowing, 90-minute conversation Monday evening at the *Quad-City Times*, they seemed to share a concern that the rhetoric they hear creates unattainable expectations. This group has expectations, and

VOICES | A3

INSIDE: We asked *Quad-City Times* readers if they could talk to the candidates, what would they like President Bush and Sen. Kerry to know. Check out the two full pages of readers' responses. Pages A6-7

"We have to leave Iraq better than we found it. Like if you borrow a car, you always leave more in it than ... when you got it."

— RICK KISLIA, LeClaire, Iowa

"How in all reality will you lower the national debt so our grandchildren aren't paying for our deficit?"

— DIANE FLAHERTY, Davenport

Voters equally divided

By Ed Tibbetts
QUAD-CITY TIMES

When President Bush and Democratic challenger U.S. Sen. John Kerry, D-Mass., converge in the Quad-Cities today, they will do so in a metro area that is sharply divided, according to a new *Quad-City Times*/KWQC-TV6 poll.

Bush holds a 49 percent to 47 percent lead over Kerry, according to the poll, which was conducted from July 31 through Aug. 2. Just 4 percent said they hadn't made up their minds yet.

The two-point difference is within the survey's 4.8 percent margin of error, but it also was conducted on the heels of the Democratic National Convention in Boston. Bush campaign officials, citing nationwide polls, argued Tuesday that Kerry failed to get the post-convention bounce he should have

POLL | A3

Q-C poll results

From July 31 to August 2, Personal Marketing Research, Inc., conducted a poll among Quad-City voters. The random sample of 531 residents, commissioned by the *Quad-City Times* and KWQC-TV6, was equally split by gender as well as a stratification of political party. The margin of error is 4.8%.

Q: How likely is it that you will vote in the November 2004 Presidential election?
Somewhat likely: 7%   Very likely: 89%

The *Quad-City Times* took advantage of coincidental Bush and Kerry campaign stops to let the candidates know what was on readers' minds. (Reprinted with permission of the *Quad-City Times*)

and Kerry if they could talk to the candidates.

Instead of making citizens spectators of the joint Bush-Kerry visit — "firing" them from the electoral process — the *Quad-City Times* put them to work as participants. "We decided it wasn't about horse races, and it wasn't about campaigns, it was about people," said John Humenik, the paper's editor at the time.[11] This was an unusual way to present the news of the day, but Humenik said no one complained about the presentation or its emphasis. Kerry actually held up the paper and praised the focus on voters.

Focusing on the election rather than the campaign changes the metaphor from a horse race to something like a hiring process, and it changes the central question from "Who's going to win?" to "Who's best for the job?" To answer this question, journalists' key role is to gather information that will help citizens make a hiring decision.

The *Virginian-Pilot* in 1996 was one of the first papers to apply this model in detail, as James Fallows describes: "Rather than giving main emphasis to the candidates' comments about each other, the paper described the duties of each office; laid out the resumes and past records of the candidates; repeatedly published information about how citizens could contact the campaign themselves; and collected questions from readers that it then presented to the candidates for their answers."[12]

Job descriptions. Qualifications. Resumes. Interview questions. These tools put the power in the hands of voters, who evaluate candidates for the job of city council member, circuit judge, state senator, or president. As the public scrutinizes the candidates' records and promises, more trivial events — day-to-day variations in the polls, TV and radio commercials, back-and-forth sniping between campaigns — take on less significance. Voters can focus on picking the person best qualified to lead them.

We'll look at how to systematically inform voters' choices in Chapter 8.

Covering process

If voters are typically sidelined from political campaigns, they're not even in the arena of daily governance. The pretense of government by the people is lost altogether as politicians, bureaucrats, and the press slip into cloistered rooms, emerging hours later with pronouncements delivered to empty chambers. With a system like this, it's no wonder citizens get bored and tune out. The issues are arcane and presented in blocks of impenetrable numbers and acronyms. The discussions are dry and cryptic, using legalistic language that rarely conveys the true meaning of the deliberation. The press portrays decisions either as polarizing contests between special interests or foregone conclusions requiring no citizen input. And extraordinarily important issues, like a congressional appropriations bill that will allot billions of dollars to schools, roads, or health research, inch forward so slowly that coverage can be painfully redundant. These are government "process stories," which were the meat and potatoes of newspaper reporting when papers viewed themselves as keepers of the community record and took pride in recording the minutiae of civic affairs. Process stories are getting less common, as new technology allows expanded civic access through government Web sites, as newspapers become noncompetitive monopolies in more and more towns, and as editors grow more aware that nobody wants to read this stuff.

A study conducted for several journalism groups found that many newspapers were shifting attention to issues with more direct impact on readers, such as health care, personal fitness, personal finance, and lifestyle and family news. "With newspapers trying to cover a greater number of topics at the same time many are reporting cutbacks in staff, there are inevitable choices to be made," the study says. "By far, the biggest loser in this equation is the coverage of government, particularly governmental process."[13] The study says three in four editors reported covering fewer routine local government and school board meetings, and one in four said they were covering fewer politics and governmental stories. More than half the editors surveyed blamed the cutbacks on staff reductions. But 28 percent said the decisions reflected shifting priorities. One editor was quoted saying, "[P]olitical pissing contests and personality conflicts — these things, unless they actually affect real people, are pointless."[14]

To the extent these choices reflect a new awareness that government reporting must provide context and relevance to be meaningful, this study is encouraging. But the overall finding that newspapers are reducing government coverage is a distressing trend. Recognizing that poorly covered government process can be boring is one thing, but retreating from the duty to

Below the surface

The Project for Excellence in Journalism Web site, **www.journalism.org**, offers some advice on treating officials as complex people, culled from several journalists under the heading "Ruts, Traps and Thinking Outside the Box." Some of the site's suggestions:

From Phil Trounstine, political editor of the *San Jose Mercury News*: …In the day-to-day of coverage it is easy to get locked into a view of politicians as being "corrupt" in some way — pandering to voters, to big business, to big donors. But part of being skeptical is being skeptical of your own thoughts and biases and considering other interpretations of the action. It is quite possible, for instance, for a politician to take a position because he really believes it, then receive money from lobbying interests for doing so, and to please his constituents at the same time. This is, actually, how the political system was designed to work. All three things can coexist at the same time. Just because the politician profits from doing this does not necessarily mean that profit is his only motivation.

From Paul Taylor, formerly of *The Washington Post*: See policy and platform as a frame to understand character. More important, and more useful, than just what position a person has on an issue, is what that position says about someone. How did they come to this position? Why do they feel this way? Have their views changed? How steadfast are they on it? How extreme or moderate? How does it differ or reinforce other positions on other issues? How does it fit into the history of thinking in their party on that issue? How does it fit into their worldview? What experiences or what in their biography led them to this? Suddenly, policy and issues come to life, become people stories and take on an authenticity that they lack in the abstract. This approach may also be the key to unlocking whether a candidate really means something or whether he or she just adopted a position for an electoral purpose or to satisfy a constituency or lobbying interest.

From Tom Rosenstiel, director of the Project for Excellence in Journalism: In reporting, be sure to dig out why actions were taken originally. Don't infer. Don't assume. It is too easy to just see the negative consequences of a policy later and propose that people were foolish or even corrupt for enacting it. That picture may not only be inaccurate, but the more complex reality is more human and more interesting.

cover it well is another. The choice shouldn't be between covering process and reporting "interesting" news. The choice must be to cover the process in new and interesting ways. It often comes down to how the story is framed — the context in which it is presented to readers. The authors of *The Two W's of Journalism* suggest that too many government and politics stories are framed as a spectacle that people can only shake their heads over, or as abuse of power that people can only endure. Using the same facts, they say, journalists instead can frame stories to position "reader-citizens" as empowered actors who can affect political outcomes. [15]

All that's required is to start with the premise that citizens are in charge of policy, and make sure both citizens and policy makers get it. Then approach policy questions from the perspective of the people they will affect. That means if there's a proposal to ban cigarette smoking in restaurants, the story doesn't begin in the city council chambers. It begins with a problem policy makers are trying to solve: concerns about unwanted second-hand smoke. We'll talk more about framing problems and solutions in Chapter 2.

The story continues at a restaurant. Follow a thread of smoke from one part of the dining room to another. Find out whether having a smoking section bothers nonsmokers. Find out what a smoking ban would mean to smokers. Talk to the owner about what the ban might do to business. These are the story's stakeholders, and we'll discuss them in Chapter 3.

As the story unfolds, don't dwell on the city council members' political strategies or on the effectiveness of each side's advocacy ads. Focus on the proposal and its alternatives, the pros and cons of each idea, the potential consequences of the various choices. Educate readers on the health effects of smoking and second-hand smoke, debunking any myths you encounter along the way. Develop a shared set of facts the community can agree on as it makes a choice. We'll talk more about these principles in Chapters 4 and 5.

Once you've identified a problem, possible solutions and the people who will be affected, and once you've educated the community on a clear set of agreed-upon facts and choices, give citizens the tools they need to get involved. Offer the time, date, and place of meetings where the issue will be discussed. Provide contact information for the officials who will make the decision. Publish Web addresses where readers can learn more, contribute money, or join an advocacy group. Giving readers information to act on is the focus of Chapter 6.

Finally, find new angles and approaches as the story develops. One of the biggest problems with covering governmental process is stories get so redundant that readers can't tell what's new after a while. Every time a proposal advances a step — from a subcommittee to a full committee to a working group to a formal vote, the story is rehashed. So you might produce a series of 500-word stories whose only difference is which committee has ahold of the proposal now, followed by canned background and quotes only slightly different from the last story. An extensive study published in 1992 concluded that people respond less to episodic, day-to-day coverage of an issue than they do to broader stories that lend perspective and a human touch. Part of the study explored how people thought about AIDS in the mid-1980s:

> Most individuals do not know much or care much about the specifics of a recent report on AIDS issued by the National Institutes of Health, but they care deeply about AIDS as a social problem, how it [a]ffects people around them and

what policies ought to be put in place to respond to the epidemic. Reporting by its nature focuses on the most recent event, frequently an official press conference where experts abound and are inclined to debate…, and not on the more personalized story of a young man or woman who succumbs to the disease.[16]

Of course, reporters need to cover issues as they develop — one press conference, one meeting, one committee vote at a time. But they shouldn't be bound by the walls of the news event. You can use graphics and information boxes to explain background and report developments, while your story explores compelling human and moral issues. By refusing to be boring, you'll enlighten more readers. We'll talk more about that in Chapter 7. First, let's close this chapter about putting people in charge of public events by thinking about how to portray those who are most in charge … as people.

Making officials 'real'

News organizations have been pushing for years to get more "real people" into their reports — to weave the voices of ordinary folks among the "experts" and "officials" who dominate news coverage. On its face, that sounds like just the kind of thing I've been talking about, and in some ways, it is.

But there are a couple of problems with the way we've gone about it. The first is that the standard for "real person" is so low that stories often quote some guy or gal who doesn't know anything about the issue but represents a demographic perceived to be missing from the paper. This often results in stilted, useless stories.

The other problem with the "real people" idea is the implication that individuals who don't appear average enough are somehow "unreal," or at least less real than the rest of us. The notion that government is "of the people, by the people," is as old as Lincoln's speech, and yet, somewhere along the line, "the government" and "the people" became distinct entities. Government became something imposed on people, rather than arising from them. And in that way of looking at things, it's easy to dehumanize the people who work for the government — even though most of them live in the same neighborhoods, commute on the same streets, shop in the same stores, pay the same taxes, and send their children to the same schools as the rest of us. An effective and welcome application of the "real people" principle would start with the recognition that the mayor, your state legislator, and the clerk at the Department of Motor Vehicles have parents, went to school, buy gas, have had their hearts broken, and dream of a better future, just like everyone else. That would give us an opportunity, when policy questions arise, to probe decision makers on the origins of their beliefs, just as we do when we talk to farmers about price supports or small-business owners about regulations or the person on the street about abortion.

Instead, we tend to approach public officials and public employees like this: We hold them to impossible standards of public and private conduct and wait gleefully for them to fail; we reflexively expect them to operate in their self-interest to the exclusion of community interest, and therefore interpret every action as motivated by greed or cynicism; or, in the case of bureaucrats, we believe them to be unthinking and inflexible adherents of silly rules and red tape. There is "us," the citizens, and "them," the corrupt, or clueless, or incompetent cogs of government.

In portraying public servants this way, we get a lot of help from the people we cover. Many bureaucrats are so wary of the press they wouldn't dream of uttering an independent opinion on their job or agency — or on the weather, for that matter. Regulations and red tape do complicate the lives of citizens and the jobs of reporters. And elected officials, so intent on staying "on-message" and avoiding spontaneous mistakes, are either inaccessible or reluctant to stray from their scripts.

The *Chicago Tribune* reported in 2004 about how difficult it was for reporters covering the presidential campaign to even *talk* with John Kerry. And the phenomenon was nothing new; the story pointed out that Bob Dole's staff had reined him in after he spoke too freely with reporters in 1996, that Al Gore once went two months without directly addressing reporters in 2000, and that George W. Bush that year would pal around with his press corps but back away from substantive questions.[17]

But even high-profile politicians can be moved from their defensive crouches, sometimes in extraordinary moments and sometimes when a reporter establishes a reputation as someone searching for the truth instead of probing for a "gotcha" moment. Daniel Yankelovich, a leader in thinking about meaningful collective decisionmaking, saw an extraordinary moment when Congress debated the first Iraq war in 1991:

> I recall Congress's reaction vividly because it was so unusual. As members of Congress spoke, instead of making the usual lawyerlike arguments for their point of view, they eloquently expressed their own torn feelings: anxiety about putting American soldiers in harm's way conflicting with the need to counter the Iraqi threat to vital American interests and world peace.
>
> If the congressional response had been the usual partisan debate, it would not have made a dent on the public's sensibilities. But when our political leaders put aside their trained adversarial tendencies and instead responded like ordinary humans, openly expressing their concerns, the impact on the public was extraordinary. Average citizens saw and heard their leaders struggling with the same mixed feelings that they themselves were experiencing. Because members of Congress articulated these feelings with clarity and eloquence — and because they also expressed their conclusions after working through their conflicting emotions — they helped the public to resolve its own ambivalence.[18]

In building a relationship between citizens and public servants, it's best not to wait for a crisis, like the eve of war. Our most challenging public decisions would be easier to address if a foundation were laid earlier, so there's already a level of understanding between a representative and her constituents.

The following story is an effort I made to depict public service through the eyes of the public servant. The story, from 1995, follows a rural businessman and former county commissioner from northeastern North Carolina through his first hours as a member of the North Carolina House of Representatives. The blanket stereotype of legislators is that they are arrogant, conniving, self-serving, and self-aggrandizing. But there are other ways to see them:

RALEIGH — At 3:20 p.m. Wednesday, with his supporters whooping it up at a nearby hotel reception, Rep. Bill Owens of Elizabeth City stayed in the House to watch the activities on the floor.

First day on the job, and Owens was already tied up by legislative business.

"It's an important day for him and his family," Owens said as he watched the ceremonial swearing-in of 38th District Rep. Harold Brubaker, the first Republican speaker of the House in North Carolina this century.

"The business of the House is more important than a reception for me," Owens added later as he walked briskly through the parking lot to his party at the Holiday Inn Downtown.

A cheer rose from more than 75 well-wishers as Owens, longtime commissioner of Pasquotank County, entered the room. Most of the greeters had made a special trip by chartered bus from the Elizabeth City area to watch Owens be sworn in as the 1st District Representative.

He succeeds Vernon G. James, who retired after decades of duty in the House.

At mid-morning, Owens had entered the red-carpeted House chamber with the energy of a first-day elementary school student. Like hundreds of members, media, staff and family that swarmed through the room, Owens bumped, jostled and greeted those he encountered while working his way to his fourth-row seat. He had spoken with pride earlier this week in announcing his seat number, 45, an assignment that placed him in subtle prestige ahead of 25 freshman Republicans. It's the second-best freshman seat in the House, a nice place to be for a Democrat in a Republican-controlled environment.

"This is my seat, right here," the beaming Owens said, patting the desk as he spoke. "Sat in it last week. Got a little practice."

Practice became reality at noon when the gavel sounded and Owens as the 1st District representative was the first to stand and pronounce "Present" in the session's first [roll] call. With his wife, Cynthia, holding the Bible engraved with Owens' name, he joined in the simultaneous affirmation of legislative duty.

It didn't take long for the House to stop speaking as one and turn to partisan wrangling. And the very first agenda item presented a dilemma for the new lawmaker from Elizabeth City.

Owens, who has said many times he will work with Republicans and Democrats alike and had indicated he would support Brubaker for speaker, was caught in the middle by an 11th-hour Democratic decision to put up Rep. Jim Black for speaker. Owens said the Democratic caucus in December had voted not to oppose Brubaker's impending nomination.

"I'm gonna vote for Brubaker," said Owens, adding that he needed to stick to his pledge of bipartisan cooperation. Owens was one of about a dozen Democrats who broke ranks and supported the Republican.

But when it came to approving the rules for this session, Owens stuck with the prevailing Democratic sentiment. In two hours of debate, Owens supported five Democratic amendments, all of which were defeated. He voted against the rules resolution, which passed 81 to 37.

Although Owens, 47, is new — he had to ask for directions as he hurried out of the legislative building — he has many of the advantages of an old hand.

Principal among them is his secretary, Marie Sheets, who worked 15 years for Vernon James and has a reputation for knowing the ropes in Raleigh.

"She's very familiar with the constituents in the area," Owens said.

"It's good that she'll be here to guide me along."

Sheets was with Owens briefly on the floor before the session opened, going over last-minute details as the jumbled din of the other settling lawmakers surrounded them.

When Owens broke free from the session and entered his reception, he thanked his supporters for making the trip to Raleigh and pledged to do his best for them.

"I know I'll make some mistakes," Owens said to a crowd of elected officials, local party leaders and community activists, "but I'll certainly be here to represent you as you want to be represented."[19]

This account could have focused on the legislative business of the session's first day — a process story about the politicking that went into passing House rules favoring the majority Republicans. It could have been a multi-source story evaluating Bill Owens' opening-day performance, with political experts weighing the pros and cons of his breaking with his own party to support a Republican speaker. My choice, instead, was to help Owens' constituents see the day through the eyes of their representative — as a hectic, humbling series of events and choices that would help set the tone for his term of office. There would be plenty of opportunities to gauge his performance as a legislator — his effectiveness advocating for his district, his ability to continue keeping his word, his deftness for dealmaking. This story, I hope, gave readers insight into the man who would be tested and scrutinized as he acted on their behalf for the next two years.

By offering this example, I don't mean to suggest a touchy-feely approach to covering officials. Reporters seeking to engage the public must aggressively question motives and official pronouncements, check whether actions match up to promises, monitor use of public funds and campaign contributions, and otherwise fulfill the news media's watchdog role. But it's important to direct this scrutiny toward a complex *person*, not a machine or a target.

If we approach public affairs journalism as the work of the people — beginning with the collective choice to hire the most qualified representatives to solve our common problems; continuing with governmental process coverage that emphasizes the effect on human beings; and then tearing down the perceptions that divide "the government" from "the people" until citizens and officials can face community challenges as partners — then we can change the way journalists, citizens, and government view the vital processes of democracy. In the following chapters, we'll build on how the people, once re-hired into the governing process, can get on with the work of self-government.

How to put people in charge

■ Judge every official action by Lincoln's standard that government is "of the people, by the people, for the people." In every story, answer the questions: Who are the people responsible? Who are the people affected? How can people get involved?

■ Cover elections as a collective hiring process, with voters as the ultimate authority. Describe the job each candidate is seeking and his or her background and qualifications. Determine the primary challenges of the office and insist that candidates answer how they will meet them — whether the candidates want to talk about it or not. Judge stories' value based on how well they help voters make a decision. Place less emphasis on horse-race polls, sniping between candidates, and superficial stories that distract from the substance of the campaign.

■ Help readers see the importance of day-to-day governance by making the impact of policy questions clear from the outset. If a certain meeting, policy, or debate has little impact on people, find a better story.

■ Introduce readers to political leaders and public decisionmakers as people, to provide a frame of reference for their decisions and break down divisions between the "governing class" and "citizen class."

For thought and action...

1 Find a published story about the latest election in your community. Write a one-page critique examining the story's emphasis. What metaphor does the story seem to rely on: the horse race or the job search? How much information is devoted to helping readers make a good choice? How much is devoted to less meaningful issues? How could the story have been approached better?

2 Find a newspaper story on a government meeting that seems dry and uninteresting. Rewrite the whole story as though you were explaining it to a friend. Don't worry about making it worthy of publication; only worry about holding your friend's attention and getting the point across accurately.

3 Interview a political leader who represents your community in local, state, or national government. Focus your questions on how this person grew up, his or her early jobs, what steered him or her into politics, and three specific things he or she would never compromise on. Write a profile describing how these personal attributes influence the way the politician works.

Chapter 2

Report Problems *and* Solutions

Most of our communities' failures are rooted in complex problems. A truly excellent newspaper will spend most of its investigative skills on explaining those circumstances. We misdirect readers if we concentrate on narrow problems and inflate their significance.
— Frank Batten Sr., former publisher of *The Virginian-Pilot*[1]

Conflict, real or contrived, is the highest coin in the journalistic realm. Journalists love it and defend their ardor on the grounds that readers also relish it. Clearly, people are drawn to conflict, but where obviously contrived or transparently partisan conflict stands in the way of resolution of important problems, citizen tolerance for it — and those who convey it — becomes strained.
— Davis "Buzz" Merritt, *Public Journalism & Public Life*[2]

In the early months of 2003, the state of Michigan faced a whopping budget deficit projected at $1.7 billion, its worst fiscal crisis in 40 years. A new Democratic governor and a Republican-controlled legislature were struggling to get out of a hole created by a sagging economy and poor planning.

A *Detroit Free Press* story predicted that "[t]he biggest battle over taxes in a decade may be shaping up" among political leaders and interest groups with different spending and cutting priorities.[3] An Associated Press story placed a group called the Red Cedar Coalition "[o]n one side" of the battle, with the Taxpayer Protection Caucus "[o]n the other side."[4]

Reporters and editors at the *Lansing State Journal* looked at the numbers, looked at the looming battle, and decided to tell the story differently.

"$1.7 billion is a huge number," *LSJ* political editor Chris Andrews said.[5] "We wanted to put it into a context that people could understand as policy makers were figuring out what to cut or where to find more money. ... We wanted to provide a collection of ideas that could be part of the discussion. [Editor] Mickey Hirten suggested that we scrutinize the budget, talk to experts, and work to come up with 50 or 100 ways to cut the budget."

So Andrews and reporter Stacey Range spent a month doing just that. They interviewed dozens of government experts, analysts, and citizens, collecting ideas that ranged from privatizing state services to squeezing more revenue from tax policy. The paper hosted a summit of Michigan financial experts, which was broadcast on government TV. The result was a front-page package that jumped to a two-page spread under the headline "100 ways to cut Michigan's 1.7B deficit." In a brief introduction, the reporters laid out the problem:

> Short-term fixes have been used. One-time money pots: empty. And higher taxes will be a blip in the equation. The only solution, economists say, is to find new ways to control spending. [...]
>
> The Lansing State Journal looked to analysts, budget experts, lobbyists, lawmakers and think tanks to compile a list of ways to cut. Some, such as dropping prescription drug coverage for seniors, are harsh. And some, such as selling the fairgrounds, could forever change Michigan's landscape and heritage.
>
> "We have to ask, 'What's best for the citizens ... in the long run?" said Rep. Leon Drolet, R-Clinton Township. "That's what will guide us."[6]

The 100 ideas followed. Andrews explains:

> Each item required considerable research — including many that ultimately were scrapped. We wanted to include big ideas and small ones. We tried to provide enough context and information in each item to educate readers and help them decide whether the idea was a good one. For instance, we noted that the beer tax hadn't been raised since 1966, and we showed that the savings from a cut in lawmakers' pay would be a relative drop in the bucket. ...
>
> We knew that some of the ideas would draw criticism — state workers certainly didn't like the idea of giving up their pay raises. At the same time, we wanted to make the package enjoyable to read, so we injected attitude into the writing. But we were not intending to be advocates. ...
>
> We received numerous calls from regular folks providing other ideas and critiquing some of ours. The Michigan League for Human Services put a copy on the wall to refer to as the debate over the budget unfolded. The Mackinac Center for Public Policy, a free-market think tank, posted it on its web site. The governor's office said it gave the project a thorough review as it was developing its budget-balancing proposal. Ultimately, many of the ideas — or variations of them — were part of the budget solution.[7]

The *Lansing State Journal* could have reported on Michigan's budget problem in a number of ways. Political issues like a budget deficit often are set up as an opportunity for warring political parties or ideologies to clash — hence the "battle" metaphor and the "one side, other side" positioning of leaders.

But the paper chose a more constructive method: Identify the problem, explain it, offer potential solutions, and provide a forum in which those solutions could be discussed. In *The Two W's of Journalism*, Davis Merritt and Maxwell McCombs liken this approach to asking "democracy's core question, 'What shall we do?'"[8]

The way journalists address these public questions, and the way they position citizens and political figures to confront them, has been called the "frame" they choose for the story — in essence, the point of view through which the story's facts are presented. Every public challenge can be framed as an opportunity for officials to abuse their power; as a polarizing conflict whose combatants will never find common ground; or as a problem with a range of solutions the community must sort through.

The first two frames can create a sense of disenfranchisement. By framing the story solely as a competition, journalists portray what could be a solvable problem as an intractable one. On the other hand, Cheryl Gibbs and Tom Warhover say in *Getting the Whole Story*, "If a reporter writes not only about a problem but also about its possible solutions … citizens are much more likely to see ways they can get involved in helping to solve the problem."[9]

Ways of framing

The Virginian-Pilot took this idea to heart in the mid-1990s. Accepting that journalists always frame stories, whether or not they're aware of it, the staff resolved to make conscious choices. Reporters and editors thought through and redefined the purpose of their beats, setting priorities for how those beats would explain the world to readers.

The police and courts beat took on a "public safety" orientation, meaning a story's news value would be judged in part on whether it showed readers how safe they were in their community and what they could do to be safer. Sensational crimes were still big news, but the public safety frame also required putting big crimes into context. A triple homicide one day did not necessarily mean the city of Norfolk was less safe than it had been last year or five years ago. So in addition to reporting the crime as a matter of public interest, the reporter would add statistics about how many murders had been committed in the city that year versus recent years. The paper ran full-page maps breaking down crime rates by neighborhood or census tract, so citizens could see whether things were getting better or worse where they lived.

You can see the empowering nature of these choices. Suddenly a beat that seemed to be all about shootings and stabbings and rapes and murders can be about much more. This approach builds in accountability for the people who run the justice system, and it delves into the impact of crime for the whole community, in addition to individual villains and victims. On top of reporting WHAT, WHERE, and WHEN crime happens, it seeks to describe WHY.

The framing process also helped the paper focus its education reporting on the question of how the community was preparing its children for adulthood. Rather than concentrating solely on school administrative issues — taxes, construction, labor-management relations — this frame forced the paper to study how schools actually worked, how classes were taught, how effective tests were, how children developed in the classroom, and broader questions of government's role in education, including vouchers, charter schools, and home schooling.

In essence, the frames mandated an approach to public issues that more closely mirrors the way readers and citizens look at the world — a perspective that can bridge the divide among government, journalists, and citizens. An extensive 1992 study on how people construct meaning from the news noted a gap between news media and citizens' perception of news stories. The study found that while the news media emphasized conflict in 29 percent of its reporting, nonjournalists tended to view issues as conflicts only 6 percent of the time.

News audiences were far more concerned with the human and moral aspects of stories than journalists were.[10]

"Regardless of the medium in which they work, journalists eschew the moral frame which figures prominently in the public's understanding of issues," the study says. "The public, in contrast, relished and drew out the moral dimension in the human impact of issues, and underscored the moral dimensions of public policies."[11]

The "moral values" perspective gained popular attention in late 2004, when polls revealed morals to be the single most cited motivator among voters in the presidential race, if the war on terror and the war in Iraq were viewed separately. Journalists began a round of hand-wringing about a disconnect with the public, but evidence suggests the disparity has existed for some time. Social researcher Daniel Yankelovich points out that most people tend to *feel* their way through issues as much as they *think* through them:

> In public judgment, facts and values are indistinguishable from each other. Average Americans judge whether a policy makes sense without differentiating sharply between practical and moral considerations. In making a judgment, people take into account the facts as they understand them *and* their personal goals and moral values *and* their sense of what is best for others as well as themselves. For example, in weighing the pros and cons of decriminalizing drugs, people tend to make their judgments on whether "it is the right thing to do" and not only on whether it might reduce crime rates.[12]

While most people view controversy through this moral lens of right and wrong, news people tend to shy away from these questions, partly because they are difficult to address on deadline and partly for fear of tying their own beliefs and emotions into the story. But the quick-hit, traditional frame of conflict, which allows journalists to passively report on ugly partisan battles without shedding any light on the problem, helps explain why many people are turned off by or uninterested in news reports: The story is framed in a way that excludes their priorities and perspectives.

Overemphasizing winners and losers can determine not only how a story is played, but also whether it's reported effectively. *The New York Times* broke a story about a week before the 2004 presidential election that tons of specialized explosives had disappeared from a munitions depot in Iraq. John Kerry's campaign grabbed the story in an effort to make the Bush administration appear incompetent, and it immediately became a campaign issue. Reporters following the story focused on the impact it would have on the election — and *not* on what it meant for national security. After the election, an analysis in *CJR Daily* noted, the story seemed to dry up:

"Has anyone in the press since asked … how the Pentagon's fact-finding mission is proceeding and what's been turned up to date? Or are reporters permitting the entire matter to recede — because the Kerry and Bush camps are no longer out there trading accusations about it, because the what-will-the-missing-explosives-mean-for-the-presidential-election angle is now moot…"[13]

In other words, once the political angle disappeared, so did the story, though questions of how much materiel was taken and who was responsible remained unresolved. In a striking parallel to the government's possible failure to secure weapons it once controlled, the news media failed to follow through adequately on a national security story that it had exposed — because it was using the wrong frame.

Choices and consequences

So let's adopt the problem-solving frame, instead of political winners and losers, as the default approach to covering public affairs. After all, what are government and civic organizations for but to take care of problems that individuals and private organizations can't or won't?

We can quickly come to terms with almost any public initiative by asking the question *The Virginian-Pilot*'s Dennis Hartig uses to get to the heart of an issue: "What is the problem you're trying to solve?" Though officials debate, propose, and act for a variety of reasons, not all of which are in the public interest, most newsworthy initiatives aim to fix something that's broken, ease something that's difficult or stop something that shouldn't be happening. Asking what problem officials are trying to solve forces clarity on the issue, exposes ulterior motives and enlists citizens in the quest for the best solution.

Laying out a range of potential solutions, and the possible consequences of each choice, is the next step. *The Journal Times* of Racine, Wis., captured consequences efficiently when it found a person whose circumstances illustrated both the positive and negative effects of a proposal to make Wisconsin drivers carry auto insurance.

"[R]ather than running stories about the statistics and the committee hearings, we tried to help readers relate to the issue in very local, personal terms," *Journal Times* Editor Randolph Brandt said.[14] "One of our reporters remembered a police accident report from a couple weeks before in which an uninsured motorist had been hit by an uninsured motorist. So, we tracked down the driver and asked him how he felt about the state mandating insurance coverage.

"It was perfect. Here was a young man (in our 'target audience' of young adult readers) who demonstrated both sides of the issue in really, really personal terms. On one hand, he couldn't afford auto insurance and pay his rent, but on the other hand, here he was with his truck damaged and no recourse from the other driver who hit him. It really summed up the conundrum, and we could present it in a compelling, reader-friendly way with great storytelling. Oh, we ran the statistics, too, in an accompanying breakout."

Here's part of the story:

> RACINE — David T. Boehler is just the kind of person that a proposed bill, to make mandatory car insurance the law in Wisconsin, would help.
>
> Boehler is also just the kind of person it would hurt.
>
> Boehler, 20, was driving his 1989 Ford F-150 pickup on Saturday afternoon when another driver pulled out from a stop sign and hit his truck in the intersection at North Memorial Drive and Albert Street.
>
> Since the accident, Boehler's knee has been leaking fluid and may need surgery. His truck is a mess, too. The wheels no longer sit straight in the wheelwells, and it's hard to drive it straight.
>
> Boehler figures either the frame or the axle is bent. Either way, he figures it

will cost at least $1,500 to fix it.

Here's how mandatory car insurance could help Boehler: The driver who hit him was uninsured, so it's still unknown if she'll be able to pay the costs to fix his truck and knee. That wouldn't have been an issue if she had carried insurance.

Here's how it could hurt him: Boehler, too, is uninsured. "They're asking crazy high prices," Boehler said, and he can't afford car insurance. That's why he doesn't support the idea of making it mandatory.

"Because there's people like that has a child to support and has to work for a living," Boehler said. "And the only way I have to get to and from work is my vehicle, and I can't support my child if I can't get work, and I can't afford car insurance."

Wisconsin is one of only three states that doesn't have mandatory car insurance. New Hampshire and Tennessee are the other two. State Rep. John Lehman, D-Racine, wants to change that.

He has written a bill, and is circulating it for co-sponsors, that would require drivers to carry liability car insurance or face a $500 fine.

"I think there's a presumption out there from motorists that when you're driving down the street, the other guy is insured," Lehman said. "And it seems to me, that if you're going to be getting in the car and getting behind the wheel, you should ensure that vehicle is insured. The burden shouldn't be on somebody else's insurance policy."[...]

Insurers are against mandatory car insurance. Their reasons include:

■ The law is difficult to enforce.

■ It may raise everybody's premiums because insurers would have to take on high-risk drivers they might otherwise avoid.

■ It unfairly punishes poor people who can't afford car insurance.[...]

People like David Boehler.

Boehler earns $8 an hour, 40 hours a week, working for a company that sterilizes and disposes of medical waste. He pays child support for a daughter he can't afford to visit in California. Car insurance would cost him between $130 and $160 a month, which he said wouldn't leave him much money to keep his truck running.

Boehler's just waiting to see if the other driver can pay to fix his truck. Boehler summed up his options if she can't.

"If anything," he said, "I'm pretty much S.O.L., if worse comes to worse."[15]

The first lesson from this story is that heads-up reporting leads to creative journalism. Editor Brandt notes that the story's main character was discovered because a reporter connected the insurance issue to a routine accident report he had read earlier. That shows how paying attention to little things can pay off in bigger ways. The next lesson is that this story, which could have dwelled on legislators and lobbyists in the state capital, instead focused on a local driver whose life will be affected by a political proposal. This makes the story personal and tangible — it's about dollars in and out of people's pockets. The story continues by laying out the pros and cons of mandatory insurance — reporting each side's best substantive arguments instead of focusing on political strategies. Then it returns to the local driver. Bringing the problem home in concrete terms means local readers can respond; this is part of their world, not some unapproachable political realm.

WHEN THERE ARE a lot of choices with a lot of consequences, a different approach can be effective. As the nation looked at looming deficits in the Social Security trust fund in 2005, the Associated Press put together a package of options for solving the problem — from raising taxes to reducing benefits to investing part of the trust fund in the stock market instead of U.S. Treasury bonds. Each option noted how the current system functioned, what would change, how much money it would save, and the best cases for and against the proposal.[16]

The package clarified choices with detail that no politician could describe in a speech or interview; it demonstrated that there were many different ways to attack the problem, not just a few oversimplified catch phrases people were hearing on TV; and it showed that every choice had advantages and drawbacks to consider. In a clear and easy way, the story broadened readers' perspectives on a complicated problem.

Competing values

Politics is a key part of resolving public problems, but it is not the only part. Public disagreements involve practical and ideological concerns as well as political motivations, and helping people work through important issues requires reporting in each of these realms. Ultimately, a political solution is only possible after people identify the problem, sort through their values, and weigh the pros and cons of possible solutions.

One common mistake in reporting on public debates is focusing on the people who take extreme, and often irreconcilable, positions. These people are the most vocal and active on an issue, so they're easier to find, easier to quote and more likely to make news. But they also are unlikely to reflect your readership, most of whom will be less engaged with the problem and feel more ambivalent about it. A focus on the extremes can make a problem seem unsolvable and frighten away people inclined to more civil deliberation. Expressions of ambivalence and opportunities to test ideas, as opposed to polarizing debate, help people engage in public affairs.[17] So it's important to seek out people who can see both sides, who are wrestling with competing proposals. The clash of two positive values can lead to disagreement without creating good guys and bad guys. Most people support some level of environmental protection, for instance, but most people also support the right of property owners to use their land as they see fit. People who believe in both of these values can disagree on a specific question about a specific piece of property. Rather than forcing people to choose sides between progress and protection, reporters can help show that well-meaning people exist on each side of the question.

Former *Virginian-Pilot* reporter Karen Weintraub stumbled on this lesson while covering the resort city of Virginia Beach. In a 1997 article for the *Kettering Review* and later in an interview, Weintraub described covering a public forum where city officials and property owners were arguing over how much the city should pay for taking residents' land to build an industrial park. She began reflexively framing the story in her head as a case of stingy city officials trying to screw poor landowners out of money they deserved — the "David vs. Goliath" formula — when a new perspective dawned on her. She asked herself: "What if everybody's right?"

The question led Weintraub, after she had filed for publication, to rewrite her story as an exercise in three different ways — one framing the landowners as victims of official greed, one framing city council members as vigilant stewards of public money, and one with the nuance to portray *both* sides as well-meaning groups with different perspectives.[18] By spending some time in everyone's shoes, Weintraub, who later became an editor at *The Boston Globe*, believes she became a more sensitive, more accurate reporter. "The end result is you come up with a truer story," she said.

Here's how a reporter for *The Tampa Tribune* presented the competing values raised by a civic question:

> RUSKIN — Residents weighed their fears about rampant development against their worries about higher taxes at a town hall meeting last week about whether to incorporate Ruskin into an independent municipality.
>
> About 100 residents were evenly divided as they listened to a consultant explain details of a study on the pros and cons of incorporating Ruskin.
>
> Joe Mazurkiewicz Jr., who has done similar studies for 14 other Florida communities, said only two have chosen to incorporate. "It's not an easy process," he said.[19]

The story goes on to describe what might happen if the town incorporated. Taxes would probably not go up for the first four years, according to the consultant, but might increase after. The tax base would likely increase also, bringing in more revenue, but residents might begin to demand more costly services. There are pros and cons, and people have different priorities. The story is about choices and ambiguity, which leaves room for people to seek common ground.

Making strategy a sideshow

The methods people use to get their way are interesting. Most novels, plays, and films depict characters beating obstacles to achieve their goals. Sports are all about devising strategies to confuse or overwhelm the opponent. So is war. These are the dramatic models embedded in our cultural psyche, and so it's natural that we employ these themes as we document the public drama of governance. Our reporting on a referendum campaign emphasizes how each side deploys rhetoric and ad dollars to win the fight, instead of examining what the proposal would achieve, what it would cost and how it would change lives.

Our legislative coverage dwells on arm-twisting and dealmaking instead of how a law will help or hurt constituents. Strategy and salesmanship attract more attention than detail and analysis. But emphasizing strategy takes our eye off the ball. The key question for citizens, and therefore for journalists, should be: Who's got the best idea? Not, who's got the best game plan? It's not who will win, but "What shall we do?"

A powerful and deeply values-laden story from early 2005 signaled to some journalists an opportunity to break out of the political battle mode and into a national conversation.

Terri Schiavo, a 41-year-old woman who had been in a persistent vegetative state since 1990, was in the last stages of a legal battle over whether to keep feeding her mechanically or to let her die by withholding nourishment. Her husband, Michael Schiavo, insisted that Terri would not have wanted to live in her artificially maintained state. But her parents were committed to keeping her alive and fought through every level of Florida state courts to continue her care. In March 2005, when Terri's parents' state legal options were exhausted and the feeding tube was removed, the U.S. Congress intervened, hastily passing a law requiring federal courts to hear the case. President Bush flew from his Crawford, Texas, ranch to Washington to sign the bill into law.

The case had carried political overtones for years, becoming a symbol of the cultural battle over end-of-life issues. But more powerful for many Americans than the simplistic "sanctity of life" and "death with dignity" arguments, and the legal and political maneuvers surrounding them, was their own personal confrontation with these questions. According to surveys, the case launched millions of kitchen-table conversations about how people wanted to be treated if they were in Terri Schiavo's position, and thousands of people established living wills instructing loved ones and doctors on what to do if they became incapacitated.

Poynter Institute faculty member Kelly McBride saw an opportunity for journalists to help audiences work through these questions. In writing about the case and discussing the definitions of disability, she invoked her own older brother, who "has an IQ somewhere around 50 and bags groceries at the Piggly Wiggly. ..."

> In conversations about the Schiavo story, we find that the words we use to characterize another lead us back to ourselves. I think about my brother's life. You might think about your grandfather's death. ... In the struggle to do what's right for Terri Schiavo, we are really trying to do what's right for all of us. ...
>
> If journalists can help people give voice to our reservations in the same breath that we declare our convictions, we can make progress. If we can learn to ask questions of one another on a story like this — and then listen to the answers — perhaps we'd discover an open and civil society within our grasp.[20]

Still, much of the coverage sidestepped the universal moral problem that the country was trying to figure out. In reporting the twists and turns of the Schiavo case, the issue of political strategy and consequence dominated, along with polarizing commentary.

A Cox News Service story focused on how the case had allowed Republicans to flex their social conservative muscles in an effort to slow Democrats' momentum on other domestic issues. But the story noted that those efforts could backfire politically, pointing to poll results showing most Americans objected to congressional and presidential intervention in the case.[21] Meanwhile, a *Kansas City Star* story featured Republican and Democratic lawmakers trading barbs over "a culture of death" and "bold inconsistency" in political positions.[22] The personal side of the story — the honest assessment of beliefs and misgivings that Kelly McBride called for — did not appear in these stories.

And yet several reporters did find a way to connect Terri Schiavo's story to the struggles of their own readers. *The Jersey Journal* told of Sister Alice McCoy, the director of a local hospice group who had wrestled with her own mother's illness years earlier. Rather than have a malignant tumor surgically removed from her aging mother with no guarantee that it would help, McCoy and her mother chose to manage her pain, and McCoy cared for her mother in the parish until she died. "'Right to life' means 'What kind of life?'" the paper quoted McCoy saying. "To draw these lines that the only way you are going to love Terri Schiavo is to put a feeding tube into her is overly simplistic."[23]

The *Daily Camera* of Boulder, Colo., found a mother who had rejected a medical panel's recommendation to disconnect life support from her 18-month-old daughter, left in a persistent vegetative state similar to Schiavo's after a car accident. The mother, Linda Shepherd, had since spent 17 years caring for her daughter, who lived at home in a bedroom equipped with a respirator and a lift to help her change positions. Shepherd's daughter, Laura, could be fed with a spoon and make some facial gestures. "If someone were to tell me today that she is not viable, that her life is not meaningful, that would be unthinkable," the paper quoted Shepherd saying. "Quality of life to me is being alive and having love in your life. Terri Schiavo had both of those, and so does my daughter."[24]

Though politics intervened in the Terri Schiavo story, it was not a story about politics. The actions of Congress and the president needed to be covered, and their motivations needed to be evaluated — something we'll re-examine in Chapter 4. But ultimately, the most effective journalism was about people — how their own circumstances shaped their opinions on the Schiavo case, and how Schiavo's plight influenced their perspectives on the meaning of life and death. Those perspectives are part of the great working through process of morality, law, and policy. They make important news interesting.

How to report problems and solutions

■ Define and portray politics as predominantly a means of solving common problems, rather than a way for elites to exercise power.

■ Be conscious of how you frame stories — how you identify what's important (who's winning, or what's at stake?), how you portray the issue (a battle for supremacy or a moral question to be sorted out?), and how you position readers (passive victims or potential actors?). Figure out how your readers interpret and respond to issues, and try to meet them on that level.

■ In reporting on conflict, pay as much attention to people who feel ambivalent about the issue as those who feel strongly. Challenge people's assumptions, pushing them to explain the beliefs and values they bring to the argument.

■ Identify and present a range of choices and consequences, not just two irreconcilable positions.

■ If strategy is part of a public battle, report on how various groups are working to get their position heard. But subordinate that reporting to a thorough examination of whose ideas are more practical and meaningful. Don't take sides, but lay out, point by point, how each group's proposals will address the problem. Rely on the expertise of independent observers, and don't be afraid to use your own common sense.

■ Provide a forum for people to respond to your coverage and offer their own suggestions.

For thought and action...

1 In a brainstorming session, identify the top problems your school or community faces. Assess whether and how people are addressing these problems. Are they getting any attention in the news media? If so, how are the problems being framed? If not, why not?

2 Find a news story about a local conflict between competing interests. Re-report the story, using the same sources if possible, through a problem-solving frame. Ask: What problem are you trying to solve? Then ask sources to honestly discuss the pros and cons of their position, and to acknowledge the pros and cons of others' ideas. Ask them where there might be room for compromise.

3 Find a news story about a polarizing issue like abortion, affirmative action or gay marriage. Assess whether the story approaches the issue from a moral frame — discussing what's right or wrong — or a political frame — discussing who's winning or losing. Does the story offer an opportunity for an exchange of ideas between the opposing parties? Is there any expression of ambivalence? If the story is primarily political, re-report it, using the same sources if possible, through a moral frame. Don't take a position yourself, but push your sources to explain why their position is morally right. Identify the competing values at play.

4 Go to several key decision makers in your community — the mayor, school superintendent, city council members, etc. — and ask them about their approach to solving problems. When presented with a conflict between values or priorities, how do they decide on the right thing to do? What steps do they take? Where did they learn to approach problems this way? Who are their role models? Write a story comparing the leaders' personal styles in working through public problems.

Chapter 3

Let Stakeholders Speak

If the point of journalism is to write about truths, I think it's more true to write about more people.

— Karen Weintraub, *The Boston Globe*[1]

When we talk about putting the people in charge of solving our collective problems, it's important to remember just how many people are involved. The very idea of positioning citizens as the ultimate power in a democracy broadens the discourse from a few elected officials to the great variety of individuals who make up a community. Identifying public choices and explaining their consequences requires a broad perspective, because for every choice, there are people with something to gain and people with something to lose. Finding people with different stakes in the outcome of a public question, and telling their stories well, gives citizens a chance to see the issue from several perspectives beyond their own. That creates empathy, which leads to understanding.

When citizens in Virginia Beach, Va., were asked to vote on whether to pursue a $1 billion commuter train line between their wealthy, suburban, ocean-bounded city and the urban center of downtown Norfolk, *The Virginian-Pilot* set out to cover the issue through the eyes of many stakeholders: commuters whose grueling daily drive between the two cities could be eased by the new "light rail" line, residents whose neighborhoods might be disrupted by noise and traffic, businesses that might profit from being near a rail stop, public officials eager to ease a growing traffic burden, taxpayers concerned about government waste. All these groups were contributing openly to the debate over how to proceed.

But as the story developed, it became clear to some *Pilot* journalists that one big aspect of the discussion wasn't being addressed — at least not out loud. Here's the beginning of the story written to tackle the issue:

> VIRGINIA BEACH — Talk to most people about light rail, and you'll hear the same questions again and again.
>
> Will enough people ride it? Is it worth $1 billion? Will it help solve the region's traffic problems?
>
> A concern you won't hear much about, at least in public, is the one that Kim McDonald ventures to raise.
>
> McDonald, a 40ish white Virginia Beach resident, voices anxieties about

inner-city black people riding the proposed commuter link between Norfolk and Virginia Beach.

She has tried to keep an open mind, she says. She even plans to support light rail in the city's Nov. 2 advisory referendum.

Yet she continues to worry that black people, especially young men from low-income urban areas, could become disruptive on the commuter line, at the Oceanfront and on the streets near station stops in Norfolk.

"Even if it's an incorrect perception, it's still a perception," McDonald said. "You're going to have a hard time coaxing white middle-class people onto the light rail to go downtown, if that's what they feel, that they're going to be in danger."

McDonald says she'd like to talk with African Americans about her perceptions and hear theirs in order to better understand. Only she doesn't know how to have such a conversation, McDonald says.

The proposal for a light rail system between downtown Norfolk and the Virginia Beach Oceanfront has been debated for nearly 20 years. The public discussions, the speeches, the forums, the letters published in newspapers have been dominated by arguments about costs, taxes, efficiency, convenience and development.

But many, like McDonald, contend that there's another important conversation about racism that washes through all the other words and actions, a discussion that few leaders and citizens are willing to publicly acknowledge.

This is a dimension where "race" comes into play, as it does in so many divisions in American society.

Some say Virginia Beach and Hampton Roads have matured beyond letting racism influence the decision-making abilities of leaders and citizens. Others contend that long-entrenched racist beliefs and their wounds have only become obscured by changes in language, or code words such as: those people, young rowdies, criminals and drug addicts from the city.[2]

Kim McDonald, the woman quoted at the beginning of this story, meets all the criteria we've established for engaging public affairs coverage. She's a traditionally defined "real person," operating in no official capacity, speaking only as a concerned citizen. She's joined a discussion of people aiming to solve a community problem — overcrowded streets that make driving a daily frustration. She's not raging on one side of the debate or the other, but rather is expressing feelings of ambiguity and uncertainty.

She's also raising a topic that is highly sensitive — race — in a manner that many would legitimately find offensive. She's worried about poor black people coming into her community. Having her say this in a front-page story angered a lot of readers, reporter Mike Knepler said, especially white readers who thought the paper was falsely injecting racism into a debate that shouldn't be about race.

And yet, the story — which goes on to quote several other black and white citizens, activists, and political officials — proves that for at least some people who would ultimately decide the fate of light rail, race *was* an issue. For better or worse, like it or not, people uncomfortable about race were among the stakeholders in the debate.

The paper could have ignored those people and their concerns, which are easily dismissed as inappropriate, ignorant, or personally affronting. But that wouldn't have made them go away, and it wouldn't have kept them from acting on their prejudices. Instead, *The Virginian-Pilot* examined its community, discovered an issue that, beneath the surface, had some impact on the conversation, and brought that issue to light. If journalism is about telling the truth, then all points of view — even hidden ones, even ugly ones — are fair game.

It's worth noting that Kim McDonald, with the reporter's help, is reaching out. She accepts that her perceptions might be incorrect. Better yet, she'd like to talk with African Americans about her concerns and theirs, but she doesn't know how. "I thought that was very interesting how she was very frank, very candid in her thoughts and in her general struggle with the issue," Knepler said.[3]

Most people with strong feelings about an issue are less likely to be so candid. People with a vested interest in a debate protect their positions by ignoring the flaws in their own views or the strengths of their opponents'. This prevents people who might have overlapping interests from recognizing middle ground, and it prevents people who are narrowly informed from broadening their understanding. Conflict-oriented journalism feeds into this polarization. But a journalist with the sophistication and civic good will to help people of diverse viewpoints understand one another can break this impasse.

This is accomplished by writing honest and compelling accounts of how people come to believe what they believe, how they will be helped or hurt by the issue at hand, how even someone whose point of view may be altogether different from yours is nonetheless a human being.

Kinds of stakeholders

When *The Virginian-Pilot* introduced the term *stakeholders* into its journalistic jargon, the paper's staff identified three major categories of people who had a stake in the outcome of a given story:

■ Official stakeholders — people with power granted by government or other institutions.

■ Civic stakeholders — people or groups working in what they perceive to be the public interest, either for change or to protect a way of life they value.

■ Personal stakeholders — people or groups who could be directly affected physically, financially, or emotionally.

The staff also laid out a set of standards for ensuring that various stakeholders are covered:

1. Early in the reporting of continuing stories, we should identify and describe all the key stakeholders and their stakes, to build the widest possible audience for the evolving story.

2. Our coverage should be in proportion to the needs of the key stakeholders. For example, in the coverage of education, we should pay significant attention to the stakes of the primary stakeholders, the parents and children depend-

ent on public schools for their education.

    3. Stakeholders and stakes should be prominent in our writing, editing and page design.

    4. Our readers have to see their stakes reflected in our coverage. They do not necessarily have to see themselves as sources or commentators.[4]

Some of this might seem like common sense, but sometimes defining the obvious is the only way to make it happen. The purpose of highlighting stakeholders is to help journalists internalize the notion that many more people are affected by public issues than those we most commonly quote — officials, pundits and power brokers — and to help citizens recognize the many ways people are helped or harmed by public policy decisions. The local government story that quotes only the mayor and city council members may be fair and accurate. But it is not complete — and often it is not relevant — without also quoting the people in the community who are participating in the issue, and those who will be affected by the outcome. Once this expanded idea of sourcing becomes routine, its execution is simple enough. But it requires breaking through what *Columbia Missourian* Executive Editor Tom Warhover calls "Rolodex reporting," the habit of returning to the same sources over and over, without thinking about other possibilities.

"We know institutionally through survey after survey and study after study that the same Rolodex tends heavily toward institutional figures, tends heavily toward people in power, tends heavily toward middle-aged white males, tends against minorities, young people, old people, people of certain geographic areas," Warhover said.[5] Good reporters, he said, can see beyond these routines and stereotypes.

"You think about something as simple as putting a crossing at a school. Well, you know the obvious stakeholders there are the kids crossing, and the teachers and the crossing guard. But then you start to say: the motorists who drive that route every day, and who are busy on the way to work, and the parents of those children and the PTA and the local school board and the taxpayers of that city who have to pay X amount for the crossing guard, and the police who have to enforce it or not enforce it. ...

"It's amazing how little we do that exercise internally, consciously or otherwise. ... It makes for more complicated reporting, and that's why folks don't want to do it. It means you've got to make five more phone calls than you would otherwise. It means you can't just rely on the mayor proposing and so-and-so gadfly opposing. You've got to get a little more complicated. But it's not a complicated process. It's a real simple process."

The Gazette Telegraph of Colorado Springs followed this process in 1996, when the community was considering a school bond issue. The paper identified four major groups with a stake in the referendum and gave each of them a chance to speak out. Here's how the paper explained the series to its readers:

    Everyone has a stake in public schools.

    Because they're so important, the Gazette listened to people from four different groups as they discussed education in light of Colorado Springs School District 11's two tax measures on the Nov. 5 election ballot.

    We asked parents, students, teachers and taxpayers about their feelings toward the district, what they'd like to see changed and whether new money would address their concerns. The idea was to produce a series that goes beyond traditional election coverage.

We found plenty of common ground although each group comes at issues from different perspectives.[6]

One story representing each group ran on each of four consecutive days. Accompanying the stories was a summary of all four perspectives — identifying the top priorities of the people the paper had interviewed. For both parents and teachers, the No. 1 priority was reducing class sizes. Students most wanted their buildings repaired. Taxpayers without children, the largest voting group, wanted schools to teach the basics and be more fiscally accountable.

Ultimately, 54 percent of voters passed the two property-tax increases that had been proposed for the district — the first time in 12 years that an increase for the schools' budget had been approved.[7]

Emphasizing diversity

Kelley L. Carter, a black entertainment writer for the *Detroit Free Press*, tells the story of a white colleague who looked at her braided hair and asked if it was styled in corn rows. He was curious because his 8-year-old son wanted corn rows, and he didn't know what they were or how his son got interested in them. The family lived in a mostly white Detroit suburb, and Carter's co-worker said no one in his son's school wore his hair that way. What was influencing him?

Carter knew that corn rows were a popular style among hip-hop artists, whose influence extends well beyond the urban communities that many come from and sing about. And she was happy for another opportunity to show how "news that happens elsewhere affects what happens in your own neighborhood."

"My job is to write to the white father of the 8-year-old boy in Oakland County to explain why his son would want to get corn rows," Carter said.[8] More broadly, Carter sees her responsibility as educating all sorts of different people about diverse cultures, lifestyles, and ways of understanding the world.

The topic of diversity — in newsrooms and in news coverage — has been one of the main subjects of journalistic introspection in the past decade. There's a growing recognition that news organizations must do better reaching out to diverse communities if they hope to grow — or at least stop shrinking. There's also pushback from some journalists and readers who believe that seeking diversity is a way of contriving coverage — creating news that isn't there, or blowing stories out of proportion, or neglecting the traditional white male for the sake of appeasing minority populations.

Like almost any other worthwhile effort, diversifying coverage can be done well or poorly, constructively or shallowly, to good effect or ill. Carter disagrees with the practice of tracking down a representative of a random racial or ethnic group to comment on a city council or school board story, just for the sake of diversity. "I think it's wrong to try to force it," she said.

Rather than trying to fit specific minorities into specific situations, reporters must break from their comfort zones as a matter of habit — approaching people who don't look like themselves and learning new ways of seeing things. By establishing relationships with people across demographic lines and building a much broader Rolodex than the white, male, middle-class version Tom Warhover describes above, reporters can draw regularly from a strong, expanding pool of informed and concerned sources from a variety of backgrounds.

One healthy way to look at diversity coverage, rather than thinking of it as pandering or political correctness, is to view it as an accuracy issue. If a news organization is committed to covering its whole community, all of its stakeholders, then it must cover the diverse populations that make up the community. A paper that covers almost exclusively white people because they happen to hold the major elective offices and control the public purse strings, even though 30 percent of the population is black and 10 percent is Latino, is inaccurately reflecting its community. And it's giving 40 percent of its potential readers little incentive to pick up the paper.

Diversity is a stakeholder issue because minority populations are community stakeholders who are often overlooked or undercovered by the mainstream press. Any time a reporter asks herself "Who am I missing?" as she considers potential stakeholders, she must look beyond public officials, civil servants, taxpayers, and businesspeople, and think about people of diverse backgrounds.

Reporters also must take care not to fit people of certain backgrounds into the same roles again and again. After Hurricane Katrina, during which the overwhelming majority of people left to weather the storm and its chaotic aftermath were black, Roy Peter Clark of The Poynter Institute noted a propensity to portray survivors too narrowly: "It's become too easy in this crisis to depict African-Americans as either the purveyors or victims of violence. In fact, black Americans will play out all the dramatic roles that make this story so vivid: not just criminal or victim, but protector, parent, child, law-enforcer, politician, soldier, reporter, friend. Our job is to capture all these roles to tell the fullest and fairest story."[9]

Diversity is not limited to race. The Maynard Institute for Journalism Education describes five "fault lines" of background that help shape the way people see the world: race, economic class, gender, generation, and geography.[10] By considering a range of factors that drive people's perspectives, we can take a more complex look at how people interact with their neighbors and with public policy. Teenagers of different ethnicities are more likely to agree with each other on the quality of popular music than with elders from their own racial or ethnic group. Wealthy suburbanites of many colors might have more in common with one another than with poor people who share their skin tone.

One college newspaper, *The University Daily Kansan*, introduced its primarily student readership to a stakeholder rarely considered by that audience — an older permanent resident — in a story about neighborhood relationships:

> Arly Allen examined the beer bottles, cigarette butts and the red Budweiser trash can and shook his head. Allen, a Centennial neighborhood resident, recalls the history of the home and the family that used to live in it.
>
> Allen, who has lived in his neighborhood for 30 years, is fighting to keep his neighborhood clean and family friendly.
>
> "Students are into wild, raucous living," Allen said. "When they live next to an elderly couple, it's a clash of cultures."[11]

It's a gutsy call for a student paper to cover a story from this perspective. The story may or may not change young residents' minds about how they should interact with their neighbors, especially those old enough to be their grandparents. But at the very least the *Kansan's* readers are exposed to a point of view they aren't likely to consider every day.

Letting people speak

The only real tricks to enriching your journalism with a variety of stakeholders are committing to do it and then making the effort. The less obvious stakeholders — for instance, those who might be conflicted about a public issue — are often the hardest to find. Public officials are in the phone book. Activists show up to all the meetings. Experts are available through university PR departments. But regular folks who can see both sides of a question and are struggling to make the right choice take a little more work.

How did Mike Knepler find the perfect person to lead his story about the racial tensions underlying debate over a commuter train? He went to the same kind of meeting where reporters find the usual suspects, but as citizens arose to ask questions and make comments, he opened his ears to new perspectives.

"You go out to the community meetings, and you listen closely to what people say and then go up and ask them questions to ferret out a little bit more," Knepler said.[12] The woman in Knepler's lead "had raised a question or two during a community meeting on light rail. … (S)he had asked some questions I believe about the security issue. … I can't remember exactly what the wording of her question was, but it made me go up after the meeting to ask her to elaborate."

With sensitive issues such as race, extracting honest answers can be a challenge. Here, persistence is key, along with trust.

"Some people were more direct, forthcoming, and others beat around the bush," Knepler said of sources for his light rail story. "You just kind of have to ride with them and ask them what they mean by this or mean by that, or listen carefully to their answers and continue to try to ask them questions to get them to clarify.

"You just have to stick with them sometimes; you're not always successful. But … you just try to build a rapport with whoever it is."

A way of building rapport and earning trust is to demonstrate to sources that their point of view won't get short shrift in your story — that a single quote won't be taken out of context, and that they'll have a chance to develop their argument. Knepler returns to Kim McDonald toward the middle and end of his light rail story. We learn that her best friend at work was a black woman, with whom she could talk about many things but did not discuss race relations for fear of damaging the relationship. The story ends with a quote from McDonald: "There's no simple answer, for sure. … So it all comes down to that person you look at in the mirror every morning."

ON COMPLEX STORIES that develop over time, the best way to help readers understand where people are coming from — including people they disagree with — is to let those people speak without interruption. In other words, write an unfair, unbalanced story from only one person's perspective. Let him make his case. Then, write an unfair, unbalanced story from another perspective. Do this with as many major points of view as you have time and space to lay out, as *The Gazette Telegraph* did with the 1996 school bond. It's a great way to let readers judge for themselves. The *Detroit Free Press* took this approach as part of a package of stories about gay marriage, in advance of a 2004 state referendum on an amendment to ban homosexual unions. Here's the front-page introduction to two stories that ran, side-by-side, inside the paper:

> Kristina Hemphill and Judy Fertel Layne are not political activists. They are professional women and moms. Neither professes to know much about homo-sexuality.
>
> But they are deeply involved in the campaign over Proposal 2, a proposed amendment to the Michigan Constitution that would define marriage as the union of one man and one woman, effectively banning same-sex marriage or marriage-like arrangements between same-sex partners.
>
> Hemphill, 35, is a public relations and development specialist. Her life revolves around family, church and a self-help group for women she helped organize in Detroit. Since late summer, she has been the chief spokeswoman for Citizens for the Protection of Marriage, the campaign that collected a half-million signatures and put Proposal 2 on the ballot. Hemphill says she thinks its passage would signal that our society still supports the traditional family.
>
> Fertel Layne, 41, is an estate attorney in the Bloomfield Hills office of one of Michigan's top law firms. She considers herself a committed liberal.
>
> But she's never been much involved in politics — until Proposal 2, a measure so odious to Fertel Layne that she spends most of her spare time fighting it.[13]

In reporting on the gay marriage issue, *Free Press* reporter Dawson Bell had gotten to know Kristina Hemphill and thought she would make a good story. At the same time, he and his editor had been talking about ways to "personalize" the gay marriage debate. Social issues like gay marriage, abortion, and gun rights "tend to excite interest in people who aren't ordinarily politically active or involved in public policy on a regular basis," Bell said.[14] "When there's a campaign like that you get people who are sort of drawn to it and become involved." Bell thought Hemphill was a good example, and then found Fertel Layne, someone similarly motivated by the issue, but on the other side. Running parallel stories on each woman seemed a natural way to go: "You can get a clearer understanding of what the belief system is of somebody involved in a campaign like that if, instead of sort of going through the he-said, she-said or the on-the-one-hand-this and on-the-other-hand-that, you get closer to reality if you just focus on a single perspective at a time."

Here's a glimpse of each story:

> …[Kristina Hemphill] says part of her support for marriage between one man and one woman is based on the experience of growing up with divorced parents.
>
> Her mother and father were wonderful and supportive, she says. Both remarried, and the stepparents that came into her life were loving.

"But the desire of every child is to live in a home with their mother and father," she says.

Hemphill says problems with marriage and well-documented increases in divorce and single parenthood, "doesn't mean we can't aspire to a model we know works for children."

"I don't want to be in anyone's bedroom. But I am interested in how our culture affects my family and my children and my community. We have all these studies showing […] divorce is bad for children. But when it comes to gay marriage we turn around and say that one of the child's parents isn't important," she says.

She doesn't believe Proposal 2, as some of its detractors have suggested, is a religious overreach into public affairs. Consider what motivates the opposition, she says.

"They are fighting for a value system they think the culture should embrace.

"So are we."[15]

Like many of those on the other side, [Judy] Fertel Layne frames the issue of same-sex marriage in the language of right and wrong. But for her it is a more generalized, golden rule kind of right and wrong rather than a religious teaching (her family observed conservative Judaism, but she attends synagogue only on high holidays).

"It is hurtful and wrong" to exclude gays and lesbians from the institution of marriage and its benefits, she says.

She also says it's bad for everyone else.

During her lifetime, she's seen a growing acceptance of gay and lesbian relationships, she says, and that [is] a good thing. Children who grow up with an awareness and appreciation that not all families consist of a mother and father are more likely to learn the virtue of tolerance, she says.

And she is skeptical about the argument made by Proposal 2 proponents that children are most likely to prosper in a home with their own mother and father.

Two parents are better than one, she says.

"But I'm not sure it has to be a mom and a dad. If our society didn't treat homosexuality with the disdain that it does, I don't think it would be a problem."[16]

The two profiles obviously don't cover the full range of stakeholders in the gay marriage story, but this was just a piece of a four-day series on the issue. The package got a lot of reaction, Bell said — mostly from people with entrenched points of view, but also from some who admitted they learned something: "There were a few people who said things like, 'I hadn't considered it in precisely the way she expressed it before, and I think I understand it a little better, even though I don't agree.'"

The more stakeholders you let speak, the more understanding you spread.

How to let stakeholders speak

■ Before reporting a story, take a minute and list every type of person who could be affected by that story — not just the officials debating policy but the people who have to carry it out, the people who have to pay for it, and the people who will have to abide by its rules. Don't think of some stakeholders as doers and others as passive recipients. Think of every stakeholder as a potential actor with a different interest and perspective. As you write, consider the subject again and ask, "Who am I missing?"

■ In addition to seeking out people with different stakes in an issue, look for people with different backgrounds. The Maynard Institute identifies five "fault lines" that help shape an individual's perspective: race, age, class, gender, and geography. Often, reporters look for people like themselves when hunting for sources. Successful reporters will try hard to find people unlike themselves — people of different colors, ages, social class, etc. — to glean perspectives they otherwise would have missed.

■ Push stakeholders to fully explain how they feel, both in terms of their own interests and the community's. Don't assume people will always behave selfishly. Remember that people often process policy issues in moral terms, so find out what perspective of right and wrong they bring to the discussion. Gently test their conclusions and challenge their factual assertions. If someone says abolishing capital punishment is "just the right thing to do," ask why. A personal story will often follow. If someone makes a factual claim, ask where they learned the information. If you know it's wrong, tell them so and ask if that changes their opinion.

■ When possible, give each stakeholder a chance to air his or her views without immediate rebuttal from the other side. Be fair about giving various viewpoints a similar amount of space, but let people who disagree speak for a while without being interrupted. This doesn't always require separate 20- or 30-inch stories; a single story about a proposed zoning change could also include a mug shot and quotation from a city council member who supports it, one who opposes it, the developer who wants to use the property, and a neighbor who will have to live nearby.

■ Present disparate viewpoints not as a confrontation but as a meeting of ideas. In *The Magic of Dialogue*, Daniel Yankelovich offers a number of strategies to help foster meaningful communication. Among them are to "[f]ocus on conflicts between value systems, not people," which makes disagreements less personal; to "[e]rr on the side of including people who disagree," which means telling a lot of stakeholders' stories; and to "[f]ocus on common interests, not divisive ones," which gives people a chance to compromise.[17]

For thought and action...

1 Find a news story about a local controversy. List every stakeholder represented in the story, then come up with a list of stakeholders who are not represented. Interview one of those stakeholders and rewrite the story to include the new point of view.

2 Get an agenda for a local government meeting (city council, planning commission, school board, etc.). Choose one agenda item and list as many stakeholders as you can think of. Write a paragraph for each stakeholder, explaining their interest and how they might be able to influence the issue's outcome.

3 Pick an issue currently in the news and interview five people about their opinions on it. None of the people you interview can be the same age, race, or gender as you. Write a story about their opinions. Compare it with other stories in the class.

4 Do a content analysis of your local paper, with an eye on diversity. Determine if reporters are talking to enough different kinds of people in different communities, or if they keep going back to the same people in the same places. Can people of different backgrounds see people like themselves in the paper each day, in a variety of contexts that transcend stereotypes? How could the paper improve its diversity coverage?

Chapter 4

Take Citizens' Side

Some things are objectively verifiable, true, and not just a matter of opinion. And when a government official at any level says something that is objectively untrue, we don't need "a different viewpoint," we need to say that what the official said is untrue and ask him why he said it.

— Lex Alexander, Greensboro *News & Record*[1]

While disparate groups play wide-ranging roles in confronting public problems, there remains a single, broad category of people for whom journalists are out working each day: the citizens who make up our communities. Tied down by daily entanglements with partisans and activists — the most informed and invested stakeholders — journalists often lose sight of their obligations to the general public, the great majority who rely on the news media to help them sort out what's important, what's true, and what's possible. Successful journalists are constantly mindful that their constituency is this broader citizenry, and that their ultimate task is ensuring that issues are presented clearly, transparently and honestly. In the messy process of conducting a democracy, journalists must take citizens' side.

This stance requires an emphasis on clarity — not simply in language, but also in the struggle to present a clear picture of reality, helping citizens decipher a world that's often packaged to deceive them. This expanded view of clarity broadens reporters' obligation from ensuring that their own prose passes the transparency test to enforcing the same discipline on the people and institutions they cover. Politicians, or anyone in public life, can't be allowed to manipulate facts and opinions to blur reality. When a partisan throws mud against the windshield of public discourse, the journalist must be there with a squeegee.

One of the greatest criticisms of the press during the 2004 presidential election was that it failed to hold campaigns accountable for distortions and half-truths aimed at misleading voters. A Committee of Concerned Journalists survey in October 2004 quoted one professional saying: "Find the truth with your own independent reporting and research and state it. Do not report two conflicting claims and let readers sort them out. This kind of journalism is terribly vulnerable to manipulation. It also confuses and alienates citizens."[2]

Taking citizens' side requires a manifold approach to clarity — explaining your role as a journalist, writing for meaning and understanding, and cutting through sources' attempts at obfuscation.

Clarity of purpose

The Elements of Journalism, which draws on surveys and conversations with hundreds of journalists to boil down the profession's key obligations into nine principles, says, "The primary purpose of journalism is to provide citizens with the information they need to be free and self-governing."[3]

This elegant statement should drive every decision journalists make; it's the standard for judging all your efforts. Communicating the values of informed self-government to readers and asking them to hold you to this standard creates a partnership between journalist and citizen that can withstand a great deal of mischief by those who don't have the public interest at heart.

Elements author Tom Rosenstiel says the citizen-focused statement of purpose fosters a sort of "demand-side journalism," where the reporter is constantly evaluating what citizens need to know and is therefore less beholden to the "supply side," which relies on press releases, official pronouncements, and staged events for news. The demand-side mindset helps journalists "by turning them to the citizen first and not to the newsmaker first. … The second thing that it does is it turns you away from the institutions, the buildings — and more, I would hope, towards problems."[4]

Assessing the public's demand for news is not as simple as market research on tennis shoes or mouthwash, Rosenstiel cautions. "Our product changes every day. News is what hasn't happened. You can't market research a demand for the unknown." What journalists need to do, he said, is learn about how people live their lives. How far do they commute? How long is their workday? How much time do they spend with their kids? These and other questions reveal the kinds of information citizens need, and they make people the focus of public affairs reporting.

As we saw in Chapter 2, a story's frame profoundly affects the way it's received, and a simple shift from a supply-side frame to the demand side can make important news a lot more interesting. Approaching your work with clarity of purpose can help shape the nature of your journalism into something that citizens see as clearly relevant to their lives.

Clarity of language

The idea of demand-side journalism clarifies not only your purpose in reporting but also your language in writing. It's easy, when an assignment takes you into the realm of news suppliers, to adopt the complex cadences and opaque arrangements of their words and ideas. This can prompt well-meaning reporters to return from government meetings with leads like this:

> The six-month controversy concerning the existence of an outpatient facility in Bloomington was clarified Wednesday night when the Bloomington City Council amended the municipal code to alter definitions concerning the words 'hospital' and 'outpatient care facilities.' The debate began in February of this year when a for-profit specialty hospital was proposed by Dr. Kamal Tiwari. The debate sparked many within the Bloomington community to voice concerns about competition between the Bloomington Hospital and a new facility. Mark

Moore, president and CEO of Bloomington Hospital, said he opposed the option of building a new hospital and maintained another hospital would have had a negative impact and not provide the best possible care to its patients.[5]

This windy paragraph answers the five traditional W's we ask of reporters: There's Who — the City Council; What — amended the definitions of health care facilities; When — Wednesday; an implied Where — City Hall; and Why — to settle a controversy over a proposed outpatient facility. But for people not directly involved in this controversy, the lead fails to answer more fundamental, and more significant, questions: "What does this mean?" and "Why should I care?"

Was a new medical center approved or denied? What effect will the City Council's action have on patients in the community? How about doctors? And taxpayers? These questions are left unaddressed. Just answering the five W's, without reporting impact and meaning, does not lead to clarity.

COMMUNICATING CLEARLY is a matter of will. It requires empathy for people outside your head. YOU know what you mean, so you're the last person to think about as you write. You have to think of the reader.

When you do, the difference is remarkable. Sentences get shorter. Jargon gives way to common language. Tone shifts from stiff to conversational. Readers are invited to join you on a journey through the story.

Here's the beginning of a story about the Michigan State University student government, or ASMSU, considering a change in its structure. Technically, it's a story of procedure, but the reporter recognized that the bigger story was about identity. So he started it like this:

> Your undergraduate student government charges you $13.75 every semester.
>
> This year it's lobbied against Proposal 2, fought drinking game bans, spent almost $36,000 on upgrades to its offices, voted against opening the Red Cedar River to fishing and questioned administration officials on the new residential college that was slated for the 2005 school year.
>
> So, the perennial question on ASMSU representatives' minds is: Do students know what we do?
>
> Well, do they?[6]

Scott Cendrowski, who wrote this story, says he thought a lot about how to begin it. "During the whole story process, I knew what the body of my story would look like: opposing sides duking it out for the rights to call their system of student governance best," Cendrowski said.[7] "What I didn't know was how I was going to get anyone to read it. ... The most important part of the story was students on ASMSU saying it was ineffective because of its structure, but unless I did something in-your-face, I never thought I could get anyone to take a glance at it."

With these concerns in mind, Cendrowski started the story reminding students that their money supported student government, then questioning its relevance. Only after establishing these ideas did the story ask whether the government should merge its student and academic assemblies into a single unit. Because Cendrowski took the time to explain the student government's significance early on, readers might be primed to stick around for the details of how the government could be more effective. This is writing for citizens.

Clarity of fact

Americans were wrestling with some big questions ahead of the 2004 presidential election. The biggest was whether the United States had done the right thing by invading Iraq in March 2003. The invasion had gone as well as military planners could have hoped; Saddam Hussein's regime was toppled within weeks. But some 18 months later, tens of thousands of U.S. troops were still battling for control of the country. Many Americans were asking whether the war was worth the human and financial costs. In a poll released just before the election, 74 percent of respondents agreed the war would be wrong if Hussein's regime did not have chemical, biological or nuclear weapons and was not aiding al-Qaida, the terrorist group responsible for the Sept. 11, 2001, attacks on the United States.[8]

By this time, experts like the national Sept. 11 commission and the chief U.S. weapons inspector had concluded that Iraq had no chemical or biological weapons, or any significant nuclear weapons program. And President Bush had acknowledged a year earlier that there was no evidence Hussein was part of the Sept. 11 attacks.[9] And yet, the poll reported by the Program on International Policy Attitudes found that nearly half of Americans believed Iraq had weapons of mass destruction or a major program. Fifty-two percent believed Iraq was providing substantial support to al-Qaida. A *Newsweek* poll released on Sept. 4, 2004, found that 42 percent of registered voters thought Hussein was directly involved in the Sept. 11 attacks — nearly a year after President Bush said he wasn't.[10]

It's OK to argue that invading Iraq was the right thing to do, that taking down dictators who wish us harm is the best way to protect the country. It's OK to argue that Iraq was a bad idea, that pre-emptive war is a poor way to keep the peace. And it's OK to suggest that the war could have helped both Americans and Iraqis if it hadn't been botched by incompetent administrators. There were compelling arguments for all of these views as this book was written, and it's citizens' duty to consider competing arguments and make political choices based on their conclusions.

What's not OK is for Americans to support a policy based on false conclusions they believe to be true. Going to war based on untruths may be the worst possible outcome of the democratic process.

It's journalists' job to provide citizens with a shared set of facts they can use to make decisions, but this has been difficult in recent years. One reason public discourse is so poisonous is that there's no agreement on the facts that underlie our policy debates. People on each side present information that serves their ends, whether it is selective, misleading, or patently false. Journalists — either too lazy, too overwhelmed, or too concerned with maintaining an effected "balance" between disagreeing parties — have been largely unable to help the public figure out what's true. This criticism was rampant during and after the 2004 presidential campaign.

Dan Froomkin, a columnist for washingtonpost.com and deputy editor of the Nieman Watchdog Project, summarized critics' arguments this way: "Out of fear of appearing too partisan or adversarial, the press failed to sufficiently demand answers to important questions, failed to prevent outright falsehoods from gaining currency, failed to uncover deception, malfeasance and incompetence in our most powerful institutions, failed to pierce the façade of cynically stage-managed events, and failed to demand accountability from our leaders."[11]

We have to do better than this. Citizens aren't served by clear language that distorts reality. Taking citizens' side means reporting established fact, even if it contradicts official claims. The fear of alienating people who will read bias into factual assertions is baseless. Partisans will always try to discredit journalists whose reporting challenges their point of view. But the public is more likely to trust journalists who consistently tell them the truth, rather than just reporting opposing parties' half-truths and spin.

"Striving for fairness and balance does not mean we can't adjudicate the facts," Bryan Keefer wrote in an influential 2004 mid-campaign analysis. "When the truth is knowable, the press should not hesitate to point it out. When it is not knowable, reporters need to include anything they can to help the reader understand a given issue or situation."[12]

In his book *Public Journalism & Public Life: Why Telling the News is Not Enough*, Buzz Merritt likens journalists to referees, "fair-minded participants" whose knowledge gives them authority to keep the players honest.[13] Sports fans generally accept referees as neutral arbiters of right and wrong in athletic contests. The officials' job is not to support one team or another, but to ensure that the game is played fairly. When one team commits a penalty, the referee throws a flag. The team that breaks more rules is penalized more. Reporters and editors should be no less serious about refereeing public affairs — calling fouls as they see them.

Journalism critic and blogger Jay Rosen called the willingness to add a reportorial voice to the debate between political adversaries "he said, she said, we said" journalism. The press, Rosen wrote, "should draw defensible conclusions, and make its way forward by defending, explaining — publicly justifying — those conclusions."[14] Here's an example, cited in a *CJR Daily* story that called for more rigorous fact-checking. It comes from a *New York Times* story that challenges a claim made by Defense Secretary Donald Rumsfeld:

> [Rumsfeld] contended that the decision on troop levels was largely "out of my control," since he was following the advice and requests of his regional commanders, first Gen. Tommy R. Franks and now Gen. John P. Abizaid and Gen. George W. Casey Jr.
>
> While that may be technically true, Mr. Rumsfeld approves all decisions on troop levels in Iraq, and his commanders and top civilian aides have indicated that he routinely demands detailed explanations for troop increases and movements."[15]

In another example, the Colorado Springs *Gazette Telegraph* discovered in its reporting of a local school referendum that many community leaders believed a bloated education administration was consuming too much money. It was a reason for many people to oppose the referendum seeking tax increases for the school district. The paper wrote a story to put the administration's expenses in perspective:

It's one of the biggest perceptions out there: Colorado Springs District 11 spends too much money on administrators.

School officials say it's all a misconception, fueled by chronic district critics but rarely backed up by facts.

But voters don't make decisions based solely on data the district provides. They make decisions by talking with neighbors, reading the newspapers and watching TV, and weighing their own experiences and beliefs.

School officials acknowledged that some of these shared beliefs — that there are too many administrators with too many perks — will sway some voters against the tax increases.

But they complain it's a tough reputation to shake because so few people offer specific suggestions on exactly what positions or departments they think are expendable.

[...]

D-11 Chief Financial Officer Robert Moore argues that there isn't much administrative fat to cut, pointing to a 1993 study of district spending by the U.S. Chamber of Commerce.

The voluntary study found that 91.4 percent of the D-11 budget was spent at school sites; the remaining 8.5 percent was spent on the central office.

Moore argues that's pretty lean, considering the scope of district operations: 3,431 employees to manage, 1,000 classrooms to supply, 3.9 million square feet of space to clean and maintain.

Many school districts use different accounting procedures, different budget presentations and different ways to classify their employees, making comparisons between districts difficult.

But here are a few facts provided by the district. Decide for yourself. [...]"[16]

The story goes on to list information about the central office duties, staff, and budget. Accompanying the story was a summary of the bond issue and the views of key stakeholders, as described in Chapter 3. Note that the story doesn't take a position on whether the district spends too much on administration, but it does challenge conventional wisdom of rampant spending with facts and context.

Then there was Hurricane Katrina on the Gulf Coast in 2005, which exposed such widely acknowledged failures across all levels of government that reporters working among abandoned, sick, and starving people showed an assertiveness that Americans had not witnessed in years. Reporting from third-world conditions in their own country gave journalists the confidence to challenge officials who didn't get it yet. In one of the most widely quoted moments, CNN's Anderson Cooper upbraided a Democratic U.S. senator who was engaging in the usual political pleasantries while discussing the government's response.

"I got to tell you," Cooper interrupted, "there are a lot of people here who are very upset, and very angry, and very frustrated. And when they hear politicians … thanking one another, it just, you know, kind of cuts them the wrong way right now, because literally there was a body on the streets of this town yesterday being eaten by rats because this woman had been laying in the street for 48 hours. And there's not enough facilities to take her up. Do you get the anger that is out here?"[17]

CNN also posted an item on its Web site allowing readers to contrast officials' claims that everything was under control with completely contradictory accounts from local witnesses and victims.[18] The news media's sense of urgency after Katrina, and the feeling that reporters were truly speaking for citizens, provided at least a temporary boost to the profession in late 2005.

Here are some ways to ensure that facts are clear and meaningful:

Leave no assertion unchallenged

The best way to hold sources factually accountable is to refuse to take their word for anything. Very few sources really know what they're talking about on any given subject. Political operatives are paid to portray their side in the best possible light. Regular folks are likely to spurt out whatever they've heard from a neighbor or Web site. Even well-informed and well-meaning people can exaggerate for effect or make up a fact — consciously or not — to support their argument.

You have to leave no assertion unchallenged. When a source makes a claim, you have to ask: How do you know? Where did you get your information? Why do you believe it? Regardless of whether these answers are satisfactory, you should later double-check the claim with other sources.

This might sound off-putting — especially if you're talking to a VIP like a mayor or a senator. You don't want to sound like you're accusing these people of lying. But enforcing this discipline on people who play loose with facts will keep both you and them out of trouble, and it will keep people honest, which is a big part of your job.

The State News wrote a story in November 2004 localizing a debate over whether the abortion pill known as RU-486 was dangerous. Concerns had been raised over the death of a California woman in January of that year, and the FDA strengthened warnings on the pill on Nov. 15 in response. *The New York Times* reported that the coroner's report blamed the California death on a different medication, but the FDA insisted RU-486 was to blame.[19]

The State News quoted the student leader of a campus pro-life group saying the drug was "very dangerous to women's health." Then it paraphrased an officer of the Mid-Michigan Planned Parenthood Alliance saying the death was probably "due to the abortion itself, not the drug used." The story didn't refer to the information from the coroner's report that *The New York Times* had reported.[20]

Before publishing these assertions, the reporter needs to ask what qualifies either source in Michigan to speak on what killed a patient in California whose death is disputed by medical experts. By citing these sources, the reporter cues readers to accept their opinions as well-informed. What's more likely is that both sides are drawing conclusions based on their beliefs, not direct expertise. Reporters should not give the sheen of knowledge to just anyone willing to express an opinion. Medical disputes are best left to medical doctors with direct knowledge of the case; political activists are free to make judgments based on what's known, but they shouldn't be elevated to adjudicators of specialized facts.

A key reminder of the importance of skepticism occurred in early 2006, when 13 miners were trapped underground for more than a day after an explosion at the Sago Mine in West Virginia. Around midnight of the second day, word made it to the church where the miners' families had gathered that rescuers had found 12 of the 13 men alive. Jubilation erupted, church bells pealed, and even the governor of West Virginia stepped out to confirm the good news.

Newspapers, bumping up against their deadlines, rushed to remake pages with bold headlines trumpeting the miners' survival, despite the lack of official verification from the mining company. Some of these papers hedged their bets, attributing the news to family members. Many others took no such precautions. A couple of hours later, company officials made the devastating revelation that there had been a tragic miscommunication — in fact, 12 of the 13 miners were dead.

Many papers around the country, especially those on the West Coast, were able to get the right story into at least some editions. But millions of people awoke to inaccurate headlines in their morning paper, leading to significant corrections and editorial explanations the next day.

It was debated whether reporters on the scene and editors at their desks could have performed better on a tight deadline. As Poynter's Bob Steele wrote, "Frankly, when the Governor said they were alive and when the church bells started ringing and the families started celebrating, it would have been extremely difficult — if not impossible — to 'hold the story' pending more verification."[21]

But even if reporters acted reasonably under the circumstances, acting *skeptically* might have averted much pain and embarrassment. Scott Libin, in the same Poynter article, observed: "Even when plausibly [reliable] sources such as officials pass along information, journalists should press for key details — respectfully and courteously, but assertively. Mr. Mayor, tell us more about how you found out. Chief, can we talk to the officer or officers who actually responded to those rapes? Governor, you tell us 'they' say 12 are alive; who, in this case, are 'they?'"

Journalists' willingness to test assertions tends to peak during heated political campaigns, when intentional truth-stretching also tends to peak. Media watchers at *CJR Daily* noted that news people did a lot of fact checking in the 2004 campaign's final months, "regularly measuring candidates' claims and charges against the yardstick of known truths."[22]

The month after the campaign, though, Thomas Lang of *CJR* noted a significant drop-off in fact-checking features, as though only elections presented the opportunity to hold public people accountable for their claims. Lang called on news organizations to launch permanent fact-check features, noting that:

> [R]eporters and editors at every outlet that we checked with affirm that, during the election campaign, the readers ate up the fact checks, sending in e-mail after e-mail thanking reporters for their candor and commitment to the truth.
>
> If reporters like it, and readers like it, what then is standing in the way?"[23]

Report, report, repeat

Journalists have long believed that once they uncover a truth, they need to move on to new questions — that as soon as a fact has been published it becomes part of the public's knowledge. I had many conversations with senior editors who wanted to get something in our paper where my response was, "We've already reported that."

That's a fine answer if a newspaper's goal is to put important truths on the record for historians to discover and analyze years later. If the newspaper's goal is to build a smarter, better informed community equipped to make important decisions *right now*, then reporting a fact once simply isn't going to do the job. If the information is important enough, the only recourse is to publish it again and again, until it enters the public consciousness. Take the example of Americans' misperceptions about Saddam Hussein's weapons programs and involvement with al-Qaida, well after numerous official reports and pronouncements had removed doubt about the truth. It behooves journalists, once aware that the public clings to inaccurate conventional wisdom, to repeat the truth as often as necessary to correct the misconception. Publishing a daily info box about Hussein's lack of chemical and biological weapons might rub some people the wrong way, but it would be worth it if the next poll showed people knew what was going on.

It bears repeating that however these efforts to clear up misunderstandings are taken by partisan readers, they shouldn't be represented in a partisan way. To report what's actually going on in Iraq isn't to argue for or against U.S. policy, only to make sure that the arguments are based in reality. Let proponents and opponents of any policy present their best cases, on honest terms.

Be clear on what you don't know

Often, important stories develop in haphazard ways that preclude immediate understanding. Reporters don't like to have gaps in their stories, and the instinct is often to write around them and hope readers won't notice. The better practice is to share with readers what you don't know, just as you share what you know. This helps set a direction for both journalists and citizens moving forward, trying to eliminate unknowns as they go. And, often, it puts pressure on people who *have* information to be more open.

In early September 2004, two sexual assaults were reported in the same area of Michigan State University's campus. University officials were slow to release details of the crimes, and *The State News* held off reporting them for a few days, waiting patiently for enough information to write a complete story. Eventually, though, the staff realized that waiting for sensitive information was not the best strategy. The paper published a story with the meager details that had been released about the crimes, and then turned to the broader context of the community's response, including hurdles faced by reporters:

> MSU police are investigating two reported sexual assaults in or around Emmons Hall late Sept. 2 and early Sept. 3.
>
> The incidents were the two first reported cases of sexual assault on campus this semester.
>
> Both attacks were posted as first-degree criminal sexual conduct on the police blotter section of MSU's Department of Police and Public Safety Web site. First-degree criminal sexual conduct involves forced sexual penetration.
>
> According to the site, the first incident happened at 10 p.m. on Sept. 2 and was originally listed as happening in or around Emmons Hall, but the site later reported a student sexually assaulted on campus. The second was listed as a 1

a.m. attack on a student by another student in or around Emmons Hall on Sept. 3.

The two alleged assaults happened within three hours of each other, but students living in the residence hall were not notified as of Thursday evening.

University spokesman Terry Denbow said police officials decided it was premature to do any mass notifications because information gathered so far hasn't led officials to believe other students are in danger.

"The investigation is extensive," Denbow said. "At any moment when it's determined that there is a clear and present danger to students in a residence hall or beyond, immediate notification will be made."

MSU police Sgt. Florene McGlothian-Taylor said police reports of the assaults were unavailable.

MSU police Lt. Alan Haller said the report would quickly have been made public if there was an immediate danger to the community.

"If it was a situation where it was a stranger rape and it needed to go out, it would have been flagged by the detective bureau and sent out immediately," Haller said.

McGlothian-Taylor said officers still could be interviewing witnesses, and said the department didn't want the reports publicized yet because "it may confuse (witnesses) in terms of the days," she said, adding that police officials wanted possible witnesses to remember the incident from their own memory, not from what they read.

Several Emmons Hall residents said they hadn't heard anything about the reported assaults.

There are about 425 students in Emmons Hall, said Brody Complex Director Diane Barker, who declined further comment.

Emmons Hall Resident Director Quiana Smith also declined comment, but said she had been in touch with MSU police. She asked State News reporters to not talk with residents in the Emmons Hall lobby Thursday.

But Denbow said students could make their own decisions about talking with members of the media, as long as they are approached in a public space, such as a lobby or entryway.

"For a common area, students can choose whether or not to talk with The State News," Denbow said.

McGlothian-Taylor said the department won't have a report until it's finished investigating.

"It's not anything we're hiding," she said.

Henry Silverman, vice president of the Lansing branch of the American Civil Liberties Union, said police are entitled to withhold specifics of a crime while they're under investigation, but the public should have been told about the incidents.

"When they're doing an investigation, they have the right to keep things quiet, but I think the university's entitled to know information about crimes on campus," Silverman said. "How else can the community defend itself?"

Haller said neither of the alleged attackers were strangers to the victims, otherwise the public would have been notified soon after the incident.

Emmons Hall roommates Erin Wiltse and Ashley Brewer said they hadn't heard of the assaults through an e-mail, floor meeting or through the grapevine.

Brewer, a history freshman, said she would have liked to learn about the assaults, regardless of whether it was a stranger or not, because it could have been someone she knew.

Wiltse, a mathematics freshman, said she agreed. "People should be made aware anywhere, because it could have happened in any hall on campus," Wiltse said. ...[24]

Journalists don't have subpoena power like a court or arrest power like the police, but they do have the power of influence. By bluntly pointing out when officials are hoarding information, journalists can mobilize a community, multiplying the number of voices seeking answers.

Sometimes officials have legitimate reasons for withholding information, but those cases are rare. The pattern of government, especially in recent years, has almost always been to say, "We know best. Leave us alone." But governments that are left alone are not democratic, and they're typically not very competent. Often, when reporters stand up to stonewalling efforts by reporting them prominently, the will to stonewall begins to erode in the face of public curiosity. People keep secrets because it's easier than sharing information. When the opposite becomes true, behavior can change.

Eventually, about a dozen sexual assaults were reported at Michigan State that semester, many more than usual. Some people attributed the increased reporting to the attention the newspaper had given the issue. By the end of the semester, informational meetings were held in student residence halls, and a campus task force was created to combat sexual assaults and relationship violence. When a student was mugged outside a dorm the following semester, university officials sent an e-mail to inform 4,000 students living in that part of campus. An administrator described the e-mail as part of a new policy, adding, "We like to keep residents informed..."[25] *The State News*, by aggressively reporting what it didn't know, almost certainly helped bring about these developments.

Clarity of motive

I argued in Chapter 1 that it's destructive for journalists to pursue every public person as though he were a criminal just waiting to be exposed. I argued in Chapter 2 that public questions should be addressed on their merits — the pros and cons — more than on their strategic or tactical impact on politics.

But neither argument should deter reporters from aggressively discerning the motivations of people who spend public money, speak on the public's behalf, or make decisions the public has to live with. Giving people and issues a chance, presenting them in a light that citizens can understand, is not an invitation to be manipulated. And when a person of authority uses her position for personal or political gain under the guise of serving the public, journalists have to point it out.

The motivation behind any proposal, vote, or position can result from a variety of factors, including genuine feeling, constituent demand, pressure from special interests or political donors, and party obligations. Often, several factors come into play. Your challenge isn't to ignore political strategy or sneakiness or official cynicism, or to pretend that motivation isn't intertwined with political action, but to give readers the same understanding of what's driving a debate that you have.

In Chapter 2 we looked at the case of Terri Schiavo, the Florida woman in a vegetative state whose feeding tube was removed after 15 years of court battles. The point of the example was to demonstrate that such an elemental question of life and death must be pursued journalistically through a focus on the lives and choices of people in our communities — reporting that helps people understand the complexity of end-of-life matters and sort through their own feelings. Reporting exclusively on how the case had been seized for political purposes would tarnish that important conversation and distract from its most vital, and most personal, elements.

But at the same time, elected officials thrust themselves into the case, and their actions and motivations must be scrutinized.

Republican leaders in Congress interrupted Easter recess to call a vote on legislation requiring the federal courts to hear the pleadings of Schiavo's parents, who wanted to keep their daughter alive. Most Republicans supported this measure, despite its clash with the conservative principle that the federal government should stay out of state matters. In addition, a memo surfaced detailing how the Schiavo case could help Republicans in the 2006 elections. "This is an important moral issue and the pro life base will be excited," the memo, written by a Republican Senate staff member, said. "This is a tough issue for Democrats."[26] Citizens witnessing Congressional moralizing over Terri Schiavo's fate were entitled to this political context.

President Bush flew to Washington from his ranch in Crawford, Texas, to sign the bill. In explaining his actions, he said it was important for the government to "have a presumption in favor of life." He didn't say that, as governor of Texas, he had signed a bill allowing hospitals to take patients off life support — even against the family's wishes — if doctors deemed that further care would be useless. Even as the Schiavo case was peaking, a baby boy died after being removed from life support against his mother's will under Texas' futile care law.[27] Citizens have a right to review Bush's statements on Schiavo in the context of his earlier actions.

Meanwhile, when Congress voted, many Democrats stayed out of the fray, presumably to avoid having to take a position at all. Just three Democrats were on the floor for the Senate's voice vote, in which the loudest side carries and individual votes aren't counted for the record.[28] In the House, where a roll call was recorded, more than 100 Democrats abstained.[29] Citizens should be aware that when the going got tough, some of their representatives turned chicken.

When motivations for political acts seem to depart from the rhetoric, journalists need to root them out and put them on the record. But at the same time, selfishness and cynicism must be recognized as impediments to good government, not irrevocable side effects of a corrupt system. Ulterior motives should be highlighted not to foster citizens' sense of helplessness, but to inform their own participation in the debate.

Journalists also must come clean with readers about their own motives. This starts with being honest with yourself. Why are you going after a particular story? Is it really to serve readers, or are you pursuing your own agenda? Are you chasing a little gotcha story because the mayor's a crook, or because making him look bad over a single $75 lunch is a notch in your belt? Are you taking a particular angle on an issue story to help the people you agree with? If your own motivations aren't pure, you need to reconsider what you're doing, and why.

Clarity of method

One of the best ways to make your own motives clear to readers is to be transparent in your methods. We talked earlier about the importance of journalists reporting what they know to be true, even if it conflicts with a source's assertion. This practice invites charges of bias, which is a risk many journalists will take if it means properly informing readers rather than playing patsy to a sham.

The way to preserve credibility while calling things as you see them is to employ what Kovach and Rosenstiel call an "objective method" in your reporting, a "discipline of verification" that separates aggressive journalism from aggressive advocacy. Kovach and Rosenstiel believe objective methodology is the historical origin of what has been distorted into "objectivity" — the impossible, and potentially detrimental, standard of balancing every conceivable viewpoint equally in a single news story.

> In the original concept … the method is objective, not the journalist. The key was in the discipline of the craft, not the aim.
>
> The point has some important implications. One is that the impartial voice employed by many news organizations, that familiar, supposedly neutral style of newswriting, is not a fundamental principle of journalism. Rather, it is an often helpful device news organizations use to highlight that they are trying to produce something obtained by objective methods. The second implication is that this neutral voice, without a discipline of verification, creates a veneer covering something hollow. Journalists who select sources to express what is really their own point of view, and then use the neutral voice to make it seem objective, are engaged in a form of deception.[30]

Your obligation is to tell readers where your information came from, how reliable it is, and how it leads to whatever conclusions you draw in the story. If you grant anonymity to a source, for instance, readers are entitled to know why and under what conditions. Transparency also requires reporters to explain their sources' qualifications, as noted above. If you're talking to an economist from the Brookings Institution, Rosenstiel said, you should be clear about her expertise, and note that Brookings is generally a liberal-leaning think tank. The goal is "to provide the audience with enough information to assess for themselves what to think about it. Don't trust me, a reporter whose name you don't know, that this source is an authority. Show me why this source is an authority, and then I will trust you more as a reporter."[31]

An interesting case of reporting methodology arose in December 2004 when a reporter for the *Chattanooga Times Free Press* embedded with a Tennessee National Guard unit in Iraq coached a soldier who asked an embarrassing question of Defense Secretary Donald Rumsfeld. The reporter, Lee Pitts, had been told that only soldiers could question Rumsfeld, so he reviewed two soldiers' prepared questions and asked the sergeant in charge of the microphone to make sure they were called on. One of the soldiers asked why he and other military personnel had to dig through trash bins for scrap metal to armor their vehicles, which drew cheers from the military crowd.[32]

The story about the question and Rumsfeld's answer got big play across the country, but it took a turn when word got out that a reporter had helped the soldier prepare. Pitts and the soldier took some criticism for "staging" the event, though the response from the audience had been spontaneous, and both Rumsfeld and President Bush acknowledged the problem. Many journalists congratulated Pitts for finding a way to get an important question answered despite limited access to officials, but were concerned that Pitts, in his original story, did not own up to discussing the question with the soldier ahead of time. In a letter to the *Chattanooga Times Free Press'* readers, the paper's publisher and executive editor, Tom Griscom, defended Pitts' reporting but acknowledged a failure to make his methods transparent.[33]

One way many newspapers share their methods with readers is through the position of ombudsman, or public editor — a person usually independent of the newsroom whose job is to respond to reader complaints and questions. Public editors often write columns addressing controversial issues or explaining the processes that lead to news decisions. Many editors themselves have taken to writing columns periodically explaining their thinking to readers, either on potentially controversial matters or simply to introduce new approaches to reporting. One virtue of this type of transparency, Rosenstiel said, is that "If you can't explain it, you probably haven't thought it through. ... If the explanation seems silly, maybe what you're doing isn't the best thing to do."[34]

TAKING CITIZENS' SIDE in public affairs puts great responsibility on journalists, whose job is to help readers navigate a morass of confusing, conflicting, and misleading information. Equipping citizens to take charge of democracy and tackle common problems requires that they have a shared set of facts to work with, that they understand the motivations of public actors, and that they can judge the purpose and merit of the journalism producing this information. But even these efforts aren't enough for most readers to make good decisions. You also have to provide enough background and context to help citizens interpret the latest facts. As we'll discuss in the next chapter, you have to be prepared to teach.

How to take citizens' side

■ Be clear in your own mind on the purpose of your work, which Kovach and Rosenstiel define as providing citizens with the information they need to function in a democracy. Focus your efforts on meeting this purpose.

■ Write with empathy — constructing sentences, paragraphs, and stories for a reader who is likely unfamiliar with the subject. Don't write for yourself, your sources, or your editors.

■ Translate official jargon and complex language into terms that non-experts can understand and relate to.

■ Debunk "conventional wisdom," information everybody "knows" that isn't true. If you discover a public misconception, refute it whenever possible with the best available facts.

■ Have the courage to tell readers what's true, if the truth is knowable, rather than equally reporting both sides of a lopsided argument. Just as referees can call a foul without taking sides in a game, reporters can expose a lie without being partisan.

■ Leave no assertion unchallenged. When any source makes a claim, ask: How do you know? Where did you get the information? What makes you believe it? How does that influence your point of view? After the interview, check the assertion with an independent source.

■ Repeat important information. Don't assume that facts presented once will become common knowledge. If the community needs to be aware of something, find a variety of opportunities to present it.

■ Come clean on what you don't know, both so readers don't feel they've missed something and so the community can come together on what questions need to be answered.

■ Be upfront about motivations — your own and your sources'. Give readers the background they need to understand why people are acting the way they are.

■ Be transparent in your methods. Explain where your information is from and how you got it. If you don't name a source, explain why. Don't use the phrase *experts say* when you only talked to one expert. In sensitive cases, explain your news decisions and ethical reasoning.

For thought and action

1 Critique a news story about a government meeting. What does the lead say? What questions does it answer? Who would be inspired to read the second paragraph? Are the questions "What does it mean?" or "Why should I care?" answered? Overall, is the story clear about what's important?

2 Pick one of the more complicated news stories from today's paper, take it out to the street, and ask five people to explain it to you. How did they do? Rewrite the story for clarity and take it to five more people. How did *you* do?

3 Find a story about a controversial issue. List every source and the assertions they make in the story. Are those assertions supported by direct knowledge or sufficient reasoning? Did the reporter double-check or challenge them? Is the story ultimately believable?

4 Create a fact-check feature allowing you to monitor public statements for their truthfulness. You can fact-check a mayor's luncheon speech, a superintendent's "state of the schools" address, an activist group's direct-mail pamphlets, a member of Congress' Web site. Make it a platform for keeping officials honest.

5 Think of a common misconception you hear regularly in your community about the way government, business or the newspaper functions. Figure out a way to correct that misconception through sustained coverage.

Chapter 5

Use News to Teach

Citizens do need to be more engaged in politics, but the reasons for paying attention need to be clearer to them, the benefits of stronger citizenship must be more evident, and the opportunities to learn about politics more frequent, timely and equitable.
— Michael X. Delli Carpini and Scott Keeter,
What Americans Know About Politics and Why It Matters[1]

The people we're writing for not only don't know a lot of the process about public affairs, but shouldn't be expected to know. That's not their job to be experts in it.
— Tom Warhover, *Columbia Missourian*[2]

Can you find Iraq on a map? How about New Jersey? If you answered yes to both of those questions, you're smarter about geography than the overwhelming majority of young Americans. Even as Iraq dominated the news and Congress was authorizing the president to attack Saddam Hussein's regime in late 2002, only 13 percent of Americans aged 18 to 24 could find Iraq in a *National Geographic* survey. That's one out of seven.[3]

As for New Jersey, it was identified by 30 percent of American respondents. Just over half could find New York.[4]

In a different survey, this one from the presidential election year of 2000, only 15 percent of respondents from all age groups could name a single candidate for the U.S. House of Representatives from their own district. Just over one in 10 knew William Rehnquist was then chief justice of the United States — the most powerful judge in the land. And other studies suggest that Americans lack not only specific political knowledge — names and titles — but also a basic understanding of how their government works.[5]

These types of surveys, which seek to identify and often exploit ignorance, probably aren't the best measure of how smart people are. But the results certainly suggest that a lot of Americans don't know much about where things are, who runs what, or how the world's people and places affect their own lives. As the authors of a whole book on this subject summarize, "a majority of people lack even the most basic political information."[6]

Given that reality, how many readers are likely to be moved by a story like this:

UNITED NATIONS — The top U.N. envoy to Sudan urged the world's most powerful nations to use their political clout to ensure that the Sudanese government and southern rebels end their 21-year civil war as promised by Dec. 31.[7]

This isn't a bad lead; it's a typical one. People who had been following Sudan's troubles through 2004, which included a religious civil war between northern and southern factions and a genocidal massacre in the country's western Darfur region, could easily fill in the background from memory to create meaning from this lead.

For everyone else, though, there's no invitation to learn about Sudan and its troubles, or to contemplate the country's moral and political relevance to people in the United States. There is only the name of a place that could be anywhere and a reference to a war whose combatants are as faceless as bees in a hive. This story is useful for the already engaged, and essentially worthless for the uninvolved.

The problem with the typical lead is that the news is supposed to be written for everybody. Its aim is to give citizens a base level of shared information to help them carry out their lives — private and public. And yet, considering the limited knowledge of politics, processes, and boundaries that many readers possess, we're letting a lot of people down. City council stories assume people understand the relationship between the elected council and the hired city manager; legislative stories assume people know how a bill becomes a law; international stories presuppose knowledge of where the news-making country is and how it relates to the United States.

Writing and editing from these assumptions, newspapers package information that has little chance of making a difference to the average reader. The access points are for people who already know, already care, already understand their stake in the story.

Tom Rosenstiel of the Project for Excellence in Journalism says this kind of coverage "strikes people like a cocktail party they came to in the middle." The hapless socialite misses the beginning of the discussion, barely gets a glance from the chattering clique, and can't discern the subject from "just catching snippets in conversations and never engaging in any of them." So rather than try to understand, the confused partygoer simply walks away.[8]

If journalists want their work read, talked about and acted on, they must start reaching out to their audiences, these casual eavesdroppers on public life. The way to do it is to explain how things work, without pandering or belittling.

In other words, we have to teach.

When I presented this notion to a group of college newspaper editors, one student scoffed at the prospect of journalists teaching basic civics or geography to lazy readers. It was the same gut reaction I would have had 10 years earlier, because it's the arrogant stance of the old-school, come-and-get-it reporter: If people aren't paying enough attention to know where Iraq is, or what the mayor does, or how a millage translates into dollars, that's their problem. But "their problem" is our problem, because the people who don't know the name of their congressman aren't going to rush to the newsstand to find out what he said yesterday. We don't help ourselves by leaving these folks in the cold. What do we gain by shutting the geographically unschooled — the six in seven young people who can't find Iraq — out of the conversation? What do we lose by reaching out with the context and background that might connect a city resident with a budget debate? Journalists need to remember that it's their job to be experts on public affairs, says Holly A. Heyser, state editor for *The Orange County Register*. It's not fair to expect someone who makes her living as a mechanic or a mail carrier to be as well informed. "Other people aren't paid to understand [public affairs], they're paid to understand their own thing," Heyser said.[9] "We can't look down on people who don't understand politics as well as we do." Stories need to be framed in a way that makes them part of the conversation.

Audiences want this kind of help. In a report aimed at goading news organizations to overhaul the way they present news to younger, more diverse audiences, Northwestern University's Readership Institute says people's *experiences* with newspapers — more than their opinions of them — influence how regularly they read. One of the key motivating experiences is a feeling that the newspaper makes readers smarter — helps them get more out of life and learn new things. A common reader reaction to the news, Readership Institute managing director Mary Nesbitt said during a workshop in 2005, is, "I'd like to be more informed about these things, but I don't have the background."[10]

Teaching through news isn't a one-shot deal. Journalists can't run a single map of Indonesia or describe the city budgeting process once a year and think they've made readers smarter. Civic knowledge builds over time, through repeated exposure to background, context, and explanation. News audiences appear to learn relatively little from individual stories — even in experimental settings where people are motivated to pay attention. One study concludes that "learning from the news has to be understood as a gradual, incremental process."[11] Daniel Yankelovich, in a 1991 book that inspired many new approaches to public affairs journalism, identifies three stages through which citizens come to understand and resolve public issues. The first is the consciousness-raising stage, in which people become aware of an issue through personal experience or media reports. In the second, or "working through," stage, people process the issue, developing opinions as they encounter new information, and consider ways to resolve it. This requires active involvement in thinking and talking about a problem, not just passively receiving information. The third stage, resolution, comes after people have learned about, debated, and reached conclusions on an issue. Resolution requires people to confront not just what they think about a subject, but how they feel about it, and the moral implications of their choices.[12]

In the mid-'90s, *The Virginian-Pilot* adapted those ideas to help define its public affairs coverage. The adapted terms for the three stages of understanding were "literacy, utility, and mastery," and the paper recognized that to help readers reach conclusions on key issues, it must build their understanding on all three levels over time.

Literacy, utility, and mastery became shorthand for categories of stories targeting readers with various levels of interest in an issue. A literacy story introduced readers to a concept — identifying the major questions and the key players involved. Utility stories, most helpful during the working through process, showed readers how to get involved by attending forums, contacting officials, joining activist groups, or finding more information. Mastery-level stories tended to be deeper pieces detailing the choices and consequences facing the community.

Yet another way of defining involvement in public affairs is Kovach and Rosenstiel's "Theory of the Interlocking Public." They identify three levels of engagement on every issue: an "involved public," an "interested public," and an "uninterested public." Every citizen spends time in each category, depending on the issue. A suburban Detroit autoworker might be oblivious to agriculture or foreign affairs, but could know a lot about labor issues and workplace safety, might have kids in local schools that draw his attention to education, and might be concerned about pollution where he fishes. On a wide range of subjects, he has varying levels of interest. A second example concerns a Washington, D.C., lawyer who is regularly quoted on Constitutional issues and follows political news carefully, but has no interest in technology and, with grown children, is unconcerned about local schools.[13]

The point is that you can't assume what a person is interested in just by looking at her age, address, and education level. More significantly, you can't assume that the smartest, most connected people are interested in everything and less knowledgeable people with menial jobs aren't interested in anything. Rather, depending on their backgrounds, their family situations, and their personal tastes, demographically similar people might be intrigued by altogether different issues, and people who would appear to have nothing in common might be moved by the same story or subject. Casting aside stereotypical prejudgments about who might be interested in a given story requires journalism that appeals to people at different levels of engagement.

"You don't assume that a story is only written for the most intensely interested," Rosenstiel said.[14] "The only vaguely interested person might still read the story if you can build in near the top things that they might want to read. ... Some parts of the paper have to speak to the people who are kind of interested but not well informed and want to become better informed."

For instance, many readers following a debate over Social Security might know that money gets deducted from their paycheck and that it's eventually supposed to come back to them, but they might have all sorts of questions about what the program actually is, when it started, how it works — "the question that you're almost afraid to ask because you're afraid you'll sound dumb," Rosenstiel said. "Journalism should be answering that, over and over and over." When the nation began debating President Bush's proposed Social Security overhaul in early 2005, some news outlets did provide this literacy-level information about the program. The *Lansing State Journal*, for instance, ran a front-page package headlined "Social Security 101," a blend of graphics and short explanatory paragraphs defining the president's proposal and breaking down the pros and cons.[15] The Associated Press, in addition to the extensive lineup of Social Security alternatives I mentioned in Chapter 3, also produced stories exploring Social Security's history and impact on American society.

In this chapter, we'll look at methods of getting beyond the day's news with information that helps people understand it.

Civics 101

Most high school graduates have passed some sort of government class, skimming over the three branches of government, balance of powers, the Bill of Rights, qualifications and terms of elected office, the life cycle of legislation, etc. It's also hard to get through school without at least one field trip to City Hall or visit to the School Board. So most people have crossed paths in some way with the institutions that support their citizenship.

But few encounters with these institutions manifest the partnership a healthy democratic government must forge with citizens. Many civics classes are a hodgepodge of Trivial Pursuit questions (how many justices on the Supreme Court? What's the term of office for a state senator?), and the field trips are show-and-tell, not interactive. So, for people born without a political junkie gene — that is, most everybody — the people and processes and even the ideas behind government drift through the consciousness as transiently as the elements of the Periodic Table and the conjugations of French verbs. Without relevance, the rights and responsibilities of citizenship are just another set of facts to learn for the test and then forget.

The disadvantage for schoolteachers, and the advantage for journalists, is the fluctuating nature of the "teachable moment," a confluence of circumstances that primes people to learn something important because it's important to them, now. Many school curricula must follow a schedule, whether anything related to the instruction is going on or not. But journalists can follow the news, which means there's a sense of urgency attached to the information they present. Reporting that carries the message "this is important, it's happening now, and we're going to explain it to you" can awaken the uninterested.

So when covering public concerns, to return to Rosenstiel's cocktail party analogy, the journalist must be ever poised to grab the arm of the casual observer and catch him up on the topic. The story of the day might be the fifth this month about state budget negotiations, but it's in your best interest to assume the reader has missed the other four, and furthermore doesn't know the name of her state representative and has no clue how many roads you can fix with a $3 billion highway budget.

You bring this reader into the conversation by smiling, offering him a drink and hors d'oeuvre, and doing journalism that says, "We were just talking about X, and here's why we think it's valuable." You can accomplish some of this with background writing in the story itself, but you don't want to bore or drive away those who are already in the conversation. This is where sidebars, graphics, and fact boxes come in, whispering in the new participant's ear even as the story moves the conversation forward.

Time and space permitting, here are some of the interesting boxes you could create for the story on the state road budget debate (this information is made up):

■ A "Background" box, describing the state's historical role in transportation: "The Transportation Department was created in 1872 to ensure the safe passage of rail cars and horse-drawn carriages from city to city. It now maintains the state's roadways and is responsible for new construction."

■ A "What's going on" box, summarizing the debate in the context of the larger budget. It could say something like: "State lawmakers are trying to figure out how much to spend on road construction next year, as part of a debate over the $35 billion state budget. Some people are calling for an increase to $3 billion to help ease traffic congestion around big cities, including new lanes for Main Highway downtown. But others want to keep spending steady to keep taxes low and pay for other services."

■ A "How it works" box, explaining the legislative process: "The governor asked for $2.7 billion for roads in her budget proposal last month. The legislature uses that proposal as a starting place, but can change the budget however it wants. Transportation committees in the state House and Senate came up with their own figures, and then each house voted on them. Now a committee of lawmakers is trying to agree on a budget that both houses will approve and send back to the governor. She can sign the budget into law, reject it with a veto, or use her 'line-item veto' to approve the overall budget while cutting out specific expenses she dislikes. It takes a two-thirds vote of the legislature to override a veto."

■ A "What's that mean?" box defining important terms like bill, committee, appropriations, veto, override.

■ A "Key players" box with short bios and job descriptions on the governor, the House and Senate leaders, the chairs of the legislative conference committees, and leading citizen activists involved in the process.

■ A "Pros and cons" box that outlines the good and bad parts of major proposals, including which road projects would be funded, whether taxes or fees would be raised, what other services might be cut, etc.

■ A "Contact" box that tells readers how to get in touch with their representatives to make sure their interests are carried into the debate.

All this work entails is thinking carefully about the questions a person would have about the process, issues and people involved, and answering them. None of this information gets in the way for people who pay a lot of attention. And none of it insults or talks down to people who don't know, although throwing out too much at once could be overwhelming.

Making a regular effort to educate does require an investment of space that can lead to tighter stories or slimmer selection when news hole is at a premium. But when the choice is between presenting news that readers understand and respond to or merely dumping raw data onto a page, a smaller count of more meaningful stories serves readers better. And remember your Web site offers unlimited space to share background information that doesn't make it into print.

The day after the 2004 vice presidential debate, the *Lansing State Journal* reached out to the uninterested public with an info box headlined "Why you should care." The box, which ran with the wire story covering the event, offered several reasons why the debate was an important part of the campaign, including the vice president's growing influence on public policy, the possibility that a VP could ascend to the presidency, and the effect the debate could have on the campaigns' momentum.[16]

Here's a box from *The State News* that same fall, laying out the issues on a state referendum over gay marriage:

Proposal 2

"The union of one man and one woman in marriage shall be the only agreement recognized as a marriage or similar union for any purpose."

Reasons people will vote yes:

■ To reiterate [...] the definition of marriage as a union between one man and one woman

■ To help ensure children have parents of both genders

■ Some religions oppose same-sex couples

Reasons people will vote no:

■ To help protect the future of domestic-partnership benefits

■ To help ensure children of unmarried couples receive health-care benefits

■ To support the LBGT community and same-sex couples.[17]

The word choice for those headers — "Reasons people will vote yes," as opposed to "Supporters say" or similar wording — is a very clarifying way to deliver the arguments. The structure invites readers to decide: Which reasons best reflect my point of view?

When Indio, Calif., was searching for a new city manager, *The Desert Sun* realized that many readers might not know what a city manager does. So the paper ran a box explaining the job with a story on the City Council deciding to pay a consultant to find candidates. The box listed the manager's duties, including enforcing the city's laws, supervising department heads, advising the City Council, and preparing budgets.[18] Armed with that information, the casual reader can better understand why it's important to hire the right person.

It's unwise to expect most readers to understand developing political news without giving them a primer on the basics. Showing how things work at the same time you tell what just happened means more people can join the conversation.

The Q&A

One of the best formats for educating readers is the question and answer. Rather than trying to impose a false story structure on basic information, the Q&A simply anticipates what newcomers to the issue would want to know, and fills them in. This format predated the now ubiquitous "frequently asked questions" features on Web sites, but the FAQ has probably helped legitimize the traditional Q&A.

The *Detroit Free Press* has made frequent use of this format, including on its front page. In many cases, the reporters putting together the Q&A assume the role of expert, presenting the questions and answers with minimal quotes or attribution. "We call it writing with authority," said former *Free Press* Publisher and Editor Carole Leigh Hutton.[19] Hutton said the question-and-answer format works best when "a subject is complicated and you can help readers understand. … The Q&A format allows you to maximize the information in limited space. You're not worrying about transitions and quotes, just details. You can also write them in a more conversational style, which is the way readers digest them best."

Dawson Bell, whose coverage of the gay marriage issue we explored in Chapter 3, also did a Q&A about Proposal 2, the ballot question seeking to define marriage in Michigan as only between one man and one woman. The story answered such questions as what the amendment would say, what it would do and why people thought it was necessary.

In coming up with the questions, Bell got feedback from his editor and others in the newsroom. Staffers wanted to explain the issue thoroughly, Bell said, because though it was a controversial topic that most people had an opinion about, not everyone understood the details and potential consequences of the proposal. "While they were vaguely aware this was going on," Bell said, "… an awful lot of people didn't have a very firm understanding of what it was at all."[20]

Bell's Q&A was written with the authority Hutton mentioned above, quoting the occasional expert but relying primarily on his own knowledge and synthesis of the issues. "We're relying on readers to trust us a little more than maybe we would for other kinds of things in which we do directly quote experts," Bell said. "I think it's easier to read and understand than having a thicket of boring experts."

Maps and bio boxes

In 2004, the *Chicago Tribune* published a project exploring radical Islam and its impact on the West. The 12-installment series took readers to places they had never been, or even heard of, and described how these places, their people, and their cultures made a difference in Americans' lives. Here's an editor's note introducing one of the stories, which was reported from Araouane, Mali:

> It's doubtful that most Americans could find Mali on a map. Racked by poverty, decades of dictatorship and illiteracy, the West African nation is hardly a name on everyone's lips. There are two reasons why Americans should pay attention to Mali, though. It is one of the few places in the world where Islam and democracy prosper together, and it is the newest but least-known theater in a global war on terrorism and Islamic extremism. In this 10th part of an occasional series, a Tribune correspondent finds a U.S. ambassador in Mali who battles militants with wells and pumps.[21]

Accompanying these stories were beautiful maps, placing the unfamiliar location in a geographic context readers could understand, along with text explaining the characteristics of the country and its region. A map of Iran also explains the difference between Sunni and Shiite Muslims and breaks down Iran's population, government type, literacy and poverty rates, industries, and economic output.

Maps might be the single most underused tool journalists have for helping people understand the world. A map that shows a story's location in relation to a larger region — along with why-should-I-care information about who lives in the country, its relationship with the United States, and what issues the two countries are trying to work out — can build knowledge and help readers understand the value of international news.

The *Chicago Tribune*'s daily news-lite tabloid, *RedEye*, which I'll talk more about in Chapter 15, runs maps at the top of its news pages labeled "F.Y.I Nation" and "F.Y.I. World." Numbered stories correspond to numbers graphically pinned on the U.S. and world maps, so readers can spot where the news is taking place.[22] Another paper that does it is *The Bay City Times* in Michigan, which runs a small map of the world atop its "Global report" briefs package, and keys each brief by number to a spot on the map.[23]

Late 2004 was a major occasion for maps, as towering waves resulting from an Indian Ocean earthquake killed an estimated 200,000 people in about a dozen countries. A few days after the earthquake, as the death toll was still mounting, the *Lansing State Journal* ran a four-column-wide map on its front page showing the nations struck by the waves, from Indonesia, Malaysia, and Thailand to the African nations of Somalia, Kenya, and Tanzania. Different colors highlighted the affected nations and the worst-hit areas. Under each country's name was its population and the known number of dead at the time.[24] As is often the case with devastating news stories, this disaster became a powerful moment to teach about the geological forces that created the tsunami and a vast geographical region unfamiliar to most American readers.

But foreign nations shouldn't be the only places mapped out in the newspaper. From the survey at the top of this chapter, it's clear that many readers need help placing states and

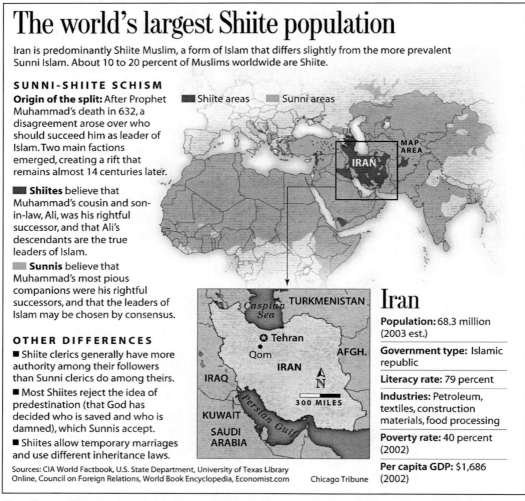

The world's largest Shiite population

Iran is predominantly Shiite Muslim, a form of Islam that differs slightly from the more prevalent Sunni Islam. About 10 to 20 percent of Muslims worldwide are Shiite.

SUNNI-SHIITE SCHISM

Origin of the split: After Prophet Muhammad's death in 632, a disagreement arose over who should succeed him as leader of Islam. Two main factions emerged, creating a rift that remains almost 14 centuries later.

■ **Shiites** believe that Muhammad's cousin and son-in-law, Ali, was his rightful successor, and that Ali's descendants are the true leaders of Islam.

■ **Sunnis** believe that Muhammad's most pious companions were his rightful successors, and that the leaders of Islam may be chosen by consensus.

OTHER DIFFERENCES

■ Shiite clerics generally have more authority among their followers than Sunni clerics do among theirs.

■ Most Shiites reject the idea of predestination (that God has decided who is saved and who is damned), which Sunnis accept.

■ Shiites allow temporary marriages and use different inheritance laws.

■ Shiite areas   ■ Sunni areas

IRAN

TURKMENISTAN

Caspian Sea

● Tehran

Qom

AFGH.

IRAN

IRAQ

N

300 MILES

KUWAIT

Persian Gulf

SAUDI ARABIA

Iran

Population: 68.3 million (2003 est.)

Government type: Islamic republic

Literacy rate: 79 percent

Industries: Petroleum, textiles, construction materials, food processing

Poverty rate: 40 percent (2002)

Per capita GDP: $1,686 (2002)

Sources: CIA World Factbook, U.S. State Department, University of Texas Library Online, Council on Foreign Relations, World Book Encyclopedia, Economist.com   Chicago Tribune

The *Chicago Tribune* used graphics to teach readers about Muslim populations throughout the world in a 2004 series. (Reprinted with permission of the *Chicago Tribune*)

cities in their own country. So a map locating and describing, say, the state of New Jersey, would help at least the 70 percent of young Americans who couldn't find that state when prompted.

Teaching the newspaper

After a session of my Michigan State ethics class in October 2004, a student approached and asked me to explain how *The State News*, MSU's student newspaper, could claim to be fair and nonpartisan in its election coverage when its editorial page had just endorsed John Kerry for president. She was incredulous, after all our class discussions about journalists avoiding conflicts of interest and refraining from any public support for politicians, that a newspaper staff would announce its preference for one candidate.

I explained to her that most newspapers endorse candidates for office, using a process —

and usually journalists — entirely separate from the news gathering and presentation process. I pointed out that newspaper opinion pages take sides every day on something the paper's news reporters had covered without expressing an opinion or showing favoritism for one side. I said the institutional voice of a newspaper offers an informed perspective on important issues that helps readers reach their own conclusions.

I don't think I convinced the student that editorial endorsements are a good idea, which is fine; the effectiveness and propriety of newspaper endorsements is debated at least once every four years. What was surprising was her lack of knowledge about how newspapers work — about the care nearly all papers take to separate news gathering from editorial writing, about the distinct functions of the news and opinion pages, about the plain normalness of a political endorsement in an election year. And this wasn't a person coming in off the street. She was a senior in journalism at a major university.

Just imagine how little the average person knows about how newspapers work, about all the processes that newspaper people take for granted. Half a century ago, newspapers explained themselves less than they do now — partly because they had a different attitude toward readers but primarily because newspaper reading was part of the culture, and the idea that news goes on the front page and opinions go on the editorial page and advertisements play a different role than news copy were passed from parents to children and absorbed in the same way young people today learn to use a computer mouse.

But a majority of people no longer read newspapers every day. And it's a big mistake for news people to assume that readers intuitively grasp subtle differences in content from the front to the back of the A-section — or even the values that journalists bring to their work. Part of the reason for so much distrust of journalists these days may simply be a lack of understanding of what journalism is, what it's for, and how it works.

So newspapers should take the same stance toward educating readers about themselves as about other important institutions. They should regularly explain their processes and methods, identify the purpose of news and opinion pages, talk about the role advertising plays and its separateness (we hope) from news decisions. When the newspaper makes a difficult or controversial decision, when it chooses to identify a rape victim or not identify a government whistleblower, when it decides to run or withhold a controversial photograph, its editors should take the time to describe the decision-making process and justify the decision.

Explaining how the paper works can be as simple as a daily reminder about the functions of certain departments. The *Wisconsin State Journal*, for instance, runs this statement in the box listing its editorial board on its editorial page: "Opinions above are shaped by the board, independent of news coverage decisions elsewhere in the newspaper."[25] That's not going to make readers newspaper experts overnight, but it's useful guidance.

Here's how Ed Ronco, *The State News* editor in fall 2004, responded to reader questions about the paper's endorsement of John Kerry:

> We at The State News have received a lot of feedback regarding our Oct. 27 editorial endorsement of Democratic Sen. John Kerry for President of the United States.
> Some of your letters have expressed dismay at how the editorial board could

Singing the First Amendment
Q&A with Gene Policinski, director of the First Amendment Center

Policinski hosts "Freedom Sings," a raucous touring show that blends live musical performances with education about the five freedoms — religion, speech, press, assembly and petition — protected by the First Amendment. The project grew out of an annual concert The First Amendment Center puts on in Nashville and the lectures on freedom that Policinski and former center director Ken Paulson were called upon to deliver. Paulson wrote a script merging the history and meaning of the First Amendment with a series of censored and controversial songs from American culture, and the show developed into a program that spreads the word about free expression. In November 2004, I talked to Policinskii about how journalists can adapt the spirit of Freedom Sings to help educate audiences about democracy. Here is part of our conversation, edited for length and clarity.

What is the feeling that you want people to leave "Freedom Sings" with?

I think we want them, first of all, to recognize and sort of get re-energized about the whole idea of freedom, and free speech, and free expression. We know from our annual State of the First Amendment survey only one out of 100 Americans can name all five freedoms unaided, and this year [2004] showed one out of three thought the First Amendment goes too far in the rights it guarantees. We want to point out to people … what they would have lost had they not been able to hear these songs, if someone had been able to censor these words or these ideas. I think by pointing out that gospel music is religion and songs like Stevie Wonder's "Happy Birthday," which was a call for the nation to recognize Martin Luther King's birthday, is a form of petition set to music — I think they get an appreciation of all five freedoms of the First Amendment, and they leave excited about it and they see the value of it.

What can somebody who writes for a newspaper do to promulgate that same spirit?

Well I think we can look for opportunities to … point out when the public has been served by open records or open comment. I think we can rigorously defend the right of newspeople but also the public to attend public meetings. I think we can occasionally celebrate the diversity of our society, the diversity of religion, the diversity of voices. I think newspeople sometimes only see the First Amendment in light of a free press and forget there are four other freedoms that are all sort of hanging together.

You worked for *USA Today* for quite awhile. … Can you think of things in your own experience as a newspaper person where you or people who worked with you endeavored to apply this kind of spirit?

No, unfortunately I think it's just the opposite. … I look at my journalism career and I'm embarrassed that I didn't make more of the opportunities I had to talk about free expression. ... I'm not the first one to say this, of course, but I think Americans take our personal freedoms, individual freedoms for granted. And I think celebrating those, talking openly about where there are problems, where there needs to be a balancing of the right of free press and fair trial, to pull out an example — we need to talk about that more. And what we create is a climate of ignorance and fear when we don't educate about it, we don't talk about it. And I think the First Amendment loses right off the bat if that's the climate.

It seems like a lot of newspapers are working a little harder on the education aspect.

I think newspapers are getting it, and I think in part because they've seen numbers like our surveys where consistently [nearly four out of 10] Americans say the press in America has too much freedom. ... And that's just an incredible number. Part of it is I think they don't understand the role of a free press. For example, they don't understand why we're there at trials. They may see us, because of several high-profile trials, as kind of headline-mongering, insensitive ambulance chasers. They don't understand the founders put that in there because they came out of an environment where there were star chambers, and manipulated courts, and they wanted a free and independent press to be in that courtroom to balance in some way the power of government. But we don't talk about that.

Is there a way that reporters — say you're a city council reporter — can approach news stories about city council that would do more to engage an unengaged public?

I think everybody is concerned about where their tax money goes. I think everybody would like to know if anybody's getting any special treatment in some area. I think ... people would love to know about the successful things government is doing. When we talk about auditing or watch-dogging government, I think there's a correlating responsibility to say, you know, there was a million dollars wasted on this bridge project, but I think you need to say also this child-care effort is really succeeding and 15,000 kids have got hot meals every year because of this program. ... All of that is a watchdog on government; it's not always negative.

Can you imagine anything that could show up in a newspaper that would have the kind of emotional impact that Freedom Sings does? Can you envision a kind of project or presentation or something that would have that invigorating impact on people?

I think celebrating diversity and celebrating the multiplicity of voices in most communities, having a program or a show that just says, this is who we are and we all live together, and we can all get together, and we celebrate our diversity — I think that's one way. I don't think every editor ought to go out and get a band and go touring, but I do think that editorials recognizing people who speak out — maybe there's an annual award or awards dinner for a group of people who have taken a leadership role in public life, like speaking out, and celebrate their powerful voices. I think there are a number of those kind of ... things that could be done. I think newspapers just need to get off their collective behinds and do them.

endorse Kerry over President Bush. We welcome that dissent and respect that opinion.

But much of the correspondence we have received has been from people concerned we would endorse a presidential candidate at all, and that doing so compromises the integrity of State News journalists and the newspaper as a whole.

Many readers have told us that by coming out in favor of a candidate on our Opinion page, our news coverage is forever tainted.

I, and we at The State News, wholeheartedly disagree, and here's why:

The State News, like many newspapers in the United States, has issued endorsements — again, contained only and ever on our Opinion page — in many races. We've shown support for Rep. Mike Rogers, R-Brighton and State Rep. Gretchen Whitmer, D-East Lansing. We have backed Proposal 1 and vigorously opposed Proposal 2. Readers have agreed and disagreed with each of those decisions. Only upon our endorsement of Kerry did we receive feedback questioning the very notion of the endorsement itself.

The State News editorial board operates independently of our news desks. As editor in chief, it's my job to oversee the newsroom side of The State News. I have final say over all content in the newspaper. But I delegate news selection duties to the managing editor, Brian Charlton, and the section editors.

At larger newspapers, the editorial board is completely separated from the news staff. Smaller newspapers, The State News among them, often have employees who serve dual purposes.

We ensure that those on the editorial board remove themselves from conversations that could enter their area of coverage.

If anything, our news coverage has been criticized by both sides of this election. I have taken phone calls from people who feel we are a blatantly pro-Kerry newspaper, as well as those who feel we are leading a clear-cut campaign to ensure the re-election of President Bush.

So why do editorial boards endorse candidates at all? Well, just as a primary role of an Opinion page is to provide a forum for discussion, an equally important role is to help readers make informed decisions.

Our newspaper has resources that can do just that. The State News editorial board invited candidates for the 8th U.S. House, the 69th State House and the MSU Board of Trustees to interview with us. As a newspaper, we have easy access to the candidates and can listen to their views and make an informed decision ourselves.

Obviously, chances were slim that President Bush and Kerry would visit The State News offices for an endorsement interview. For the presidential endorsement, we sat down and talked about the candidates' platforms based on research from their respective Web sites, which both campaigns point to as a comprehensive list of each candidate's views on major issues.

Newspapers across the country are making their own voices heard. According to Editor & Publisher magazine's Web site, by Thursday afternoon,

291 newspapers across the country had issued endorsements in the race for the White House.

Endorsing a candidate is a common and old practice for newspapers.

Aly Colón is the ethics group leader at The Poynter Institute, a Florida-based nonprofit organization for the education and development of journalists. He said it's easy for readers to misunderstand the separation between the Opinion and news sections.

"When you have this kind of division in one institution, it can be a little confusing to wonder, 'How can you have an opinion about something and say you can be fair?'" Colón said.

For that reason, he said, it's important that newspapers make the difference abundantly clear. "The key thing is that people understand that there is this separation and that the institutional voice of the paper is not something that will be reflected or of influence to the news portion," Colón said.

My hope is that The State News makes its division abundantly clear and that our Opinion page can continue to get all of you talking about the issues. There are two editions left before the polls close for 2004. Will you be heard?[26]

One powerful way of educating people about the inner workings of the newspaper is to try what *The Spokesman-Review* of Spokane, Wash., is doing on its Web site. The paper started an "Ask the Editors" feature, inviting questions that are then answered by senior editors online. The feature, whose topics range from why the newspaper identifies criminal suspects to why it shows "favoritism" for one high school team over another, gets a couple of hundred page views a day, said Ken Sands, the paper's online publisher.[27]

But "Ask the Editors" was just the beginning. In spring 2005, the paper also launched a blog, or running online journal, in which five readers critique the daily paper. "That will be controversial," Sands said before the blog launched. "I hope it lasts." And, to really bring readers in on the daily conversation of what makes news and how to present it, the paper began blogging its news meetings — revealing its story lineup for the next day's paper and inviting readers to offer feedback in real time. That brings the education loop full circle, as *Spokesman-Review* editors can learn from their readers even as they make news decisionmaking more transparent. We'll talk more about how the Web is transforming communication between journalists and readers in Chapter 14.

IT'S NOT AN OVERSTATEMENT, and it's not an insult, to say we should present the news as though potential readers know very little about the issues, people, and processes we're covering, or the structure and function of the medium it's packaged in. If readers are turned off of the news because it seems we're talking to someone else, we may be able to turn them on by talking to them — not down to them, but *to* them.

After all, we're here to help.

How to teach

■ Don't just *cover* public affairs news, *explain* it. Use facts boxes and graphics instead of bogging down the story. Be willing to use this background information over and over.

■ Present information for people with different levels of knowledge, at different levels of engagement with an issue. Plan important stories first to build awareness, then to help people understand a range of views, and finally to provide detailed information for people who've come to master the issue.

■ Run a lot of maps. Show the location of the story in its geographic context, ideally in relation to where your readers are. Include political and historical background, so people understand how this place affects their community.

■ Run bio boxes of organizations, countries, and people you're writing about. Doing a story on Indonesia? Run a little encyclopedia-style box with its size (compare it to the size of the United States or an individual state), its population, the status of its trade and political relationship with the United States, principle languages and religions, and whatever else seems appropriate to the story. Writing about your state's secretary of state's office? Run a box explaining the office's responsibilities (often things like driver's licenses, voter registration and other record-keeping duties), its annual budget, number of employees, and maybe local office locations.

■ Use the question-and-answer format — an age-old way of sharing basic information popularized by Web sites' frequently asked questions. Q&A's work best when you're presenting an overview or introduction to a complex issue, rather than reporting on a newsy development. Q&A's with newsmakers are a good way to let important people speak at length on an important issue.

■ Explain the unfamiliar using familiar terms and images: A *State News* story on homelessness, a problem foreign to most college students, made sense of the number of homeless people in Michigan — an estimated 39,000 to 43,000, by saying, "Almost as many people are homeless in Michigan as attend MSU..."[28]

■ Help readers understand your news organization. Explain how different parts of the paper operate, reminding readers of the separation between news, advertising, and editorial departments.

For thought and action...

1 Interview a professor of education or psychology about how people learn. Ask him or her what journalists can do to build readers' knowledge about public issues and institutions.

2 Think of an important issue in your community. List as many information boxes as you can think of to help people learn about the issue.

3 Take an informal poll of non-journalists about their understanding of newspapers. Ask questions like: What is a newspaper's primary purpose? What is the purpose of a news story? What is the purpose of an editorial? What is the purpose of an advertisement? Who writes the editorials? Collect and discuss the answers. Based on the misconceptions you hear, think of ways for newspapers to explain themselves better.

4 List the major government and civic institutions in your community, including the city council, school board, planning commission, chamber of commerce, service organizations, significant charities. Compile a short bio box about each organization, describing what it is, what it does, and who's in charge of it, that could run along with stories about the organization.

Chapter 6

Help People Act

What good is a bunch of facts if we don't know what to do with a bunch of facts?
— Nicole Schilt, Michigan State University journalism student[1]

Every day, readers of *The Journal Times* in Racine, Wis., are confronted with a question. They don't know what it'll be, but they know they'll be asked to step up and consider it:

Should students be involved in politics on school time?

Should it be illegal to hunt live animals over the Internet?

Should communities ban smoking in workplaces?

The questions come in the form of front-page headlines and stories that take an issue of the day and turn it into a conversation piece. The philosophy behind this feature, "Debatable," is a simple, active invitation to readers: Take this issue. Learn about it. Stake out a position. Defend it.

Here's what one of these stories looks like:

> MADISON — With gas prices hovering near record levels, two state law-makers on Monday announced they'll try to do something about it.
>
> They want to allow gas stations to sell gas at cheaper prices, even if it means undercutting smaller stations and putting them out of business. To make this happen, the state would need to repeal its minimum markup law that regulates gasoline prices.
>
> The act would allow more competition, but small gas stations oppose the proposal because it would favor larger stations that could charge less and make-up the difference by selling more. One example: Wal-Mart uses this model to steal home goods business from competitors.
>
> Should the state repeal the minimum markup? At issue is a law, also [known] as the unfair sales act, which requires wholesalers to mark up their prices by at least 3 percent and retailers by at least 6 percent. Consumers could save more than $50 million a year on gasoline purchases under the proposal...[2]

"Debatable" takes a routine news story — usually an issue being considered by public officials — and thrusts it into the hands of the people. It functions on the presumption detailed in Chapter 1 that every citizen has an equal share of political power in a democracy, and it lobs one hot potato after another into the laps of everyday folks. The idea is a great stride for participatory democracy, and it also builds on research showing that people are more likely to read a paper regularly if they believe reading makes them smarter and gives them something to talk about. In an effort to create those experiences, Debatable frames stories in a way that "both educates and enhances discussion," said *Journal Times* Editor Randolph Brandt.[3] Brandt said the feature has gotten a good response.

"[P]eople sometimes approach us now with a story idea using the parlance, 'It would make a good Debatable,'" Brandt said. "We ask readers to respond to our Debatables with a little break-out directing them to our Debatable page online, and Debatable is consistently one of our top hits at Journaltimes.com. We then run selected responses in the paper. "

This idea of giving readers something to talk about, and something to do with what they've learned, is part of a broader theory that news is more meaningful and engaging if readers can use it in their lives — if you give them a number to call, an address to visit, a place to send money, a forum for comment, a meeting to attend, a play to watch, a book to read, or tips to occupy children on a car trip. Adding utility to news reports is a simple way to make newspapers dynamic and broaden civic participation at the same time.

Helping readers act on the news is an extension of all the values we have discussed so far. It's the culmination of the process that begins with recognizing that people are in charge of their lives and their democracy. Information without action is an intellectual exercise, which may be personally enriching but lacks impact. Alerting people to their role in a democracy, identifying and framing public problems, helping them understand those problems and showing them choices and consequences are all ways to lead your citizen-horses to water. It is only fitting that you should invite them to drink — give them something to *do* with the facts you've reported. "[If] you feel a part of this report, this issue, this story, this council action, then you actually become engaged," said Tom Warhover, executive editor of the *Columbia Missourian*. "...If I'm not a passive spectator, then I might actually see a place for me in my community."[4]

Debatable

Debatables portray different sides of an issue to encourage debate around the news of the day. What do you think about today's topic? Send your opinions to Debatable, 212 Fourth St., Racine, WI 53403 or via e-mail to: debatable@journaltimes.com To vote on today's Debatable, go to: www.journaltimes.com

Gas cap?

Should state repeal its minimum markup law for gasoline?

BY TOM SHEEHAN
Lee Newspapers

MADISON — With gas prices hovering near record levels, two

The Journal Times uses its "Debatable" stories to get readers involved in public issues. (Reprinted with permission of The Journal Times.)

Every public decision offers opportunities for individuals to chime in, through public hearings, contacting legislators, volunteering, donating money, etc. As a journalist, you can assume that interested readers will find these opportunities for themselves — or you can turn your passive report into an active one. In 1996, as *The Virginian-Pilot* was defining literacy, utility, and mastery and rethinking how it packaged the news, the paper developed standards for making information useful:

> 1. In reporting and presenting every story, we should identify the range of actions a reader could take in response and, whenever appropriate, provide the who, what, when, where, why and how that supports action.
>
> 2. Information for readers' use should be easy to [find] in the newspaper — highlighted in summary boxes or in high-visibility displays. Drawing readers' attention to something they can do — watch a television broadcast related to a story, for example — could increase their stake in the story itself.
>
> 3. In covering storms, disasters, emergencies, elections, openings, closings and other action-oriented news, we should keep our primary focus on what can or should be done now and what can be expected to happen next. Recounting what happened yesterday is vital but should not overwhelm or edge out actionable information.[5]

Readers who don't get this kind of information, especially after being inspired by a story, can become frustrated. Listen to this appeal from a letter-writer responding to an editorial about the Kyoto Protocol, an international agreement to reduce global warming:

> … I'm outraged that the United States refuses to be a part of this policy. Even more bothersome is the fact that The State News has provided the reader with almost no guidance in how to support this protocol. You say, "it's up to us as citizens to do what we can to cut emissions, both on a personal and governmental level." We live less than five minutes from the state Capitol. There must be someone down the road that has some authority in regards [to] the subject matter.
>
> At the bottom of the editorial, why not provide us with information like phone numbers and e-mail addresses? As a newspaper I assume you're fairly good at acquiring information and then providing it for other people to use. If it is true that 90 percent of MSU students voted in this year's election, we obviously care about this nation. Let our voices continue to be heard by giving us the information necessary to make a change. …[6]

It doesn't take much to add an action component to your journalism. *The Journal Times'* "Debatable" feature takes an ordinary news story and shifts the frame just slightly — by asking a direct question — to get readers involved. News organizations can also use their resources and influence to amplify the voices of people seeking civic action. In *The Virginian-Pilot,* columnist John Warren plays the role of "Pilot Warrior," who acts as a high-profile middleman between the Citizen and City Hall. When people spot poorly kept properties, missing signs, and dangerous intersections, they call on Warren, whose highly publicized column tends to speed up government responses. The megaphone effect is heightened by a "Who's responsible?" box that runs with each column, naming the public official empowered to solve the problem and listing the official's phone number and e-mail address.

When the problem is addressed, the Pilot Warrior gives an update:

Donald Karnes of Chesapeake wrote on June 24 about the northbound off-ramp from the Chesapeake Expressway onto Hillcrest Parkway. He observed vehicles turning up the off-ramp, believing it to be an entrance to the parking lot at the new Home Depot. "Despite the fact there are 'Do Not Enter' signs posted there, not everyone is always paying attention" or being observant, Karnes wrote.

On Thursday [June 30], Chesapeake traffic engineers said they will move an existing "No Right Turn" sign back to improve its visibility, and will add "through arrow" pavement markings before the intersection to keep motorists from turning onto the ramp. On Friday, Department of Public Works spokesman Harry Kenyon wrote to say city crews were already putting down the pavement markings.[7]

That's using the power of the press to help everyday folks improve their communities. Here's another example, where journalism spotlights citizens' push to change a City Council policy:

What happens when the public's chance to comment comes at the end of Janesville City Council meetings?

Some have complained that issues are already decided by the time the council gets there.

What's ironic about that?

The council will discuss changing the public comment period Monday, but the public won't get to comment until the discussion is over.

Brad Munger, a Janesville resident, left a council meeting frustrated some months ago when he didn't get a chance to weigh in on a controversial issue. The council was deciding whether to give public funds to the Salvation Army, which has a religious mission.

"If the city council is going to act on behalf of the city, the people of the city should have an opportunity to give input," Munger said. "If we are excluded from that process, this is an independent board operating without the guidance of the citizenry."

Munger said he knew of others at that same meeting who wanted to speak but didn't get a chance before the vote was taken.

City staff is recommending that the public comment period be moved to the beginning of the meeting with one change: Residents would be allowed to address only items on that night's agenda. [...].[8]

The story also featured a box giving the time and place of the meeting and a rundown of public comment rules for 13 other cities, so readers could compare. The follow-up story, two days later, recounted Janesville's decision to change its policy, then explained the new rules in an info box. The people had spoken.

Showing the way

Generally, helping people act is a simple matter of thinking about the next step a reader can take if she's interested in your story. The extra bit of information giving the time, date and place of an event; or phone numbers and e-mail addresses of the people in charge; or tips on how to maneuver through government red tape, can add a whole new dimension to a story with very little effort.

TAX TIPS

WHERE TO FIND FORMS
■ Local post offices
■ East Lansing Public Library, 950 Abbott Road. (Costs 10 cents per page)
■ Online at **www.irs.gov**

E-FILING
As of Wednesday, Michigan had more e-file returns than any other state except for California and New York, state Treasury Department spokesman Terry Stanton said.

To file tax returns electronically, visit **www.mi.gov/treasury** or **www.irs.gov**. Depending on qualifications, it could be free.

If you send a paper return and require a paper refund check, you'll have to wait about 10 weeks for the money, said Sarah Wreford, an Internal Revenue Service spokeswoman in Michigan. Or, you can get your refund in about 10 days by e-filing. The refund is transferred electronically into a bank account.
If you don't receive your refund after the expected time, you can call **(800) 829-1954** to check the status of the refund. Your Social Security number, filing status and exact amount of refund are needed.

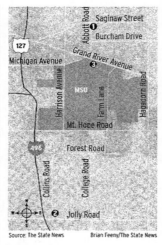

Source: The State News   Brian Feeny/The State News

EXTENSION
Extensions are only for filing, and if you expect to owe money, you must send the estimated amount with the four-month extension request, Wreford said.
File an extension request by midnight Friday to avoid failure to file penalties.
■ Get Form 4868 from **www.irs.gov**.
■ Have a copy of last year's tax return.
■ Call **(888) 796-1074** for further instructions.

TAX FILING HELP
The MSU College of Law Tax Clinic, 541 E. Grand River Ave.
■ Prepares tax returns for people

LOCAL POST OFFICES
If you're going to get your taxes in on time, you'd better get to the post office before close on Friday.

1. East Lansing Post Office
1140 Abbott Road
Hours: 7:30 a.m. - 5 p.m.

2. Lansing Post Office
4800 Collins Road
Hours: 7 a.m. - 7 p.m., today
7 a.m. - midnight, Friday

3. MSU Union Post Office
On the first floor
Hours: 7 a.m. - 5 p.m.
Note: mail pick-up time is at 4 p.m.

who use English as a second language.
■ Open from 9 a.m. to 5 p.m. today and Friday, but is only offering help with extensions.
■ There is a nominal charge to offset costs. Charges are waived if someone can't afford them, said Michele Halloran, associate law professor and director of the clinic.

H&R Block, 1122 W. Holmes Road, Suite 21 in Lansing
■ Prepares tax returns, takes appointments and walk-ins.
■ Open from 9 a.m. to 9 p.m. today and Friday.
■ Basic federal tax filing starts at $49.

Melissa Domsic

As the tax filing deadline approached, *The State News* helped last-minute filers prepare. (Reprinted with permission of *The State News*.)

Consider the *Grand Rapids Press* story about an award-winning author whose book of short stories for young people had been pulled from public school libraries after parents complained about sensitive content. Along with covering the debate, the paper ran a box listing visits the author had scheduled in the area the following month. That meant interested readers could not only monitor the debate through the news, but could meet the author and judge for themselves.[9]

It's hard to imagine a story that doesn't present some opportunity to get readers into the action, yet reporters and editors are selective about sharing these details. Ideally, no story should be considered complete until the reader has at least one tool to move forward.

Here are some other examples of ways you can help readers act on the news:

■ As winter weather settled over Michigan in December 2004, the *Lansing State Journal* devoted a corner of its front page to a stand-alone information box with the headline "GETTING HELP WITH HEATING BILLS." The box had a small illustration of a snow-covered house, a quote in large type from a 21-year-old unemployed resident — "My heating bill this month is $75 more than it was this time last year. If I don't get help, I will be sitting in the dark with blankets around me this winter" — tips on conserving energy, and a list of four programs that help people pay their utility bills, with phone numbers and a Web site for people who wanted to learn more.[10]

■ When the federal government proposed requiring Americans traveling to Canada, Mexico, and the Caribbean to present a passport to get back into the United States, *The State News* — just a 90-minute drive or so from Ontario, Canada — localized the story on its front page. With the story was a facts box detailing how to get a passport: where to go, what documentation to bring, and how much it would cost.[11]

■ Every year, homeowners all over the country get a dreaded notice from their local taxing authority: their new property assessment. Most of the time, unless the house has been abandoned or struck by lightning, its value has increased. And that means, even if nobody has raised the tax rate, homeowners will have higher tax bills. Many localities grow richer every year without ever voting to raise taxes because of appreciating property values. So for property owners, these assessments are a big deal. Many papers help readers act by walking them through the steps of appealing property tax assessments they think are too high. The Springfield, Mo., *News-Leader*, for instance, ran a sidebar to its assessment story describing where homeowners could appeal, how to set up an appointment, and what types of evidence (such as appraisals and sales data) might help make their case.[12]

Reacting to rapes
If you believe you have been assaulted or raped, do not shower or dispose of clothing, because they might be evidence.

Here are some places to turn for help:

● For assaults in progress, call 911
● MSU Sexual Assault Program 24-hour crisis line (517) 372-6666
● MSU Police Department, call (517) 355-2221 and say you want to privately make a sexual assault complaint
● East Lansing Police Department (517) 351-4220
● The Listening Ear (517) 337-1717
● Olin Health Center Information Nurse (517) 353-5558
● MSU Safe Place (517) 372-5572
● MSU Women's Resource Center (517) 353-1635
● The MSU Police Sexual Assault Response Guarantee states an officer will visit you anywhere if you don't feel comfortable coming into the station

Sources: MSU police, Olin Health Center

When a rash of sexual assaults were reported on the Michigan State campus in fall 2004, *The State News* ran a box on the front page listing eight ways to report an assault or seek support for victims. (Reprinted with permission of *The State News*.)

■ Recognizing that thousands of people in her community were eager to help victims of the Indian Ocean tsunami that devastated the eastern hemisphere in late 2004, columnist Andrea Ball of the *Austin American-Statesman* offered advice on giving — encouraging donors to research organizations before sending them a check, be wary of scams, and direct gifts specifically to tsunami relief so they wouldn't be used for other projects.[13] Hurricane Katrina's impact on the Gulf Coast in 2005 provided another grim opportunity for Americans to reach out — and another occasion for journalists to help them give effectively.

■ The *Quad-City Times* published a sample letter citizens could use to seek government information under Iowa's public-records law. This great idea enlists citizens as allies in the endless battle to keep government open and honest.[14]

■ Michigan State students were unusually primed to engage with government leaders in April 2005 after East Lansing police tear-gassed crowds following a Final Four basketball loss. MSU had a history of unruly student behavior, but on this night many witnesses said police were overly aggressive on a crowd that, by and large, was assembled peacefully to soak in the moment. In a short editorial, *The State News* encouraged dissatisfied students to let city officials know about it — and it listed names, numbers and e-mail addresses for City Council members, the police chief and the city manager.[15]

■ The *Wisconsin State Journal* invited readers to contribute comments to an online forum in a little box with a story about a proposal to require more disclosure from state contractors. The box, headlined "What do you think?" listed a Web address where readers could go and sound off.[16]

Taking the extra step to show readers what they can do, where they can go, who they can call, or how they can help create a dynamic relationship between your journalism and your audience. If you're not just a source of information but also a platform for action, your work's impact magnifies exponentially. All it takes is the sensibility to include a few extra nuggets of information, or to reframe a story so readers are encouraged to respond. Give people tools to use the "bunch of facts" you report, and they'll come back for more.

How to help people act

■ Find opportunities to involve readers in every story you write, and offer times, dates, places, Web sites, and phone numbers to help them.

■ Include public officials' contact information whenever you mention them in a story.

■ When you write about an issue that will be discussed at a public meeting, report when and where the meeting will be. Even better, add tips for how to speak at the meeting — how to sign up with the clerk, how long to talk, the best way to present a message that officials will take seriously (you could solicit these tips from the officials themselves), and how to follow up. This could be an info box you create once and run regularly with stories advancing city council, school board, or legislative hearings.

■ In stories about crimes, disasters, and social problems, provide a list of places where people can get or give help.

■ Offer readers a chance to comment through the paper, by telling them how to write letters to the editor or inviting them to an online discussion.

For thought and action...

1 Think of campus governing meetings that students can attend but usually don't: student government meetings, trustee or regent meetings, "meet the president" events. Create "how-to" boxes that explain how these events work and how a concerned person can speak up.

2 Brainstorm situations your campus paper writes about that could be accompanied by utility information: study tips to run with the story on finals week, tailgating tips to go with the Homecoming preview, advice from upperclassmen on strategies for picking classes, etc.

3 Interview five students you don't know about things they'd like to understand better about your school. What kinds of social events, academic opportunities, classes, or student groups would they be more likely to participate in if they knew more about how these things worked?

4 Identify five news stories in your local newspaper that could provide more information for readers to act on. List the questions that an info box for each story could answer.

Chapter 7

Refuse to Be Boring

It's easy enough to delight without instructing; but, boy, is it hard to instruct without some measure of delight.

— Roy Peter Clark, The Poynter Institute[1]

We need to identify more ways to drive up the cool factor. We need to go get readers where they are, not expect them to come to us where we are, which is stuck in the mid-20th century.

— Lex Alexander, Greensboro *News & Record*[2]

Being boring is unacceptable.

— Dennis Hartig, *The Virginian-Pilot*[3]

In the late 1990s, *The Virginian-Pilot* added a new line to its electronic news budgeting form, which reporters and editors use to describe and schedule stories. The earlier version of the budget line asked for a summary of the story; the name of the reporter, photographer, and assigning editor; an estimated length and delivery time; and descriptions of accompanying photos and graphics. But as the paper challenged its staff to think more deeply about getting readers interested in stories, another category of information became pertinent. So after summarizing their story at the top of the budget line, reporters now were asked: "What does it mean?"

As a metro editor, I read a lot of those budget lines and watched as the new item became a repository for wisecracks, sharp analysis, and blunt conclusions that might be useful to readers if they ever showed up in print. For the story description, the reporter would often just paste the first few paragraphs of her draft into the budget line. But in the "What it means" line, she'd get to the point. So you'd get something like this made-up example:

THE STORY: The City Council on Tuesday rescinded an ordinance requiring soft-serve ice cream vendors to submit to monthly inspections and lowered the sales tax on frozen treats to 3 percent. Councilman I.C. Creme, who sponsored the proposal, said the changes would reduce unnecessary regulations and help entrepreneurs stay in business. Opponents said the tax break unfairly advantages one type of business and the reduced inspections could create a health threat.

WHAT IT MEANS: A double-dip chocolate cone will cost less next summer, but it might make you sick.

On budget after budget, the "What it means" line would be shorter, clearer, more interesting, and more relevant than the top of the story itself. Many reporters considered the line a silly exercise, so they dropped their stiff news voice and wisecracked as a form of protest — but the result was more compelling, more readable copy. The phenomenon was so common that Editor Kay Tucker Addis brought it up in a memo to the staff: "Some of the most clever writing we do never gets published. That's because it's found in the budget lines, especially in the section asking this question: 'What's it mean?' The humor belongs in the paper, not the budget lines."[4]

The sentiment of that memo sums up the message of this chapter, and really the whole book: It's time to drop the pretenses of journalism and get in people's faces with the news. Writing like a diplomat will attract an audience of diplomats. Writing like a bureaucrat will attract an audience of bureaucrats. Writing like a politician will attract an audience of politicians. Writing like a *person* will attract an audience of people — including diplomats, bureaucrats, and politicians, but also including bus drivers, school teachers, airplane mechanics, doctors, machinists, accountants, and restaurateurs. The era of beating around the bush is over. It's time to tell it like it is. People may or may not like your take on any given story, but they will be more likely to understand it, more likely to form their own judgment — and more likely to come back for more the next day.

This doesn't mean you start calling the governor an idiot in your lead, or saying the mayor was right or wrong to suspend the police chief, or in any way inserting a partisan or policy-oriented opinion into your work. It does mean that it's OK to put a little of your personality in a story, dig down to what you perceive to be the heart of it, and tell that story. You must still be fair, accurate, and clear as the rules of journalism dictate. Credibility remains your greatest asset. But bluntly calling a situation as you see it shouldn't decrease your credibility; it should bolster the authenticity of your work. Think again of the referee analogy — a baseball umpire doesn't take sides, but every ump has a slightly different way of calling balls and strikes, or throwing somebody out of a game. Writing that's personally engaging, that communicates an impression from one human being to another, increases the chances that the important information you're presenting will be received.

I didn't always believe this about news writing. My journalism education is firmly rooted in the structure of the inverted pyramid, in which you tell the most important facts and back your way through a story until you get into details so mind-numbing that it's a crapshoot whether you run out of space before the reader loses consciousness. I believed in the importance of cramming all the five W's into that first sentence or two, getting as many facts out as quickly as possible, regardless of whether their arrangement was pleasing, compelling, or meaningful. The news was the news, not to be toyed with, dressed up, or presented in a way that would invite the uninterested reader to take a look at it.

I believed this through high school and well into college, straight through my appointment as campus editor of *The Daily Northwestern* in the spring of my sophomore year, when my co-editor at our first staff meeting encouraged the reporters to "take chances" with their writing and I blanched and balked and suggested they not take *too* many chances, hoping they wouldn't take any.

It was during that same term, when working on a research paper, that I sought out Northwestern University journalism Professor Richard Schwarzlose, a hard-nosed ethics teacher whom I perceived to be of the old school, to confirm my ideas that the journalism models of the mid-20th century were the only appropriate models for the 21st. But while Schwarzlose disparaged fledgling efforts to dumb down the news and pander to less engaged readers, he surprised me when he talked about how reporters and editors should go about their work. A purely detached news report awash in isolated facts and devoid of social feeling, democratic values, and deeper context was ineffective, he argued. "You cannot deal with complex subjects when the world is broken down in discrete quotations, and discrete facts," he said. Reporters needed the freedom to find and present the "real reality" of news, not just the "marketable reality." Each story must be written to reflect its unique circumstances, not to fit into a formula of what journalism is supposed to look like. If that meant delving into chronological narrative or a first-person account when the news called for it, so be it. Journalists had to exhibit the creativity and flexibility to bring reality home to readers who weren't necessarily looking for it, in a way that would make them pay attention.[5] That conversation was the seed of this book.

The sense of both desperation and possibility Schwarzlose expressed has manifested itself in a number of ways in the past decade or so, as newspapers have reacted to dwindling circulations and begun pursuing readers more aggressively. But the idea that vivid writing and storytelling can bring people back has not been tested nearly enough. The mentality that the most interesting way of telling the story has to stay in the "what it means" line of an internal news budget remains dominant. The exceptions prove the rule, as in fall 2004, when a *Wall Street Journal* reporter stationed in Baghdad wrote a personal e-mail to friends and family about how things were going for her in Iraq. The e-mail described in detail the fear, dread, and sense of hopelessness that correspondents and others living in Baghdad felt at the time. As personal correspondence, it was written in the first person. And it contained opinion, or at least authoritative statements, that few knowledgeable people would have disputed but which carried political weight in an election year. Here is the beginning of Farnaz Fassihi's e-mail:

> Being a foreign correspondent in Baghdad these days is like being under virtual house arrest. Forget about the reasons that lured me to this job: a chance to see the world, explore the exotic, meet new people in far away lands, discover their ways and tell stories that could make a difference.
>
> Little by little, day-by-day, being based in Iraq has defied all those reasons. I am house bound. I leave when I have a very good reason to and a scheduled interview. I avoid going to people's homes and never walk in the streets. I can't go grocery shopping any more, can't eat in restaurants, can't strike a conversation with strangers, can't go to scenes of breaking news stories, can't be stuck in traffic, can't speak English outside, can't take a road trip, can't say I'm an American, can't linger at checkpoints, can't be curious about what people are saying, doing, feeling. And can't and can't. There has been one too many close calls, including a car bomb so near our house that it blew out all the windows.

So now my most pressing concern every day is not to write a kick-ass story but to stay alive and make sure our Iraqi employees stay alive. In Baghdad I am a security personnel first, a reporter second. ...

Iraqis like to call this mess 'the situation.' When asked 'how are thing[s]?' they reply: 'the situation is very bad.'

What they mean by situation is this: the Iraqi government doesn't control most Iraqi cities, there are several car bombs going off each day around the country killing and injuring scores of innocent people, the country's roads are becoming impassable and littered by hundreds of landmines and explosive devices aimed to kill American soldiers, there are assassinations, kidnappings and beheadings. The situation, basically, means a raging barbaric guerilla war. In four days, 110 people died and over 300 got injured in Baghdad alone. The numbers are so shocking that the ministry of health — which was attempting an exercise of public transparency by releasing the numbers — has now stopped disclosing them.

Insurgents now attack Americans 87 times a day. ...[6]

When the e-mail appeared on the Poynter Online weblog Romenesko, it created a stir. Many people were critical of Fassihi for revealing her true feelings about Iraq and claimed her reporting for publication could no longer be trusted. Fassihi was vigorously defended by *Wall Street Journal* Managing Editor Paul Steiger, who vouched for the fairness of her reporting. Very shortly after the e-mail become public, Fassihi embarked on a three-week scheduled rotation out of Iraq, which allowed things to die down before she returned for more reporting.

One intriguing line of response to the e-mail, and the more prevalent one among people responding to Romenesko, was an expression of amazement that the kind of reporting Fassihi did in her personal e-mail was so much more vivid, meaningful and apparently truthful than the detached and dispassionate accounts that most newspaper correspondents were filing. There was a sense from reading Fassihi's e-mail that, yes, this must be what it's really like — which after all is the point of reporting from faraway places. A *Houston Chronicle* editorial said:

> Fact for fact, Fassihi's e-mail offers little that can't be found in published accounts. What has made it dart from Web site to Web site is the contrast of unvarnished personal expression with Fassihi's status as reporter for an establishment newspaper. What has made the piece resonate is that its voice was not meant for the public. ...
>
> In a bewildering, tragic conflict dominated by the loud sounds of polemics, the quiet tones of private communication suddenly seem to have unique credibility.[7]

Richard Schwarzlose, the Northwestern journalism professor, died in June 2003, more than a year before Fassihi's e-mail circulated, but I think it's the kind of journalism he would have applauded. Her piece reflected a sense of reality — a reality different from what many Americans stateside were familiar with or willing to accept, and a reality perhaps different from what many Americans serving in Iraq were experiencing, but a reality that reflected what many Iraqis and foreigners in that country saw and felt each day. The passage, though written from a point of view, is born of Kovach and Rosenstiel's "objective method," based on facts and experience that Fassihi and others in Baghdad exclusively held. It was an independent assessment that gave context to many official pronouncements of the time.

The e-mail's circulation and reception seemed to touch off a round of published first-person accounts from Iraq, in papers including *The Washington Post, The Philadelphia Inquirer* and, in January 2005, *The Wall Street Journal* itself, when Fassihi filed a personal account of Iraq's free elections:

> …Election Day was the most uplifting moment I've witnessed in the two years that I've been stationed in Iraq. I was here for the last Iraqi election, in October 2002, when Saddam [Hussein] held a referendum to solidify his rule. Then, there was one name on the ballot, and rejecting him meant retaliation no one dared to even ponder. …Since then, I have marked many milestones in Iraq since the war officially began in March 2003 — fall of the regime, killing of Saddam's sons Uday and Qussay, formation of the Governing Council, the capture of Saddam, the handover of sovereignty to an interim government and now the creation of a national assembly. None has captured the attention and imagination of Iraqis the way yesterday's elections did.
>
> Iraqis viewed those events with the skepticism and suspicion they always do for things forced upon them by an outside hand — in this case the Americans. It's difficult to predict what yesterday's election will mean in the coming months. The new government will continue to battle a raging insurgency, while negotiating a new constitution in hopes it will help restore the war-torn nation.
>
> But one thing is clear: Iraqis have finally broken from the past.[8]

The authority in this writing, the sense of commanding perspective born not of ideology but of observation and evidence, is one of many ways to present important news that widens the eyes of readers rather than narrowing them. We'll talk more about authority in this chapter, along with other aspects of reporting, writing, and presentation that break the boring mold of formulaic journalism.

Relevance

Here's a story:

> A woman drove herself to the hospital yesterday after feeling a sharp pain in her chest. Doctors don't know if anything serious is wrong with her. She was kept overnight for observation, which is routine. She's staying on the third floor. The room number is 322. It's a semi-private room, which means she's sharing it with one other person. The food is bland and unsatisfying. If there are no trouble signs by the end of the day, she'll be released. Otherwise, she'll remain for more tests.

Does this strike you as particularly interesting? Would you put it in the paper if you were an editor? Probably not. People get chest pains all the time. It's not clear that the woman is dying or even sick. There's no apparent value in knowing that she's on the third floor or has to share a room with someone else. These are just a bunch of facts with no connection to us.

But let's change this story ever so slightly. Go back and replace the reference to "a woman" with the name of your mother, sister or girlfriend — anyone you care about deeply — and read it again.

Is it interesting now? Do you care what the room number is? Do the quality of the food and living arrangements make a difference to you?

The answers now are probably yes. You want to visit your loved one in the hospital, so you need to know where to find her. You want her to be happy and comfortable, so her meals and her privacy are a concern.

And that, in a nutshell, is the difference between a news story that's interesting and one that isn't: personal relevance.

People want to know why the news affects them, where they fit in. The City Council vote to rezone property at the intersection of Maple and Sycamore isn't very interesting. But the fact that the rezoning will allow a new coffee shop, doubling traffic at that intersection during rush hour, makes a difference to readers who live or commute in the area. Frame the issue one way, and the square footage of the new building and the time and place of the public hearing are of no value. Frame it another way, and suddenly those details are important.

To demonstrate how a slight shift in presentation can change people's perceptions of relevance, consider a study by the Project for Excellence in Journalism, which tested the conventional wisdom among local TV news decision-makers that their audiences had no appetite for politics. The problem wasn't with the audience, the study concluded, but with the kinds of questions consultants were asking.

The standard viewer survey asked something like, "How interested are you in news reports on issues and activities in local government and politics?" In the Project for Excellence in Journalism survey, 34 percent of respondents said they were "very interested" in that topic. Twenty-nine percent were very interested in state government issues, and 36 percent in national government.[9] Those results average just about a third of viewers who said they were very interested in government reporting.

But the study found that more specific questions about government dramatically increased the number of "very interested" viewers. When the question was "How interested are you in news reports on what government can do to improve the performance of local schools?" 59 percent were "very interested." When the question was about how the government can reduce health care costs, it was 64 percent; on how government can prevent terrorism, it was 67 percent — about two out of three people.

That study demonstrates how easy it is to oversimplify survey results and draw unfortunate conclusions from imprecise questions. It's also a great illustration of how a slight shift in framing can double the number of people who find public affairs news relevant. So how do you present news in relevant ways? A couple of ideas:

Cover issues, not meetings

If a reporter heads off to "cover the City Council meeting," he's halfway to a boring story. Most meetings are dull, and are set up to be that way. The first 30 to 60 minutes of a typical city council or school board meeting are dominated by the Pledge of Allegiance, approval of the last meeting's minutes, the issuance of proclamations for Ear Health Week and certificates to honor roll students, and other routine matters that help ensure the room empties out before any real business is considered. The real business is then dispatched in language the average person is unlikely to understand. Many votes are taken without discussion because council members have already made up their minds, and when there is a debate it can be as action packed as moss growing. A story that sets out to report on this meeting is unlikely to raise readers' heart rates.

But don't confuse dullness with meaninglessness. The City Council, after its proclamations, droning debates, and jargon-laden speeches, might change hundreds or thousands of lives with a new ordinance limiting the number of pets per household, a budget that eliminates police and firefighting jobs, or a vote to allow nude dancing at a downtown nightclub. Each of these issues, and the countless other questions tackled by city government, is a problem that affects numerous stakeholders who have an opportunity to act. But covering the issue — instead of the meeting — requires reporting outside City Hall.

A good government reporter will pick up an agenda as soon as it's ready, usually a few days before the meeting. The reporter will already be familiar with issues that the board has been working on and will review the agenda to see if any of those issues are moving forward. Any intriguing new items will catch her eye, as well. She'll talk on background with the board clerk or a trusted official to learn about the most important or contentious issues. And that begins the reporting process. The next steps are asking the people behind the proposal what problem they're trying to solve, identifying and interviewing stakeholders, and getting a sense of who's likely to talk at the meeting. By the meeting's start, the story should be thoroughly reported and might be partly written. When you cover the issue instead of the meeting, a relevant story will follow.

But not all meetings involve relevant issues or serious questions, you say. Some are boring from start to finish, with procedural matters that affect few people or involve little to disagree over. How do you write an interesting story about that? And the answer is: You don't. When you resolve to cover issues and not meetings, you remove the obligation to write a story about every meeting you attend. If there's no news from a meeting, don't go back and write a 15-inch story about nothing to fill the space. Bag the story, or brief it for the record. Save your energy and newsprint for a story that is interesting, and relevant.

Don't use this as an excuse to blow off a meeting with a dry-sounding agenda — you could be surprised at any time by a resignation, a passionate citizen speaker, a last-minute proposal to raise or lower taxes or change the city's name. And don't use it as an excuse to put less government news in the paper. Use it as an opportunity to find relevant news with an impact on the people you cover — whether it originates in a boardroom, a classroom, a church meeting room, or a chance encounter at a grocery store. Cover issues, not meetings.

Cover people, not events

The State News at Michigan State University decided in the 1990s that getting a broader range of racial, ethnic, and gendered groups into the paper was important enough to create a job for it: the diversity beat. The position was a good step toward helping the newsroom and the community learn about and accept differences in people's backgrounds, beliefs, and cultures. The paper runs dozens of "diversity" stories every semester, covering a tremendous array of university groups. And yet, somehow, many of these stories — whose intention is to celebrate differences — come out sounding the same. Look at two front-page leads from a single edition, in stories about separate cultural events, "Soulful Roots" and "Latin Xplosion":

Lead 1: Wearing a traditional West African shirt called a "buba," eighth-grader Garrion Lang looked out solemnly at the audience gathered in the Auditorium on Sunday night. The crowd then went wild as he and several other classmates from Sankofa Shule Academy in Lansing beat drums and danced barefoot, filling the large room with rhythm and energy."[10]

Lead 2: Wearing a gold loincloth and sparkle body paint, Ricardo Leon blew his whistle to kick off the Latin Xplosion talent show Saturday night in Fairchild Theatre. Dressed in Mardi Gras costumes, 10 dancers followed each other down the aisles of the theater and threw candy to the audience.[11]

These leads are each OK in their own right. Both show the reporters were applying their senses and trying to place readers at the scene. But picture this style of lead repeated once or twice a day over the course of a semester, and then a year. Do these stories over time paint unique portraits of the people and cultures involved? To me, they resemble cookies stamped from the same cutter but decorated with different-colored sprinkles. The story zooms in on an individual engaged in an exotic cultural activity. It describes the wardrobe; the moves; the food, if applicable; and the audience. It says what group is hosting the awareness-raising event. It quotes people talking about the importance of awareness and heritage. And, if sensitive and accurate, it may well please the people who put on the event. But it does little to create the personal connections required to make diversity successful.

The problem with this approach is very similar to the problem with covering meetings — the focus is on structure and procedure rather than people and impact. Diversity is all about individuals striving to find their place in the world, sometimes through groups of people with similar backgrounds and ideas, sometimes in less familiar settings, sometimes alone. Our failure to embrace diversity is principally a failure to see other people as human as ourselves, a weakness that is not easily transcended through repeat coverage of parades and festivals. The way to engage readers in a story of diversity — or for that matter any of the routine event stories that interns and weekend reporters are so often sent out to cover — is to tell the story of a person.

Look at this example from *The State News*, also off the diversity beat:

> Judith Njogu smiles at strangers since her arrival to the United States from Nairobi, Kenya.

In Kenya, people are friendly and hospitable only after having their initial introduction, said Njogu, a medical technology and premedical senior.

"You don't go smiling at strangers," she said.

But Njogu said she appreciates grins from those she's not familiar with and likes to smile back.

"These days I do," she said. "I realize it's a good thing now that I have been exposed to it."

Njogu, who traveled to Michigan in December 2000, described her experiences adapting to the United States in her first place entry for the 2nd Annual International Student Essay Contest offered by the Office for International Students and Scholars, or OISS. Her essay was picked out of 145 submissions, and Njogu will be recognized today, and awarded $1,000.

Participating students described both positive and frustrating experiences since their arrival in the United States. They were encouraged to describe the high and low points of their transition, as well as events that occurred on or off campus and in the classroom.

"Being very independent and having no family in the country, you have to make big decisions for yourself," Njogu said. "If something gets really bad you can always go back to your parents' house. But here, if something goes really bad, it's just me."

Njogu said international students form deep friendships with each other early to substitute familial bonds.

One of the goals of the essay contest was to alert all students on campus to what international students go through, said Rosemary Max, assistant director of OISS.

Max said after the Sept. 11 terrorist attacks, it has become harder for international students to travel to the United States without undergoing much more scrutiny. She said reports on the students are sent to the U.S. Department of Homeland Security every semester.

The distance quickly makes the students mature and become independent, Max said.

"It's a lot farther than driving from Grand Rapids," she said. "It's a lot more of a treacherous journey these students go through. They sacrifice a lot to be at Michigan State." ...[12]

The lead in this story does two things well: It introduces us to a person, a character, around whom the story will revolve. The standard alternative would have been a lead about how "The 2nd Annual International Student Essay Contest offered by the Office for International Students and Scholars will be honoring its winners today" — which would be unlikely to capture much attention.

The other thing it does is apply the nice personal introduction directly to the point of the story. Njogu was recognized for an essay about adapting to a new culture, and her social adaptation is what we learn about in the first paragraphs. So the lead is both engaging and topical — a perfect match. The paper also ran a mug shot of Njogu, which gave readers an opportunity to see her smiling face for themselves. Portrayed as a real person, she becomes relevant.

Authority

On Sept. 11, 2005, newspapers across the country published the following story, compiled and written by more than a dozen Knight Ridder staffers:

> Two weeks after Hurricane Katrina crashed into the Gulf Coast, there is little argument that the response was botched. But an extensive Knight Ridder review of official actions in the days just before and after Katrina's landfall Monday, Aug. 29, reveals a depth of government hesitancy and a not-my-job attitude that may have cost scores of people their lives. ...
>
> [W]hat's clear is that four years after terrorists flew hijacked aircraft into buildings in New York and Washington, the United States is no better prepared to respond to catastrophe — even when it comes with days of warning. ...
>
> The Federal Emergency Management Agency, its top ranks filled by political appointees and its budget hit by deep cuts, seemed unable to grasp the magnitude of the disaster. ...[13]

A couple of things from this story are worth noticing:

■ The forceful language. Government's response to Hurricane Katrina was "botched." Officials displayed a "not-my-job attitude." The country is "no better prepared to respond to catastrophe" than before Sept. 11. The Federal Emergency Management Agency "seemed unable to grasp the magnitude of disaster." These are direct indictments of official performance.

■ The lack of attribution. Not one of the phrases above is credited to a source, official or unofficial. The strong assertions in the story aren't the opinions of other people, they're the bold conclusions of journalists who had covered the hurricane since it blew ashore in late August.

The story, which some papers labeled as analysis, walks readers through responses to the storm by all levels of government, laying responsibility on local, state, and federal officials of both political parties. It is not "objective" in the traditional sense, because the story, from the outset, dismisses any argument that officials handled the storm effectively.

Instead, it's written from a position of *authority*, in an assertive, self-confident voice that commands attention. The journalists contributing to this effort believe their reporting — not what they *think*, but what they've *observed* — supports these conclusions. As we discussed in Chapter 4, taking sides isn't necessarily a journalistic sin if the reporting relies on a disciplined approach of open-minded questioning and thorough verification. The method is invalid if the reporter is working to satisfy an ideological or partisan urge. But if you approach the story with the authoritative neutrality of a referee, intent on presenting the best possible information to help citizens understand the world, this methodology is not only defensible, but necessary.

Washington Post media critic Howard Kurtz took note of the authoritative, and occasionally combative, reporting of journalists covering Katrina's aftermath — like the CNN correspondent from Chapter 4 who scolded a U.S. senator who seemed detached from reality. "For once," Kurtz wrote, "reporters were acting like concerned citizens, not passive observers. And they were letting their emotions show. ... Maybe, just maybe, journalism needs to bring more passion to the table."[14] Passion, of course, can open journalists to charges of bias, which have become an unavoidable occupational hazard in recent years. Fear of bias accusations has sown seeds of timidity throughout the nation's reporting ranks, resulting in rampant abuse of the media by savvy manipulators. The best weapon against those criticisms is not withdrawing into a shell, but, as Kurtz suggests, asserting ourselves as concerned citizens.

Let's acknowledge that journalists have always brought certain biases to their work — and that some biases are healthy, while others are not. No good news reporter should, and almost none does, push a political agenda. But reporters have almost always acted on the bias that, for instance, crime is bad. You don't see many police stories that try to be fair to the idea that murder and robbery are OK. The same is true of natural disasters, shoddy roads, and poorly educated children. Bad, bad, bad. No one has a qualm with these obvious biases. But most journalists harbor other deeply rooted values that are both inevitable and essential for people who trade on the First Amendment. They include:

■ A bias toward openness and against secrecy. When officials try to keep information from the public without an extraordinarily good reason, journalists go on the offensive. They should, because they are professional advocates for the flow of information to citizens. And they should be equally aggressive in targeting Democratic, Republican, and bipartisan efforts to keep people in the dark.

■ A bias toward honesty. It is not enough to report an official assertion you know to be untrue and go to bed thinking you've done your job. People who attempt to deceive the public must be confronted.

■ A bias toward citizen participation in government affairs. This bias is the foundation of what has been called "public" or "civic" journalism, but more fundamentally it's a simple nod to democratic principles almost universally held by Americans. What supporter of our system is going to say people should be *less* involved in public affairs? How is it any more an affront to proper journalism to say citizen participation in government is good than to say that burglary and arson are bad?

Putting together stories that exercise these biases — toward openness, toward honesty, toward participation — requires writing with authority.

ANOTHER ASPECT OF this principle showed up on the front page of the *Detroit Free Press*, which has run signed columns in place of bylined news stories, complete with the writer's mug shot and personal voice. For former *Free Press* Publisher and Editor Carole Leigh Hutton, breaking news is part of a columnist's job. And when a columnist has a big story — such as a major road construction project or the Dow Jones Industrial Average reaching a new low for the year — it should run on the front page.

"I love to put columnists on 1A, but usually not just because they're expressing an opinion on something," Hutton said.[15] "Readers relate to them more than to bylines. And columnists are often the best writers, which means they tell the story best. ... In fact, I think columnists probably add to a reader's understanding because they write more conversationally."

The same month Hutton commented on front-page columns, the *Free Press* ran one by Dawson Bell, the political reporter we heard from in Chapters 3 and 5. Bell was writing about the Michigan leg of a high-profile concert tour in support of Democratic causes. Under the headline "Bush bashing during shows could backfire for Democrats," Bell wrote:

> Like parents averting their eyes until a child has gotten safely offstage at a middle school talent show, the political pros behind the Vote For Change tour have to be looking forward to Oct. 12.
>
> That's the day after all their entertainer/activists conclude the battleground states tour (of which Michigan was a part Sunday) and they can count the money.
>
> In the meantime, the hours are filled with forced smiles, crossed fingers and gritted teeth. As long as the stars play lots of music and limit their political commentary to the trite and inane, everything will be OK. But danger lurks around every venue: One eight-letter chant starting with a common profanity and ending with Bush and led by an excitable pop icon might send the whole thing south.
>
> Because, as frustrating as it is for the liberal activists sponsoring the tour to acknowledge, they know most voters aren't especially attracted by that kind of message. It's even likely that a significant number of people buying tickets don't hate the president at all. They just like music. ...[16]

That's not your typical front-page campaign story, but it sure is authoritative. And it's *interesting*.

Tone and drama

Here are three leads culled from Google News on a single day:

After several proposals and adjustments, Alameda County may finally be one step closer to building a courthouse in east Dublin.[17]

A city council proposal that would require customers to show identification before buying a popular craft product is one step closer to becoming reality.[18]

The Chapel Hill Police Department came one step closer Wednesday afternoon to completing its investigation of a recent rash of breaking and enterings around Cameron Avenue.[19]

If you've figured out what these sentences have in common, you're one step closer to understanding the predictable, bland nature of the formulaic news lead. Reporters are obliged to cover the incremental phases of a proposal's life span, from the moment it's introduced through committee meetings, public hearings, amendments, and votes. By the time they've written the fourth or fifth story about the same thing, they're out of new ways to talk about it. And when the only news is that the same proposal they wrote about last time has advanced to the next bureaucratic or legislative level, they pull out the "one step closer" standby — a sure signal to the reader that there is no need to proceed.

More than 25 years ago, Roy Peter Clark took a stab at livening up a "one step closer" story:

> The action picked up in Wednesday's episode of "The Budget and How to Cut It," a continuing drama featuring the citizens' Budget Review Committee and the stars of city government.
>
> In Monday's episode we left committee chairman L. Harold Corbett frustrated by the committee's inability to make specific recommendations on how the public's money should be spent.
>
> But Corbett's mood changed Wednesday as committee members challenged some features of City Manager Raymond E. Harbaugh's proposed $77.6-million budget. ...[20]

While not as scintillating as an episode of *General Hospital*, this story is groundbreaking in its attempt to portray public affairs as a dramatic event. Long before most people began talking about it, Clark recognized that bringing wit and style to basic stories can enliven seemingly dull developments.

"That was the only city council meeting I ever covered," said Clark, who, with a background in literature and composition, had been hired as a writing coach at the *St. Petersburg Times*. "I had this instinct to try to make this interesting because the editors thought it was important enough to send me there." Clark says journalists set the bar too low for routine assignments, loping from meeting to meeting for fear of missing something, rather than "affirmatively embracing the duty both to inform and entertain. I'm using 'entertain' not in a vaudeville show sense but in a classic literary sense that the dual purposes of literature are to delight and instruct — and it's hard to do one without the other."[21]

It's not uncommon for a feature story to recreate a moment, like the point of crisis in a narrative yarn where the character has to make a life-altering choice. This technique, done well, is a gripping way to start a story and can make readers forget they're reading. But how often have you seen this method applied to coverage of important legislation, or the hiring of a school superintendent, or the innovation that saved $5 million in tax money? These aren't life-or-death matters, but they involve smart, dedicated people solving problems. And here's the place where the problem-solving model of public affairs reporting intersects with the mandate to make it interesting: A story in which characters battle obstacles to resolve a problem is the hallmark of narrative fiction. In other words, when you present public issues as problems to be solved, you offer yourself the language and structure to form a narrative plot. The facts might not be as inherently dramatic as the contents of an adventure tale, but for the people involved in your story, the drama is real. Careers and promotions and reputations and personal goals are on the line. And if you've chosen the story for its public importance, the stakes are automatically high — the drama is embedded in the story. Watching almost anybody do what they do best is fascinating, be it a fly fisherman, a lawyer (how many movies build to a climactic performance in a courtroom?), a parks and recreation director, or a classroom teacher. If you can find your way to a person in the zone, excelling at her job, meeting her calling, you can find a good story.

The trick to writing vivid public affairs stories is to break down the psychological barrier against being interesting. There are a lot of books about good nonfiction writing, and all of their advice can be brought to bear not just on the harrowing tale of the rescue from a forest fire or the inspiring story of the athlete who beat cancer, but also on the downfall and redemption of a local politician or a neighborhood's complex struggle against poverty and blight. Public affairs news will get more interesting immediately if reporters stop separating news and features in their minds and just find the best way to tell the truth.

Here are some excerpts from a story that launched a monthlong project about the future of Chesapeake, Va.:

On a sticky day last summer the Southside Civic League begins its regular monthly meeting with a prayer inside a long, narrow meeting room at the Bethel Apostolic Church. The air conditioner is on the fritz.

The civic league members are talking about the grass and what to do about it.

They are telling Jack Bider, their community police officer, about neighbors who don't cut their grass or keep their shrubbery trimmed. It is not a cosmetic issue. They don't want to give criminals any more places to hide.

A 10-minute drive up Battlefield Boulevard, in what is in many ways a world away but still is Chesapeake, Little League baseball players are making good use of the grass. They won't have it for long.

"Doogie, third base, baby! I got your number!"

The third baseman taunts the batter. They are teammates and this is just a practice, but when the batter misses a couple of pitches, the third baseman gets on his case, tells him he bats like Rafael So-and-So.

Doogie nails a solid line drive into center field, to the general approval of everyone, including his taunter.

That ball field already is gone, a morass of mud on its way to becoming another parking lot near City Hall.

Chesapeake's history is made up of moments like these. Decisions, large and small, about what to do with the grass and woods that once covered the land here, have determined what the city is today and what it will be tomorrow.

Tough decisions lie ahead.

The Chesapeake of people's dreams may not be the Chesapeake they can afford. Despite its relative affluence, the city is struggling to pay for basics. It owes $500 million borrowed to build schools, roads and other expensive necessities.

That debt isn't going away any time soon. Neither will the needs: In the next six years the school system alone has proposed more than $254 million in projects. And, unlike Virginia Beach, Chesapeake can't depend on tourism money to help pay the bills.

There are consequences with each choice. Citizens may decide, as they have in the past, that they can stomach a tax increase to pay for schools and roads, but raise taxes too much and you hurt the business climate. Hurt the business climate and you endanger the very tax base that pays for schools and roads in the first place.

[…]

Newcomers driving down Battlefield Boulevard or George Washington Highway might notice only the traffic, how the roads just aren't wide enough for all the cars.

Those who have been here a while remember how things used to be.

See that? Over there is where the old mercantile used to stand. Now it's a 7-Eleven. That over there used to be acres and acres of farm land. Now it's a development.

But you needn't have been here long to see the city change and grow.

Chances are you have an opinion about what to do with the grass.

[…]

Though it might not seem likely when you're stuck in traffic on Battlefield Boulevard, only a little more than a quarter of the city's 353 square miles is developed. There still are farms, but the owners soon may have to decide whether it would be better to grow crops or houses.

As they decide what to do with the grass, the people in South Norfolk and Indian River need to make their decisions, too. For the oldest areas of the city, the days of booming growth may have passed, but not the hopes of the people who live there. Those people worry that, as the city tries to ensure that the newcomers get what they came for, those who have been here all along might lose what they stayed for.

But they're not as alone as they might think, because it doesn't take long to become an old-timer in Chesapeake, to see your way of life change in ways small and large.

You need only have been here months to say: That used to be a ball field. Now it's a parking lot.

Pay attention.

In 20 years, even sooner, all this will be history.[22]

This is a public affairs story. It's about the policy decisions that confront a city of 200,000 people. But it's not just based on a meeting, and it's not just a jumble of facts. It's a *story*. Let's look at just a few of the literary devices that make this writing so compelling:

■ **Scene setting.** The first paragraph describes "a sticky day" in a church meeting room where "the air conditioner is on the fritz." You can almost feel the humidity and see people wiping brows and tugging at shirt collars as they try to solve problems in their neighborhood.

■ **A quick cut.** The story jumps abruptly from the cramped church to an open baseball field a few minutes away. We see a ballplayer named Doogie nailing "a solid line drive into center field, to the general approval of everyone."

■ **Dialogue**. Just a snatch of it, as Doogie gets heckled with "Third base, baby! I got your number!" The natural language lends authenticity to the scene.

■ **Foreshadowing**. We learn at the beginning of the ball field scene that the players "won't have it for long." And we learn just a few paragraphs later that even as we're reading the story, the field has become a muddy place awaiting transformation into a parking lot. The ball field appears and disappears before our eyes, a microcosm of the story's theme of a city in constant flux.

■ **Nut graphs**. After setting a couple of scenes that viscerally draw the reader into the rhythms of life in the city, the writer ties those scenes into a couple of paragraphs that reveal and summarize the purpose of the story. The transition to the nut graphs is: "Chesapeake's history is made up of moments like this. Decisions, large and small, about what to do with the grass and woods that once covered the land here, have determined what the city is today and what it will be tomorrow." Numbers and examples illustrating the tough decisions follow in the next couple of paragraphs.

■ **Symbolism**. There are five mentions of what to do with the grass in Chesapeake: specific images of a civic league wanting it neat and trimmed and ballplayers sinking their feet in it, and then general references, beginning with the nut graphs, to the larger question of "what to do with the grass in a 353-square-mile city." The grass symbolizes the decisions about whether to develop, where to develop, how to develop. Do residents preserve the grass or tear it up?

■ **Direct address to the reader**. The writer invites you to "see" the site of the old mercantile, now a 7-Eleven, and that former field, now a nest of homes. She practically grasps your arm to direct you toward these images.

■ **Authority**. As we talked about above, more authoritative stories are almost always more efficient and compelling. There are no direct attributions in the parts of the story I've excerpted, but thorough reporting is evident. The reporter was in the church. She was at the ball field. She's driven these roads and researched the statistics. The quality of her knowledge establishes her credibility and informs her writing throughout the story.

■ **An ending that returns to the beginning**. Along with the recurring grass theme, one of the last paragraphs revisits an image from the top of the story, as the writer reminds the reader, "You need only have been here months to say: That used to be a ball field. Now it's a parking lot."

This story jumped to a two-page package that included quotes from Chesapeake residents, charts showing population and demographic trends, sidebars explaining where, why and how the city was growing, and a range of choices about future development that readers were encouraged to consider and discuss. And the series continued for three more weeks. But on its own, the story is a wonderful, compact example of just how compelling public policy can be when the reporting and writing is literally down to earth, down in the grass.

Humor and surprise

John-Henry Doucette of *The Virginian-Pilot* was working on a story about how local residents could talk with their mayors. The recently elected mayor of Suffolk, Bobby Ralph, held office hours reserved just for constituents — a rare level of accessibility that Doucette thought "was kind of neat." He figured he'd take the opportunity to regionalize the story, so he'd spent some time talking with officials in nearby cities about how their mayors did it. And he and a photographer arranged a time to observe Mayor Ralph meeting with citizens.

"We kept trying to set up a day when he had people who would agree to let us in,"

Doucette said.[23] It turned out to be a day in early December. "He had two appointments that morning. We sat through the whole morning with him and he went through everything." They got more than they bargained for:

SUFFOLK — The bespectacled mayor sat behind his desk at City Hall as his assistant brought him coffee with a little cream and Sweet'N Low.

Wearing a silk peanut-patterned tie, the first-term mayor checked his messages. His 9:30 a.m. was due any second.

In walked Santa Claus.

"Little Bobby Ralph grown up to be mayor!" said Claus, who is really Ernest B. Hefferon, a paint contractor. He hadn't had time to change his clothes between Santa gigs. Ralph rose and extended his right hand. Hefferon accepted, and a bell around his wrist jingled.

Claus had arrived alone, yet joked in first person plural: "We've got a few bones to pick with the mayor. We need a bigger landing space."

Kidding aside, Suffolk Mayor Bobby L. Ralph has kept morning office hours on Tuesdays and Thursdays since this summer, when he took office and hung out his shingle at City Hall. This has brought him face-to-face with about 40 folks in a modest office on the second floor.

Ralph said he decided to hold the regular office hours to be more accessible to constituents. His predecessor also met with individuals by appointment, but didn't hold regular public hours. That's the way most mayors in Hampton Roads do business.

But Ralph, who retired from the city's Department of Social Services when he was elected to the City Council in 2002, said it's good for the public and the city staffers to know when they can catch him.

So far, he's had a good response, he said.

Developers, business honchos, neighborhood captains and gadflies have stopped by, generally by appointment.

"I've had a couple of, I guess, you call it the critics, the habitual critics of the city administration," Ralph said.

Hefferon, 43, is president of the West End Civic League.

He took a seat, as did the mayor. Ralph asked about a neighborhood traffic issue.

Seen any improvement?

Yes, Hefferon said, before adding: "We've still got these criminal activities."

Vandalism?

A recent break-in.

The mayor's cellular phone went off. He pulled it out and shut off the device.

Hefferon continued.

"One of the things I wanted to talk to you about is a federation of civic leagues," he said. "I think Norfolk does it."

"I think it would be something that's worthy of the civic leagues talking about," Ralph said.

"I'm available when committees are being formed," Hefferon said, wrapping up.

"Good enough," Ralph said.

"I appreciate your time this morning," Hefferon said.

He left.

"I had no idea Santa was coming," the mayor said. He checked his schedule. "Lets see, 10:30. ... "[24]

Doucette had one story planned when he walked into the mayor's office that morning. He walked out with a different story. "When you're covering something, and something much cooler happens, that's the story," Doucette said. "I like stories that are about people and not about stuff. ... If you wrote a story that said, 'The mayor allows people to come in and talk to him, sources said Monday,' who cares? But you got a bureaucrat hanging out and in walks Santa Claus — you've got a story."

In less than 450 words, Doucette's story accomplishes a great deal. First and foremost, it gets read. It's just a story about a mayor holding office hours, but the lead hooks you and the story carries you along so easily you forget you're reading. Secondly, it gives you a chuckle. The image of Santa marching into a mayor's office to talk about traffic and vandalism in his neighborhood is incongruous enough to at least evoke a smile. And most importantly — but unlikely without the first condition — the story sheds light on a meaningful communication between the city's top official and a concerned citizen, showing readers just how easy a partnership between mayors and residents can be. In a few hundred words, it breaks down the us-and-them barrier between the government and the governed.

Give credit to fate for putting a guy in a Santa suit in front of a reporter on what could have been a much more routine assignment. But share that credit with a reporter who was able to see how one bright moment made for a more effective story than the longer piece he had planned. And give a hand to the editors who, rather than stifling Doucette's instinct, helped him put the story together and put it into the paper. Not all reporters would see that story, and not all editors would publish it. Frankly, not every attempt to pull off a story like this will work — and people need to be willing to acknowledge a noble failure and try again. More successful stories like this would almost certainly draw more readers, not in a frivolous way, but in a way that fostered a collaborative spirit in the community.

Tom Warhover, executive editor of the *Columbia Missourian* and an associate professor of journalism at the University of Missouri, who once worked with Doucette and me at *The Virginian-Pilot*, is afraid journalism schools aren't doing enough to help reporters recognize good stories when they see them — the kind of stories that don't show up in bold print on meeting agendas or press releases, but bubble up from overheard conversations or everyday events.[25] The kind of stories Tom Rosenstiel describes as "demand-side" journalism.

The vital news values of timeliness and urgency that lead to event-driven coverage also create blinders against stories that didn't happen yesterday but affect people in unique and surprising ways. If you study newspapers awhile, it's amazing how predictable they become. A woman in a study for the Readership Institute complained that whenever she watched television news, she knew what would be in the paper the next day. Readership Institute research has found that breaking this mold, amusing and surprising people, is a good way of attracting readers.[26]

In the end, to tell important stories, you have to find an audience. If you make people work to see their stake in public affairs, they're going to find something else to do. But if you can help people enjoy learning about their communities and participating in public life, you serve your readers, your community *and* your employer.

How not to be boring

■ Cover issues, not meetings. Find the stories that affect readers, and report those stories. Represent as many stakeholders as possible, not just the officials. If there's no news from a meeting you cover, write a brief.

■ Cover people, not events. When you're writing about a rally for the homeless, a Native American powwow, a walk to fight cancer, or any of the countless quick-hit stories that reporters are sent out to cover, find people and tell their stories. Look for the details that make a person unique, and the emotions that make her just like everyone else. Use the assignment to help people understand one another better.

■ Write with authority. Get to know your beat, your sources, and your subject well enough that you can explain the news to readers in your own words. Have the courage to make blunt assertions of what you know to be true, if you can support them with facts. Do not report or write to push a personal agenda, and never withhold information that weakens your assertions; rather, report and write with a relentless aim to give citizens the best information they need to make good decisions.

■ Assert your democracy-friendly biases toward open government, honest conduct, and citizen participation in public decisions.

■ Apply the literary tools of features, sports, and creative nonfiction to public affairs reporting. Get over the notion that government and civic news has to be dry and institutional. Build characters, set scenes, create suspense, appeal to the senses, play with structure, directly address the reader. Tell stories you'd read even if you weren't paid to read them. Tell them like you're trying to make a friend listen. But DON'T make anything up.

■ Bring humor to stories, when appropriate.

■ Find stories that surprise. Broaden your news judgment beyond event-driven, institution-initiated news and keep your eyes peeled for things that are interesting. Something doesn't have to have happened yesterday to be important, and we miss a lot of big stories by insisting on a time peg. If readers don't know it, it's news to them.

■ Break every traditional rule of journalism and writing — within the ethical boundaries of honesty, fairness, accuracy, and clarity — to get readers interested in the important questions faced by our democracy.

For thought and action...

1 Go to a local government meeting and write three stories off the meeting. First, write a typical story, the one you'd expect to see in the next day's newspaper. Then, write it in the second person. Then, write it in the first person. Change the structure and emphasis of each story as appropriate, with the goal of helping the reader understand what was important about the meeting. Ask somebody who's not involved with journalism to critique all three stories. Which did he learn the most from?

2 Get an agenda for a government meeting and rank the three most important items. Report and write a story based on the issue with the most possible impact, before the meeting is held.

3 When you see a news story that's particularly compelling or engaging, call up the reporter and ask how he or she approached it.

PART 2: THE PRACTICE OF PUBLIC AFFAIRS REPORTING

Chapter 8

Elections

Everybody likes to quote Winston Churchill on the messiness of democracy ("the worst form of government, except for all the others"), but Walt Whitman took a more proactive view: "Thunder on! Stride on! Democracy. Strike with vengeful stroke!" Tuesday night, make like Whitman.

— from a *Rocky Mountain News* Q&A on precinct caucuses[1]

I think it's important to note that on election night, in newspapers across the land, there's free pizza.

— Nancy Young, *The Virginian-Pilot*[2]

Covering elections might be the single most important thing journalists do. More than any other public decision, elections capture citizens' attention, and the winners call the shots for years. If we pick the wrong leaders, the consequences are vast and lasting.

Campaigns are Machiavellian affairs, in which candidates say and do virtually whatever they think is necessary to win. The primary motivator in election cycles is money — donated by people and institutions that want something from the candidates, and spent on campaign commercials that seek to manipulate rather than enlighten voters. Aware that the public has limited time and attention for decision making, the candidates avoid complex issues and nuanced discussions. Each side market-tests a variety of catch phrases and impossible promises, seeking to win over the largest crowd. And campaigns spend a lot of time finding bad things to say about their opponents, hoping the salacious stuff will distract voters from the real questions that lack simple answers.

The press is all too easily swept up in the superficial and strategic aspects of political campaigns — focusing on spin, trivia, polls, and pundits, rather than common problems, proposed solutions, the records of candidates, and honest insight into who they really are. This short-sighted, reactionary focus plays into the hands of cynics, diminishes the value of public discussion, and ultimately turns off huge swaths of citizens, who view the process as a farce in which they have no real say and after which nothing will change. Acting reflexively to cover whichever message or smear of the day seems most intriguing, journalists turn their backs on what should be the driving question behind every election news decision: "Does this help voters decide which candidate will do a better job?"

This chapter lays out a method for covering elections that systematically supplies voters with the information they need, forcing candidates to confront the issues, and inviting citizens to take control of their decisions. Coverage that focuses on the *election*, the choice voters need to make, rather than the *campaign*, the manipulations of political professionals, comes in four overlapping stages: raising awareness, educating voters, getting people to the polls, and reporting on the outcome.

Stage One: Awareness

Planning

Elections — like any good news story — are full of surprises, revelations and drama. But the campaign calendar also is very predictable. Election Day is a known quantity, and since your goal is to build readers' knowledge over time, you've got a great opportunity to plan week-by-week coverage leading up to the vote.

Tom Warhover, who helped revolutionize election coverage at *The Virginian-Pilot*, says the first thing journalists must do in planning is establish goals — "What kind of coverage do we want our coverage to be, and why?" Elections should be about governing, not winning, he says. Campaigns should advance the conversation about problems in the community, the state, and the country. Attacking the coverage from that angle will dictate what you cover, what questions you ask, and how you frame and play stories.[3]

For guidance, turn to readers. *Oregonian* Public Editor Michael Arrieta-Walden summarized what readers told him they wanted from 2004 presidential election coverage: reporting that was skeptical of campaigns' claims, in-depth examination of issues, deeper profiles of the candidates, less emphasis on one-time gaffes, more opportunities for readers to debate on opinion pages, more consistency in the display of election information, more local context for national issues stories, and a little bit of fun.[4]

Planning that focuses on the kind of coverage readers want — which, conveniently, is the kind of coverage that will help them on Election Day — requires talking to citizens about what this election means to them. Together, journalists, citizens, and candidates can set priorities for the campaign.

Priorities

Priorities are the choices you make about how to spend your election resources. With a limited amount of time, space, and reader patience, where are you going to focus voters' attention? Elections are about finding the right people to solve the community's problems, so the most challenging problems, the possible solutions, and the candidates' qualifications to carry them out are your top priorities.

Defining the biggest problems requires your journalistic judgment, attention to the candidates' platforms, and the input of citizens. Relying only on one or two of these factors won't get you where you need to go. A political professional's job is to pick a couple of issues, craft a winning message, and remain fixed on those narrowly focused ideas regardless of the community's broader needs. Citizens have disparate concerns and interests that can be focused through journalistic and political processes to create a public agenda. In Chapter 1 we talked about how the news media help communicate priorities in two directions — from officials to citizens, and from citizens to officials. Good election coverage brings the people's problems to the candidates and insists that the candidates respond.

A few ways to get a sense of citizens' priorities are scientific surveys, extensive man-on-the-street or one-on-one interviews, and group discussions, known as focus groups or community conversations.

Big papers with a lot of resources can combine these approaches, surveying for a statistical representation of what's on people's minds and then delving into details with interviews and focus groups. Most papers don't have the cash to conduct their own polls, so they have to rely on the knowledge of their beat reporters and discussions with a lot of people. Focus groups are not random or scientific samples, so you shouldn't try to generalize conclusions to the overall population. But in talking with citizens, journalists can detect patterns and subtle concerns that help shape the way issues are approached. In ideal election coverage, Tom Warhover says, "the citizen-based reporting begins early."

For the 2004 election, the *Detroit Free Press* commissioned its own poll and also held focus groups in Detroit and Grand Rapids, big cities on opposite sides of Michigan. Bob Campbell, who headed up the *Free Press* coverage, said focus groups "are very helpful in letting you hear … what's on people's minds." The discussions tipped off the *Free Press* to the importance moral issues would play in the election: "For a number of people the issues like same-sex marriage and abortion were overriding. They were far more important than their personal financial stake in which candidate is more likely to do better by me with taxes."[5]

Community conversations might not yield stories on their own. Though they are almost certain to help reporters see issues better and set the agenda for election coverage, the discussions may or may not be newsworthy enough to report in the paper. The *Columbia Missourian* decided in 2004 that the personalities from one set of community conversations were worth introducing to readers:

> There was Meggie Smith, a Rock Bridge High School student who plans to be president of the United States in 2028.
> "You'll laugh at me … (but) I'm not kidding," she said.
> There was Vikki Salerno, a public housing representative and avid motorcyclist from Hallsville.
> There was Evelyn Tschetter, a retired nurse and midwife concerned about politicians' views on issues of life and death.
> And there was Rachel Jones, vice-president of the Young Democrats at Rock Bridge. "Does anyone here need to register to vote?" she asked. "That's my job."
> Those are just a few of the community members who gathered at the *Missourian* for a series of three community conversations last week. Their purpose: To help journalists get a handle on the issues important to local residents as the general election approaches and to develop questions to challenge candidates for U.S. Senate during a debate tonight in MU's Jesse Auditorium.
> High-schoolers who gathered for the first conversation on Oct. 5 listed as

their primary worries the future of Social Security and health care, not jobs or a potential draft. Education was a close third.

The second group, on Wednesday night, spent a great deal of time trying to define the perfect senator. They want someone with integrity, accountability and transparency.

"These things lend themselves to making good decisions publicly," Karl Skala, a city planning commissioner and MU professor, said.

Betty Cramer, a registered nurse at Boone Hospital Center, summed it all up. "The ideal senator would be a mix of all of us," she said.[6]

The story uses subheads to break the discussion into the topics of health care, education, and Iraq and the war on terrorism. While it doesn't break news, it gives readers a glimpse into what their neighbors are thinking and a sense of what's motivating the newspaper's coverage.

Introductions

Election years ebb and flow, and while most people don't start paying attention to campaigns until long after journalists are in high gear, it's important to get some information out early. If you think of election coverage as a faucet, consider dripping out a story here, a story there early on, then opening up a trickle, a steady stream, and then an all-out gusher near Election Day.

The first drips of information, especially for local elections, ought to let people know they can run for office and how to get on the ballot. In 2004, not enough candidates filed to run for the School Board in East Lansing, Mich., but unfortunately, the local press reported this *after* the filing deadline. Three people ended up running write-in campaigns. Helping citizens be citizens means helping them get involved.

After the ballot is set, it's time to introduce the candidates to voters. Remember the hiring model I brought up in the first chapter, where we treat candidates as job applicants and voters as hiring managers? Journalists in this model act primarily as democracy's human resources department, providing the decision-makers what they need to make a good choice. In fall 1996, the year of a presidential election and a major U.S. Senate race in Virginia, *The Virginian-Pilot* introduced the analogy to readers in a front-page editor's note:

> [...]The process is straightforward: Describe the job, decide the qualifications you're looking for, screen applicants for their qualifications and judge how well they'll perform through job interviews, from checking their references, even from a temporary assignment. Then make the hiring decision.
>
> Every six years and every two years, respectively, U.S. senators and members of the U.S. House of Representatives reapply for their jobs, asking you to decide whom to hire.
>
> We want to help you consider your choices. We begin that process today.[7]

The note was accompanied by a graphic spoof of a classified ad, reading "SENATOR WANTED: Must be at least 30. Must live in Va. Successful candidates should have vision, ability to negotiate and compromise, and leadership skills. Job lasts 6 years. Salary is

$133,600." Next to the note was a story describing the job of a U.S. senator and how it had evolved over the years. The front page teased to the front of the Commentary section, which introduced the two major-party Senate candidates to voters.

Then, in spring 1998, the five major cities covered by *The Virginian-Pilot* held municipal and school board elections, fielding huge slates of candidates. The paper assigned reporters to each race and set up a system for introducing the candidates with "resume" information that the candidates supplied, including their age, neighborhood, education, years living in the city, occupation, political and community service experience, and a few words about why they were running.

The next step was to do background checks on the candidates. In addition to looking through the paper's clips, reporters were assigned to check real estate holdings, criminal and civil court files, tax payment records, bankruptcy, voter registration information, academic degrees, and professional certifications. If a candidate lied about her background, was behind in her taxes, or rarely voted, the reporter would catch it. This is the kind of vetting most citizens don't have the time or the expertise to do for themselves.

The last obligation of the awareness phase is to help readers register to vote. None of the information you'll present in the coming weeks or months will be of any use to people who

How to conduct a community conversation

A community conversation brings citizens together to talk about important issues. The forum helps people share their own beliefs, listen to others' concerns, and develop a better understanding of community problems. It helps news people understand the hopes, fears, and prejudices of a community and provides a sense of direction for election and beat coverage. Here are some tips for organizing and leading a community conversation, based on a Virginian-Pilot *guide:*

■ Setting it up: Invite enough people to get a group of 10 to 12 — large enough for a range of personalities and opinions, small enough to allow for good discussion. Try to hold the meeting in a gathering place such as a library, school, or rec center — not at the newspaper office. Bring snacks, name tags, a tape recorder, and a discussion guide to help keep the conversation on track.

■ Getting started: Identify yourself and explain the purpose of the conversation. Tell participants how you plan to use the information. Set ground rules: This isn't a debate, it's more like a kitchen table discussion; explaining how you feel about an issue is more important than proving a point; respect others' views and be willing to listen to people you disagree with; expect the moderator to play devil's advocate, ask questions, make sure everyone gets a chance to speak, and keep the conversation on topic. Then go around the table and have people introduce themselves.

■ The conversation: Think of the discussion as having three parts — an introductory period where people lay out their views, a period of "testing assumptions" where you summarize what you've heard and gently challenge people's opinions, and a closing period where you try to settle on areas of agreement and disagreement. As you listen and respond, be careful not to just catch a good sound bite and move on. Let people talk about where their ideas can't cast a ballot. Any election story before the registration deadline ought to include a box explaining voter eligibility and giving street addresses, phone numbers, Web addresses, and the deadline. *The State News* ran registration information on its front page at least five times in four weeks leading up to the 2004 deadline.

Stage Two: Education

This stage is the meat and potatoes of election coverage. Once you've given readers a sense of what offices are open, who's running, and what the candidates' and community's priorities are, you can delve more deeply into issues, the candidates, and the citizens who will decide the election.

Of course, you'll also cover the events — scripted and unscripted — that occupy the majority of candidates' time. These episodic, usually predictable, and often distracting rallies, news conferences, endorsement announcements, and assaults on opponents tend to dominate election coverage because they're urgent and easy, but they're not what readers want or need most to make a decision.

come from, how they came to form their opinions. Some of the best interchange comes between participants while the moderator's mouth is shut. Here are some questions you might ask to steer a conversation about traffic problems in your city:

Introduction: What's your commute like, or what's it like to get around town? What do you see as the biggest causes of traffic congestion? What are some ideas for making it easier to get around? To draw people out, ask follow-up questions like: Why do you think that? Why does that bother you? How would that idea help?

Testing assumptions: Gently challenge people's proposals. If someone wants wider roads, ask how much more in tax money they'd be willing to pay, or whether they support the government taking property for right-of-way. If there's an emphasis on alternative transportation like commuter rail or bus lines, ask how much the government should subsidize those efforts and how realistic it is to expect people to give up driving for less convenient transportation. If people suggest toll roads, high-occupancy lanes, or rerouting traffic patterns, ask them to consider the costs and consequences of these ideas.

Conclusion: Help the group see contradictions. If there's a consensus that people want more roads and lower taxes, point that out. Help people realize that every solution has costs and benefits. See if a particular solution has the most resonance, or if the group can set priorities: Is it more important to keep taxes steady or to reduce congestion around downtown?

■ Afterward: Ask people if you can return to them for comments and feedback as your coverage continues. If someone had a particularly compelling story or point of view, consider writing about him specifically. If you get a chance, reconvene the group as the issue develops and see how their thinking has changed.

Describing key issues in depth and insisting that candidates reveal positions and proposals; painting a true picture of the candidates' lives, experience, and character; and reporting how citizens are perceiving and affecting the campaigns are the vital work of election coverage. Many of these stories can be planned weeks or months in advance and rolled out on a schedule that builds knowledge approaching Election Day.

Issues

One way to tackle big issues is to profile them, the way you might profile a person. Delve into each issue's background; explore its challenges; present the ideas proposed by candidates and experts; share citizens' opinions from surveys, interviews, and community conversations; and show people where to learn more. The key in presenting issues is to get beyond the simple rhetoric the candidates use in stump speeches and provide an independent evaluation of the problem and potential solutions.

THE JOB INTERVIEW

The Virginian-Pilot used a "classified ad" to convey its election coverage as a hiring process. (Reprinted with permission of *The Virginian-Pilot.*)

In 1996, *The Gazette Telegraph* of Colorado Springs broke down issues with weekly stories leading up to the election, beginning with "leadership" and moving through "providing for the future," "growth," "the environment," and "education." Here's the beginning of one story:

It is issue No. 1: Education.

It is such a big topic that it encompasses the most complex set of anxieties voters have as they get ready to vote.

Why? You've heard it a thousand times.

"These kids are the future of this community," says Annie Walters, president of the El Paso Council Parent Teacher Association.

Education is more important to Colorado voters than any other single issue, said a statewide survey by the Norwest Public Policy Research Program of the University of Colorado at Denver. More important than the environment, than government debt; more important than family values or abortion.

It's an issue that reverberates across all levels, from the state Capitol to countless living rooms. Lawmakers have approved statewide academic standards, and have provided avenues for school choice by creating room for charter schools. Locally, voters wrestle with crowded classrooms, and even have turned a public school over to a private company to see if it can turn out better students while also turning a profit.

Most everyone wants good schools because everyone has a vested interest in well-educated kids. A good education helps people get good jobs and stay out of trouble with the law. Good schools attract business development and raise the value of surrounding homes.

But what makes schools good? That's where people disagree. And while voters might know what they want from schools, they are uncertain about what it will take to get it. So they're asking their elected officials for some leadership.

They're asking for help with some tough questions.

Does it take more money to run good schools? If so, where will it come from? Why are so many kids forced into crowded classrooms? Why are roofs leaking or heaters not working at some schools?

The answers are no less easy. Walters understands that money for construction, maintenance and school operations has to come from somewhere. A bond issue would raise tax rates. Charging fees to developers to build schools would raise housing prices. Or if the state increased the amount it provides to school districts, it would have to raise taxes or cut back other programs. ...[8]

Note how that story mirrors the structure of a community conversation. It identifies the issue and its relevance. It demonstrates a broad agreement on the importance of good schools, then introduces points of departure. And for each suggestion of what a good school is, there are potential costs and drawbacks. Readers have a good opportunity to think through what's important to them, and then find out what's important to the candidates.

The *Detroit Free Press* did something similar in 2004, running packages on major issues alongside the presidential candidates' positions and the results of the paper's Michigan polling. Readers could learn about the issue, learn about where Michigan residents stood, and see what the major candidates planned to do about it.

The *Missourian* went deep in 2004 on an issue of local concern: the legalization of medical marijuana. The front page of the paper's NewSunday edition used this tease to a package inside:

Once again, Columbia voters will be asked whether people with serious illnesses should be allowed to use marijuana without penalty if advised to do so by their doctors. Proponents say that allowing patients to "grow their own" would save thousands of dollars spent monthly on prescription medications they think don't work as well. Opponents say there is no evidence that smoking marijuana delivers medical benefits that outweigh the hazards of inhaled smoke. Who will determine what works best: the bureaucrats or the patients?[9]

Inside is a four-page package, including a story that summarizes marijuana research, reveals disagreement among doctors, discusses the political debate, previews the local referendum vote, and closes with a broader look at U.S. drug policy. Also in the package are a graphic showing how marijuana affects the brain, the text of the referendum question, a map of states where medical marijuana is decriminalized, a timeline of marijuana's legal status, and a chart showing marijuana-related laws and penalties in Missouri. It's a package aimed at building mastery among readers who will decide whether to change the drug laws in their city.

123

Candidates

Everybody writes about the candidates during an election campaign, and yet it's rare for voters to feel like they know the people seeking office. Candidates work hard to project a narrow image of themselves that doesn't always ring true, their opponents liken them to murderous fiends, and a wide range of experts add their own analysis, creating an image that's blotchy, incomplete, and sometimes altogether different from the candidate's character. That's why it's important, at least once in a campaign, to write a story only about the candidate.

A candidate profile need not be very long, and in cases where you're covering several localities with dozens of candidates, it's impractical to expect an 80-inch story on each. But the bigger the race, the more opportunity and responsibility there is to produce at least one piece that delves into each candidate's character.

Following are a couple of examples of candidate profiles. The first is an excerpt from a long piece about U.S. Sen. George Allen, who at the time was a former Virginia governor looking to move up. See if you don't learn a little something about Allen beyond his positions on abortion and taxes:

Look at this guy.

Those cowboy boots, poking their pointy toes out from under his pant cuffs.

That bottom lip, full of snuff and jutting out.

The dark wavy hair, blue eyes, pink-hued cheeks, the friendly smile, the love of real country music like Johnny Cash and Tammy Wynette, the fondness for pickups and baseball and NASCAR.

At 6 foot 4, his figure pops out of the crowd like a movie star or a famous athlete.

"What's YOUR name?" the U.S. Senate candidate says, reaching out to shake hands.

You tell him. He chats you up. He's been to your hometown, rooted for (or against) your favorite Winston Cup driver, toured the company where you work.

You walk off, impressed, blown away. What a down-to-earth guy.

But you start thinking: the boots, the snuff, the country music, the charm and good looks. It's almost too much. Is he serious?

Can George Allen possibly be for real?

George F. ("Oh gosh, it's Felix, a family name") Allen may seem like a well-heeled Southerner, but his early years were more of a struggle. His parents were newlyweds when their first-born came along, and he watched them scrap toward a better life.

[…]

He scoots a chair up to the microphone and starts commentating, just like that, like this was scripted or something. It wasn't.

It's a July evening, and the sun is fading near Keysville, a tiny town in Southside. His 12-hour day of campaigning was supposed to be over, but then his aides found out about a Dixie League baseball game.

They whisked Allen here, shuffled him up the bleachers and straight on to a radio station.

Former Gov. George Allen has now joined us in the booth, the announcer says. What brings you here?

"We were at a fund-raiser, and they said this game was going on, and I love youngsters — THAT LOOKS LIKE A PASSED BALL," Allen says.

Football's your game, Governor, right?

"I like football, I like horse riding, but my dad always wanted me to play baseball, fewer injuries. THERE'S A HIT, up the middle, one run in."

It goes like that for 15 minutes. Baseball, Allen's views on the marriage penalty, the pitch, his take on estate taxes, the hit, the throw, the call, his take on tobacco regulations.

An aide hands him a note. Another radio station wants to put him on the air. He heads over between innings. …

Allen sticks around until after dark, presents trophies to the kids and autographs baseballs. He climbs back in his recreational vehicle and then it's time for the day's final test.

He stands in the aisle, holds his arms out, spreads his feet and crouches. If he can keep standing as the RV lurches out of the gravel parking lot, he's still strong.

He calls it "RV surfing." He only RV surfs at the end of the day, because if he crashes, that'll give his wounds the night to clot.

The RV rolls and sways, then dips into a muddy rut. Allen reels backward toward an aide, who throws out his arms to catch the candidate. Allen crouches lower, throws his arms forward and his butt back, and rights himself.

Close call.

"Good one!" he says.[10]

This 5,200-word story includes a lot of biographical information and a lot of insight into personality and character. It doesn't dwell on politics, because the rest of the coverage takes care of that. The story was written by a feature writer, who obviously had a lot of time to get to know the candidate. The result is a story demonstrating that those who wish to lead us are not only politicians, but people.

When you've got a lot of candidates but only a little bit of time and space, you can scale back your profile's scope but still give readers a meaningful glimpse into a personality. When six candidates stuck their necks out in a primary for Lansing mayor in 2003, *The State News* assigned the same reporter to interview and profile all six in separate stories. Here's the first of those profiles:

Lansing mayoral candidate Gerald Rowley doesn't have large lawn placards for his supporters to display. He's not slapping stickers on cars or passing out pins or badges.

Rowley, 42, does most of his campaigning by driving around in his gray Volvo station wagon with two "Rowley for mayor" fliers posted in the back windows. When asked how much his campaign cost him, Rowley chuckled.

"I've only invested $216 for my campaign, and $100 was the (application) filing fee," he said.

The remaining $116 bought him 500 red and white fliers he's been taking with him door-to-door every weekend, talking with neighbors and residents, making his voice heard — and he says his method is working.

"I'm running a low budget, high-profile campaign, if you can believe that," he said. "I don't consider myself a politician by any means."

Rowley will be competing against five other candidates for a spot on the November ballot at the primary election Aug. 5, the top two candidates from that race will compete for Lansing's top position at the general election, held Nov. 4. Candidates will finish out the remaining two years of former Mayor David Hollister's four-year term. Councilmember Tony Benavides filled in as mayor when Hollister left office to work in Gov. Jennifer Granholm's administration.

Rowley's plans, if elected, would to be establish better relationships between police and community members. He said he'd also work to bring more people to the Oldsmobile Park, home of the Lansing Lugnuts minor league baseball team and work to draw more independent businesses into Lansing's downtown area.

But more than anything, Rowley said he wants to eliminate the condemned houses and vacant properties found in neighborhoods like his.

Rowley said he'd also want to change the way the city is run, in terms of community input.

"Lansing's a cool town, a diverse town, it's a good area to live in," Rowley said[.] "But as far as citizens having any say in town, it ain't happening — period."

Rowley has never held political office before, but he said that doesn't make him nervous.

"What this town needs is a mayor who's going to take charge of the neighborhoods, to put money into people versus buildings downtown," he said. "That's what's going to make us a better city."

Former Lansing City Councilmember Howard Jones described Rowley as an "open and honest" worker and manual laborer in the community. But it may be rough for candidates like Rowley to compete with a small campaign budget, Jones said.

"Money is very important in our society and I guarantee if you notice who the winners are, they'll be the ones with the most money," Jones said.

A husband and father of a 7-year-old daughter, Rowley works as a drywall finisher and served 20 years as a mechanic with the Michigan National Guard.

Rowley first came to Lansing at age 22 with "a $50 car and half a bag of clothes." He worked to buy a house and raise a family, now he sees the Aug. 5 primary as his next big feat.

Rowley describes himself as "the working man's man," and said he'd even offer to take a 50-percent pay cut if elected. Lansing's top job pays $107,000 a year.

"That's way too much for me in that position," he said.[11]

This story is just over 500 words, about a tenth the length of the George Allen profile. And yet, there is enough of Gerald Rowley here to give voters a pretty good idea of who this person is: no-nonsense, frugal, opinionated. You glean that he's an underdog and doesn't care, that he works hard and says what he thinks. Whether you choose to vote for him or not, from reading this you can at least feel like you know who you're dealing with.

OFTEN LEFT OUT of candidate coverage are those representing third parties or independent movements. A lot of journalists discount third-party candidates because they generally have less financial and public support than the major candidates. While this is true, there's a chicken-and-egg argument at play. A candidate no one has heard of is unlikely to have a lot of support, but how do people learn about candidates? Through the news media.

Imagine a presidential race in which all of the dozen or so people on the ballot get identical treatment on television and in the newspapers. It's not likely that a minor-party candidate would suddenly seize the momentum and win the election, but you can bet all of these people would find more support. A lot of parties represent extremist or unpopular positions, but they are also unencumbered by the need to water down their beliefs to win over vast coalitions. That means someone from the Green Party or the U.S. Taxpayers Party is far more likely to directly address controversial issues that concern millions of people.

It's worth remembering that 40 percent of potential voters didn't participate in the highly contentious 2004 presidential race — which means the two major parties failed to energize tens of millions of people. The extremely careful nature of the Democrats and Republicans, who are often reaching out with the same bland messages to the same narrow group of undecided voters, mixed with the selective and exclusive nature of news coverage, narrows political discourse, stifles ideas, and sidelines huge chunks of the population. Even lesser-known major-party candidates can be victims of this mentality. "It's no mystery why journalists generally ignore outsider candidates," radio producer Cindi Deutschman-Ruiz wrote for The Poynter Institute amid Democratic primaries in February 2004. "We don't want to lend credence to people with no chance, while giving short shrift to those who may actually win. …What concerns me most is that in labeling candidates irrelevant we participate in and may indeed help *ensure* their irrelevancy."[12]

We need to pick winners and losers based on their proposed solutions to our common problems. To do that right, we need to hear all the available solutions. And the fact is, sometimes third-party candidates do emerge from the pack, win over the public and sweep into office. Jesse Ventura, a Reform Party candidate who won the Minnesota governorship in 1998, is the poster boy for this phenomenon. News organizations with limited staff and limited space (that is, *all* news organizations) have to figure out how to give everyone a chance with the resources they have. One great option is using the Web as a repository for all sorts of information that won't fit in the paper.

Citizens

Citizens — not political operatives, not pundits, not corporate donors, not journalists — are the ultimate authority over elections, so they deserve a big role in election coverage. News organizations are getting better at helping citizens talk to one another about issues and candidates, and the press can help citizens lead by example, by spotlighting people taking the political process into their own hands. Here are some ways to get citizens into your election coverage:

Get their reaction

Give citizens regular opportunities to respond to issues, candidates, and campaign developments. This can be as simple as conducting man-on-the-street interviews, though those quote-and-run stories tend to be shallow and unenlightening unless you take a few minutes to get beyond your subject's initial reaction and probe for nuance.

Searching for a deeper way to gauge citizen reaction, *The State News* convened a student panel to watch and respond to the 2004 presidential debates. The paper invited readers with different political perspectives to join the panel, and a reporter sat with the group as they watched each debate. The morning after, the paper ran a wire story about the debate and a local story with the panel's reactions. Readers could witness their peers' responses to the candidates and watch those impressions develop over the course of the campaign. The series wrested some control from the experts and returned it to readers, said Ed Ronco, who was *State News* editor at the time.

"[A]fter readers started catching on to what the panel was doing, we would get letters agreeing or disagreeing with their conclusions," Ronco said.[13] "I'd like to think at least some of those people decided to watch the debates because they wanted to argue with the panel. It really seemed to stir up a lot of discussion in the community, which is always good for readers. It's good for reporters, too."

Profile activists

The best way to show that people are in charge of politics is to spotlight the ones who get involved. *The State News* ran a three-part series in early October 2004 about young people playing important roles locally. Here's part of the first story:

> Now that a record number of Michigan residents have registered for the November election, Genevieve Humenay wants to change the way people think about voting.
>
> She's not concerned with party politics, nor is she fretful about whether people [subscribe] to her political beliefs.
>
> Instead, the 2004 MSU graduate wants to make sure people get to the polls to cast their ballots on Nov. 2.
>
> Humenay is the co-founder of Lansing Voters Matter, a non-partisan organization she started with her roommate Michelle Johnson, a 2003 MSU graduate.
>
> "We did some research and found that in the last presidential election, there

were 20 precincts in Lansing with less than a 50 percent turnout from registered voters," said Humenay, 26, who holds a degree in social relations.

It doesn't do a lot of good to have thousands of people registered if less than half of them turn out at the polls, Humenay said. She said having that low of a turnout undermines the democratic process and isn't representative of the people in the mostly low-income precincts.[14]

At the end of the story was information about how to get involved with Lansing Voters Matter — an invitation to act. The second part of the series was about a Michigan State graduate who volunteered for an organization supporting voters' rights. The third focused on the university's student chapter of the League of Women voters, which circulated nonpartisan information about candidates.

When people see others like themselves in the paper, taking ownership of the electoral process, barriers to getting involved become less intimidating.

Profile the uninterested

The *Detroit Free Press* in 2004 gave voice to the sizable minority of eligible voters who opted not to participate. "There's a big part of our population that turns off to the process," Deputy Metro Editor Bob Campbell said. "In our ivory towers we might think that they're not very smart people, but some of them are quite bright; they just don't see that much difference between the candidates. And we knew there'd be a good story there and we found it."[15]

Here's part of the illuminating, if depressing, story:

> They've missed elections because they were too tired from 12-hour shifts, or just too tired of chattering politicians. Or they couldn't decide, or they weren't impressed.
>
> You've heard of likely voters, right? Well, these are the unlikely voters — the four out of 10 voting-age Americans who are polling place truants.
>
> Are they likely to change come Tuesday?
>
> Sen. John Kerry and President George W. Bush can trade their barbs, trot their ads and stump their way across every inch of southeast Michigan and 10 other battleground states.
>
> The passion of the 2004 race has convinced people like Denise Bieniewicz of Eastpointe, who will vote for the first time since 1992 and for Kerry, and Bertie Lea Witte of Grand Rapids, who also has missed the last couple presidential votes and will vote for Bush.
>
> But Toni Gervasone will remain on the sidelines.
>
> The Imlay City resident said she's never voted before — not once, ever — and she doesn't plan to start Tuesday.
>
> "My husband's for Bush, and I'm for the other one," said Gervasone, 49. "If I were to vote this time, it'd be like I'm canceling out his vote."
>
> The other one?
>
> "Kerry Edwards?" Gervasone guessed.

It's not that the mother of five children and three stepchildren doesn't care. She lost her factory job in May and can't find another one. She worries the work is all going overseas. She feels the country sliding downhill.

"I really believe it's time for a change," Gervasone said. "I don't see anything getting better with Bush being there."

But she's sure her vote won't make a difference. Her husband, Richard Gervasone, 64, said the more he tries to change her mind, "the more bullheaded she gets about not getting out there."

"To her, if you had Bam Bam and Pebbles in there, she'd be happy," said Richard Gervasone, a retired factory worker and regular voter.

Even with some Michigan municipalities projecting record turnout for Tuesday's presidential election, about 40 percent of eligible Americans don't bother.

"Voting takes a certain amount of effort. You have to know enough to have opinions. You have to have views about whether the country is run well or badly," said East Lansing-based polling expert, Mark Grebner.

"The real determinants about voting aren't about politics but about individual lives."

Whether people vote can be affected by whether they've recently moved, whether their car works, whether someone will baby-sit the kids — not to mention the weather.

Janice Marie Keeler, 53, of Huron Township has voted across parties and for winners — Ronald Reagan in 1984, George Bush in 1988 and then Bill Clinton in 1992. But she hasn't voted since. And she isn't inclined to.

"The more I see them on television, the more they annoy me, and the less I want to back them up," said Keeler, a disabled former shipping clerk.

She said she wants a "real person, a sincere person."

"But sincerity and politics don't meet. I'm kind of apathetic to the whole thing. From a Republican to a Democrat, I don't see how it makes a big difference in my life," Keeler said. ...[16]

These citizens are in control of politics, just like the people who vote. The reasons why they forfeit their control are newsworthy. Journalism is about helping people understand why things are the way they are. This story helps build understanding.

Speak right to them

Partly because so many people are disengaged from the political process, several groups, including news organizations, have taken to speaking directly to potential voters in unconventional ways. *The State News* ran a story in 2004 about a tongue-in-cheek Web site that encouraged college-aged people to vote, have sex with fellow voters on election night, and withhold sex from nonvoters. The story included comments from people who thought the site was insulting, but mostly it was a way to have fun with, and maybe draw some attention to, a serious subject. The story ran on the front page, next to another story about local groups trying to get young people registered. The lead? "A new college-oriented Web site is hoping to mix voting and sex for climactic results in the presidential election."[17]

The *Lansing State Journal* had a less risqué but equally direct package aimed at young voters the day before the voter registration deadline. Under the front-page headline "just VOTE," the package had a bunch of short items that encouraged young readers to think about the election. There were numbers from a poll of young Americans; interviews with young people; a quiz about abortion, Social Security, gay rights, taxes, education, and national security to help readers determine which party they supported; and summaries of Bush and Kerry's proposals on major issues.[18] In targeting young people, there's a fine line between reaching out and dumbing down, something we'll discuss at length in Chapter 15. This package — attractive, energetic, and tightly written, but focused on meaningful information — seemed to get it right.

The *Rocky Mountain News* used humor and direct address to help explain the arcane caucus system of choosing presidential nominees. Here's part of a Q&A the paper did to educate readers, under the headline "Caucuses 101":

> Question: In 2000, we had a presidential primary election like other states. What happened to the presidential primary?
>
> Answer: It went away. Get over it. Actually, Colorado still has a primary election, on Aug. 10, for all of the other races. The presidential primary was eliminated after the 2000 election to save money.
>
> Question: But weren't the caucuses over back in January?
>
> Answer: Those were the Iowa caucuses. That's why you saw so many frozen cornfields on TV. There are all sorts of caucuses out there, including the Democrats Abroad Local Caucuses, the District of Columbia Ward Caucuses and the Maine Municipal Caucuses. Pay them no mind. You don't live there. You live here, and our caucus is Tuesday.
>
> Question: What is a caucus, anyhow?
>
> Answer: It's the electoral equivalent of Opening Day of baseball season, minus the overpriced beer in plastic cups. Despite the day's significance, however, the action is more Little League than Major League.
>
> Question: How's that?
>
> Answer: Caucuses are party politics at the most local level. Registered voters in each precinct gather to select party representatives to the county assemblies, who in turn will select people to go to the state and national conventions.
>
> Question: Yawn. ...[19]

Events

We're deep into our discussion of election coverage, and only now do we address what's most commonly emphasized: the day-to-day maneuverings, announcements, and attacks from the campaigns themselves. Debates, rallies, press conferences, polls, endorsements, and similar episodic events drive the pace and tone of campaigns. Except for debates, they also tend to be the most superficial and least meaningful aspects of the race. The daily events, orchestrated and scripted by political pros, are designed to attract media attention, dispense tightly focused messages, raise the reputation of the candidate-client, and sink the reputation of the opponent. This is the information that is spoon-fed to reporters who accompany the candidates as they crisscross the country, state, or district by air, bus, or train. The assertions made at these events usually come without context or supporting evidence. They command the bulk of reporters' attention, but they don't deserve it. If our job is to give citizens the information they need to make good decisions, then the latest stump speech, sneak attack, or silly gaffe (one or two poorly chosen words out of the thousands spoken in a given day) have to be a lower priority than defining the community's problems and assessing how well each candidate will address them.

Here are some suggestions about how to cover campaign events:

Debates: These are usually the most important events of the campaign and need to be taken seriously. Opposing candidates only end up in the same room a handful of times, and their effectiveness at defending their positions and finding holes in their opponents' is an important measure of their qualification for office. But like other events, the temptation is to focus on which candidate wins more style points rather than who puts forward stronger positions. Much post-debate commentary is about whether the candidates did better or worse than expected, based on arbitrary standards of competence. Useful analysis addresses how knowledgeably and accurately candidates answered substantive questions, how effectively they responded to challenges, and how adeptly they summed up their aspirations for office. The quality of the candidates' ties, the person who got off the best one-line insult, or the number of times one candidate blinked compared with the other might be worth noting — maybe in a fun box or sidebar — but they can't become the fundamental story of the debate.

Polls: As we discussed in Chapter 1, polls are interesting snapshots of what potential voters think at a given moment. Coverage that includes the "horse race" element of campaigns tends to interest readers more than coverage that ignores these questions. But polls can't be the end-all and be-all of campaign coverage. Voters should be encouraged to pick the best candidate for themselves, not to follow the crowd as defined by a telephone survey.

Attacks: Campaigns and their allies work tirelessly to create or exacerbate scandals involving their opponents. Most candidates aren't saints, so accusations of sexual indiscretions, tax dodging, shady business deals, conflicts of interest, or substance abuse are often credible and sometimes even true. Journalists have every obligation to chase down rumors of illegal and unethical activity; that's the point of the background checks *The Virginian-Pilot* conducted independently at the very beginning of local city and school board races.

But journalists become stooges when they take bait from political operatives and publish it before it's been verified, or let a minor misdeed dominate coverage. Character assassination is nothing new in politics, but new tools such as weblogs can turn a vapor of a rumor into a swirling cyclone before anyone responsible has a chance to prove or debunk it. As we discussed in Chapter 4, we have to be sure something's right before we go with it, and we have to be open about the affiliations and motivations of sources, lest we become hit men for political assassins. Responsible journalists who don't print what they don't know to be true will be accused of covering up for a favored candidate, but this is an occupational hazard we have to accept.

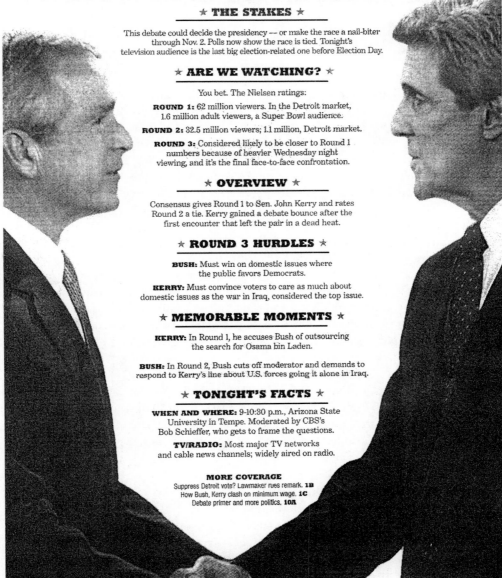

ELECTION 2004 | TONIGHT'S PRESIDENTIAL DEBATE

THE FINAL FACE-OFF

★ THE STAKES ★

This debate could decide the presidency — or make the race a nail-biter through Nov. 2. Polls now show the race is tied. Tonight's television audience is the last big election-related one before Election Day.

★ ARE WE WATCHING? ★

You bet. The Nielsen ratings:

ROUND 1: 62 million viewers. In the Detroit market, 1.6 million adult viewers, a Super Bowl audience.

ROUND 2: 32.5 million viewers; 1.1 million, Detroit market.

ROUND 3: Considered likely to be closer to Round 1 numbers because of heavier Wednesday night viewing, and it's the final face-to-face confrontation.

★ OVERVIEW ★

Consensus gives Round 1 to Sen. John Kerry and rates Round 2 a tie. Kerry gained a debate bounce after the first encounter that left the pair in a dead heat.

★ ROUND 3 HURDLES ★

BUSH: Must win on domestic issues where the public favors Democrats.

KERRY: Must convince voters to care as much about domestic issues as the war in Iraq, considered the top issue.

★ MEMORABLE MOMENTS ★

KERRY: In Round 1, he accuses Bush of outsourcing the search for Osama bin Laden.

BUSH: In Round 2, Bush cuts off moderator and demands to respond to Kerry's line about U.S. forces going it alone in Iraq.

★ TONIGHT'S FACTS ★

WHEN AND WHERE: 9-10:30 p.m., Arizona State University in Tempe. Moderated by CBS's Bob Schieffer, who gets to frame the questions.

TV/RADIO: Most major TV networks and cable news channels; widely aired on radio.

MORE COVERAGE
Suppress Detroit vote? Lawmaker rues remark. **1B**
How Bush, Kerry clash on minimum wage. **1C**
Debate primer and more politics. **10A**

The design of this *Detroit Free Press* debate package captures attention by setting up a candidate confrontation, reminiscent of a quarterback or pitching duel. The issue-by-issue primer inside then focuses that attention on the meaningful elements of the debate. (Reprinted with permission of the *Detroit Free Press*.)

Rallies, speeches, and endorsements: Candidates like visits from celebrities; it increases their chances of making news with a stump speech they give 10 times a day. Journalists can't let themselves be star-struck in the presence of an actor, musician, or athlete who comes to town to help out a candidate. Again, these events should be covered, but they shouldn't over-shadow the fundamental question (say it with me): Does this give citizens the information they need to make a good decision on Election Day? As for the candidates' stump speeches, readers don't need to hear the same message every single day. If the candidate doesn't say something new, find a way to summarize his key points and focus on something else.

Analysis

The journalist's role as referee is never more important than in covering elections. It's no joke that people will say anything to get elected, so simply reporting what gets said is no service to readers. Reporters have to get to the bottom of claims, which means constantly challenging sources on where they got their information and why they believe it's reliable; double-checking with knowledgeable, neutral sources; and having the chutzpah to tell readers the truth when politicians don't. Reporters also have to use the election rules to find and analyze information that candidates would prefer went undiscussed — like financial contributions.

The federal government and most states require candidates to disclose how much money they get and from where, and how and where they spend their money. These documents are public and create a wealth of information about who wants the candidate to win, and to whom the successful candidate will be indebted once in office. Contribution and expense forms are typically available as databases, which means journalists can crunch numbers in all kinds of ways to find patterns of giving and spending — leading to lots of interesting stories. The Federal Election Commission (**www.fec.gov**) is a great source for federal campaign data, and Investigative Reporters and Editors (**www.ire.org**) is a great group for showing you how to use it.

ANOTHER FORM OF ANALYSIS is "truth-squadding" candidates' assertions — formally fact-checking their claims. This is done especially with political ads, and a number of papers have introduced an "ad watch" feature. Here's an assessment of a presidential campaign commercial from late 2004, supplied by www.FactCheck.org and published in *The Columbus Dispatch*:

> **Ad title:** "The Truth About Taxes"
> **Advertiser**: Kerry-Edwards campaign
> **Ad text**: "Here's the truth about taxes. After nearly four years under George Bush, the middle class is paying the bigger share of America's tax burden and the wealthiest are paying less. It's wrong. We need to cut taxes on the middle class, not raise them. We also need to get health-care costs under control and lower our nation's deficit. I don't believe the wealthy need another tax cut. I believe ordinary Americans need someone who will fight for them. I'm John Kerry and I approved this message."
> **Analysis**: Actually, all income groups have seen their burden reduced.

Kerry's wording in the commercial that appeared last week could lead some to think middle-income taxpayers are paying more of the tax burden than upper-income taxpayers, which is false.

Figures from the nonpartisan Tax Policy Center show that even after Bush's tax cuts, the most affluent 20 percent of taxpayers still pay 63 percent of all U.S. taxes, including income, payroll, and excise taxes. Those in the middle 20 percent pay 10.5 percent, a much smaller share. So, strictly speaking, the highest-income taxpayers still pay the larger share of taxes than the other 80 percent.

What Kerry has said previously is that middle-income taxpayers pay a larger share — meaning a larger share than they did before, and not a larger share than more affluent groups. And it's true that the middle 20 percent has seen their share of the tax burden go up — by two-tenths of 1 percent — even as their taxes have come down. Those between the top and middle groups have seen their share of the burden go up 0.7 percent. On the other hand, those in the lowest two groups have seen very slight declines in the share of all taxes they pay, as well as in the amount of taxes they pay, something Kerry doesn't mention when talking about the burden on the "middle."[20]

Journalists are citizens' only hope for keeping campaigns honest. Thorough, independent and neutral analysis of campaigns' claims, donors, and expenditures can help readers see clearly what's at stake.

Stage Three: Get out the vote

In the first stage, you let citizens know they could run for office, you introduced them to the jobs that were opening and the candidates who wanted them, and you helped them register to vote. In the second stage, you focused on giving citizens the information they needed make good choices. Now, as the election approaches, you launch a final push to make voting as easy and meaningful as possible. This stage is high on utility, giving readers opportunities to act on the information you've provided.

The voter's guide

One of the best tools you can offer shortly before Election Day is a voter's guide. The guide explains what the election is about; reviews the candidates, their qualifications and positions; and tells readers where, when, and how to vote. If you can afford it, the voter's guide should be a free-standing section, without advertising. It should be clearly designed and simply organized. If you haven't got the newsprint for a separate section, open up some pages in the news sections of the paper. And if, for whatever reason, a printed guide is impossible, create one on your Web site. The voter's guide will help many review and reflect on what they've been learning from you for weeks. For many others, it will be their first and only meaningful exposure to the candidates and their platforms.

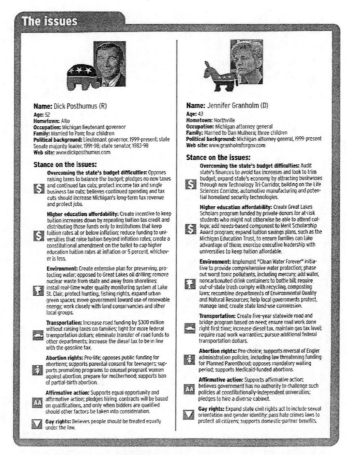

A voter's guide in *The State News* summarizes key election issues and candidates' backgrounds and positions. Issue grids, laying out questions and candidates' positions, are a simple and attractive way to organize information. (Reprinted with permission of *The State News*.)

Utility

Use the final days of the campaign to provide basic information voters need to cast a ballot: Among the details you can offer:

■ A map of local precincts, so people can see where they're supposed to vote.

■ Times the polls are open.

■ Voters' rights and responsibilities: what ID they need to bring, the questions they can expect to be asked, how to file a provisional ballot, how to stand up to a challenge of their eligibility.

■ Phone numbers and Web addresses of voting officials.

■ Phone numbers and Web addresses of groups monitoring the vote.

Stage Four: Election and aftermath
Election night game plan

Election night is the best time to be in a newsroom. It combines the anticipation of knowing something big is going to happen with, usually, the suspense of not knowing how things will turn out. It also is a tremendous test of two separate but equally crucial journalistic skills — planning and deadline performance.

A ballot of any complexity requires that a newsroom carefully assess its space and staff needs for election night. An on-the-ball election editor will have a budget prepared days in advance, with stories and lengths preassigned, a system for learning results as early as possible, reporters and photographers stationed with candidates, editors lined up to organize staff, copy and page flow, and staggered deadlines that allow for smooth copy flow.

Once the forces are arrayed, an eerie calm sets in for much of the day. Some reporters and photographers are out talking to voters, getting an early sense of turnout and mood. Other reporters touch base with sources to make sure they can get a quote when the results come in and write background material for their stories so they can focus on the news on deadline. Many staff members are working to get other parts of the paper to bed early, so the staff can bring all its energy to bear on the big story. Being in a newsroom after the polls close and before returns start pouring in is like sitting in the eye of the hurricane. Everyone is wrapping up the early day's work and waiting for information to start swirling again. Often, decisive results aren't available until minutes before — or after — deadline, requiring the very best work under pressure. That's why the game plan must be so specific and complete, so when the newsroom is under the gun, everyone knows what to do.

Reporters are often asked to write two tops for their outcome stories in advance, choosing the correct one and tweaking it when the results are in. Designers are asked to draft two or three front pages, so they don't have to start from scratch when winners are announced. Everyone needs a plan, and a backup plan, and a system for communicating surprises.

Making it meaningful

You've come too far in your thoughtful, problem-oriented, engaging election coverage to slip into a winners-and-losers mode on election night. Part of the planning needs to involve explaining what the election results mean and what will happen next. The news is not just who won, and — as day-after stories usually emphasize — *how* they won, but what they're going to do now.

Every story should remind readers what the candidate pledged to do about the problems addressed in the campaign. Every story should answer the questions: "What does this mean?" and "What happens next?" The results of each race have distinctive meanings, and often the collective results form a pattern — the retention or tossing out of incumbents, gains by one party over another, the rise or fall of a coalition with a specific agenda. Letting readers know how these collective results could change the nature of their government — the likely results of the people's decisions — is the capper on months of good journalism.

This story spends two paragraphs telling who won, then jumps right into what it means in the third paragraph:

RALEIGH — Mike Easley cruised to a second term as North Carolina's governor yesterday, turning back a Republican tide that in recent years has swept Democrats from governors' mansions across the South.

With all of the state's 2,769 precincts reporting, Easley, a Democrat, had 55 percent of the vote to 43 percent for his Republican challenger, former state Sen. Patrick Ballantine. Libertarian Barbara Howe had 2 percent.

Easley ran on a platform of increased spending on education, more support for job-training programs and calm management during three consecutive budget deficits. ...

Easley said he will follow an aggressive agenda in his second term, mostly related to education and jobs.[21]

The emphasis at the top of this story is not how Easley won the election — a recap of his campaign strategy. Instead it's on what Easley promised to do in office, setting the criteria by which citizens can judge his performance in the next four years. In other words, this story wraps up the election by focusing not on politics, but on governance, not on what happened, but on what will happen next.

Election cycles are endless. Problems rise and fall in urgency. Leaders come and go. Managing democracy by choosing our leaders is a primary duty of citizenship. Keeping citizens engaged in, and in charge of, this process requires energy, creativity, and a firm commitment to public service. Producing informed and invigorated voters is one of the best ways journalists can serve their country.

How to cover elections

■ Plan early. Define the purpose of your coverage and the values that will inform it. Then consider how to bring those values alive.

■ Figure out your coverage priorities. Use the candidates' agendas, your citizen-based reporting, and your best journalistic judgment to decide what matters most in this election. Then relentlessly pursue those priorities.

■ Let readers know an election is coming. Describe the jobs and tell people how they can run for office. After the filing deadline, introduce the candidates to readers and check their backgrounds for problems or inconsistencies.

■ Give the biggest campaign issues — education, public safety, national security, social issues, jobs, taxes, etc. — individual attention. Define and describe the issue, lay out choices and consequences, talk to people affected, and insist that candidates address the issue directly, whether it's part of their strategy or not.

■ Profile the candidates in as much depth as your resources allow. Don't let the profile be a platform for grandstanding; show the authentic person running for office — where she comes from, what motivates her, the origins of her beliefs, how she treats other people, and why she's doing this. Don't forget minor-party candidates; let voters decide who's for real and who isn't.

■ Put citizens into your coverage. Report people's reactions to policy proposals, speeches, and debates. Profile amateur activists empowered by the electoral process. Reach out to readers by showing how they can act on their own political passions.

■ Cover the episodic events that lend urgency and energy to the campaign — polls, speeches, attacks, and scandals — but don't let political professionals or other media pressure you into blowing these events out of proportion. Remember the best criteria for judging the value of campaign information: Does it help voters determine who's best qualified to solve the community's problems?

■ Provide analysis that voters don't have the time or expertise to do for themselves. Study campaign finance disclosures and bring transparency to the purchase of political influence. Test campaigns' assertions against the facts, and blow the whistle on statements that mislead or distract.

■ As Election Day approaches, energize citizens by reminding them what's at stake, who's running, and what they stand for. Tell readers when, where, and how they can vote, and who to call if they have a problem.

■ Rigorously plan for election night. Give everyone — reporters, photographers, editors, and designers — specific assignments and firm deadlines.

■ Make your post-election coverage meaningful. Remind readers of the problems, priorities, and promises that drove the campaign. Signal that you'll hold the winners accountable for their pledges, and keep readers informed about political work.

For thought and action...

1 Interview three political reporters about what they consider to be the most important goals of election coverage. Ask if they think their own work lives up to those goals. If not, how have they fallen short? How could they do better? What prevents them from delivering ideal coverage?

2 Interview three elected officials — preferably people who ran high-profile campaigns — about how their races were covered. What did they like about the coverage? What didn't they like? Would they campaign differently if the coverage emphasis shifted? Now interview the people these officials defeated, asking the same questions.

3 Hold a community conversation. Invite about a dozen people to talk for a couple of hours about the important problems they want leaders to address. Summarize the top three priorities you hear. Suggest at least three story ideas for each priority.

Chapter 9

Local News

I don't think it's correct to say we should be neutral about whether citizens should be interested in the city budget.

— Roy Peter Clark, The Poynter Institute[1]

People confront their local government every day — driving to the store, taking trash to the curb, turning on faucets, dropping kids off at school. City and county governments decide if you need a leash for your dog, how loud you can play music, what you can build on your property, how many people can stand in an elevator, what kind of furniture you can keep on your porch. School boards decide how many teachers to hire, what children must learn, what books can be used, and whether schools are bright, friendly places or drafty old shacks.

In countless moments throughout the day, your quality of life is affected by a group of elected citizens and their employees who set policy, collect taxes, regulate businesses, detain criminals, pave streets, run utilities, educate children, condemn buildings, pick up stray animals, maintain parks, and do dozens of other jobs that ensure an orderly society.

A well-functioning local government contributes tremendously, and almost invisibly, to a healthy community. A poorly run government can be a disaster. Citizens decide which government they get. And yet people are bored to tears by local government news.

The reason is that the processes behind these vital decisions are fraught with minutiae, tedium, and Latin words, and carried out in bland, institutional buildings lit by fluorescent bulbs and lined with linoleum floors. Everything about a local government says: Go away unless you want to be bored out of your mind. So people do.

That's where journalists come in. Reporters sift through indecipherable documents and sit through incomprehensible meetings and turn thousands of words of legislation and deliberation into a few hundred words of clear, compelling, and meaningful prose that helps local residents build a successful community.

The trick to making local government interesting is to resist the lure of the city attorney's cadence, the finance department head's vocabulary, and the budget director's calculator and focus instead on the values outlined in the first part of this book:

Put people in charge. Report problems *and* solutions. Let stakeholders speak. Take citizens' side. Be a teacher. Help people act. And refuse to be boring.

The news of a city does not begin in City Hall or the school administration building or the office of the police chief — though it often ends up in these places. The news begins at a dangerous intersection, in a school with 20-year-old science books, at a community's first neighborhood watch meeting. The news begins where residents encounter problems, call attention to them, and begin to solve them. Covering a city means knowing civic leaders, attending the monthly Elks lunch, checking in with the PTA, reading the Chamber of Commerce newsletter. Your job is to root out the community's problems and connect the people who can solve them — by writing and presenting the news in the way that the general public understands and can do something about.

Roy Peter Clark spotted a story in spring 2002 that exemplifies this mandate. This is the top of an advance to a budget hearing in southern Florida:

> ST. PETERSBURG — Do you live in St. Petersburg? Want to help spend $548-million?
>
> It's money you paid in taxes and fees to the government. You elected the City Council to office, and as your representatives, they're ready to listen to your ideas on how to spend it.
>
> Mayor Rick Baker and his staff have figured out how they'd like to spend the money. At 7 p.m. Thursday, Baker will ask the City Council to agree with him. And council members will talk about their ideas.
>
> You have the right to speak at the meeting, too. Each resident gets three minutes to tell the mayor and council members what he or she thinks.
>
> But why would you stand up?
>
> Because how the city spends its money affects lots of things you care about.
>
> It's the difference between whether the Walter Fuller Pool is open and heated in the winter or not. It determines whether there will be a new basketball court in North Shore Park. It determines whether the beloved volunteer coordinator at the Office on Aging for senior citizens gets laid off.[2]

Along with the story was a breakout box explaining some of the bigger budget questions (Use parking meters to raise revenue? Replace an old but beloved library?) with small photographs to illustrate them. Next to that was a box about how to e-mail council members and how to speak at the hearing, including tips: "Plan to wind up your comments before your three minutes expire, or you will be cut off."

Clark asked reporter Bryan Gilmer and his editor about the story for a Poynter Online piece. In his response, Gilmer wrote that the story's approach arose from his own boredom over covering the budget hearing. "I was, in fact, dreading it," Gilmer wrote. "It seemed like we wrote the same thing every year. Then I thought, 'Readers must really hate these stories if I don't even enjoy doing them.'"

So he came up with another way of writing a city budget advance, a way that Gilmer said helped draw twice as many people as usual to the hearing and prompted dozens of positive reader comments to the paper. Clark's essay identified four strategies the story used to achieve what he calls "civic clarity":

1. Writing with a sense of the audience as citizens who, armed with information, can take action.

2. Writing in a conversational voice, including the occasional use of the second person.

3. Writing at a slow enough pace to promote comprehensibility and learning.

4. Use of simple, but effective, informational graphics.[3]

Clark said he's since shown this story to hundreds of people. Non-journalists tend to like it better, he says, though plenty of journalists like it, too. Those who don't like it complain that its slow pace and instructional tone demean readers and cross the line into advocacy.

"Well, here's my response," Clark said: "If a thousand trees fall in the forest, and no one's there to hear them, do they make any sound? We say that these beats are crucial. We say that this coverage is central to self-governance — and we write for an audience of about six experts who already know it. ...

"I don't think that it's an illegitimate advocacy to write in a way that would inspire civic engagement or participation. What would be illegitimate is if that story expressed opinions on exactly how the money should be spent in the budget, if it really preferred one choice over another. But it doesn't do that."

As far as tone and pacing, Clark said: "On the same page, news writers will cover this issue with this horrible, incomprehensible density, while the local columnist will write it with a sort of breezy clarity. I think that we can stylistically transfer some of the benefits of the column to the news story and still write it in a way that follows the canons of neutrality. I don't think it's correct to say we should be neutral about whether citizens should be interested in the city budget."[4]

The rest of this chapter outlines some strategies for producing clear, engaging, and actionable local public affairs news.

Beat officials to the news

Mike Knepler, who's been reporting and editing community affairs news in Norfolk, Va., and surrounding cities for decades, is an expert at finding "regular folks."

While many local beat reporters habitually quote the same official sources and community leaders time and again, leading to an echo chamber of redundant stories on familiar themes, Knepler is a relentless pursuer of non-official sources — people of all walks of life who affect and are affected by the news. His street-level reporting has helped him detect neighborhood problems and priorities long before they come up for discussion at official meetings. That lets him help citizens set the agenda, and it allows him to raise issues — like the underlying question of race in a commuter train debate — that officials don't want to confront head-on.

One of Knepler's contributions is a column called the "Neighborhood Exchange," which spotlighted people tackling community problems so others could learn from their experiences. The column served as a bulletin board of best practices that got strangers sharing ideas, so civic groups across the region could learn from one another's problems and build on effective ideas. Column subjects included a volunteer mentor who began a workshop for other

Making budgets interesting

City and school budgets generate some of the most important, and least interesting, stories newspapers publish. The budget lays out how much taxpayer money will be collected and how it will be spent. It's the best measure of a government's plans and priorities. It's also vast, complicated, and overflowing with numbers. To make budget stories interesting, you have to look for the people, stories, and impact that the numbers represent. Here are some ideas:

■ Present numbers in graphic form. Too many numbers make stories dense and unreadable. Use the story to explain what the budget means; use charts and graphs to document revenues and expenses, and to compare this budget with past years'.

■ Provide context. Explain how each spending item relates to the big picture. Describe how a fight over priorities relates to past decisions. Show not just who would get the money, but how it would be used.

■ Beware the eye glaze. Remember, as you get more comfortable with budgets, that they remain boring documents for most people. Make the story about people and their stake in spending decisions. Eliminate jargon.

■ Remember the fundamental conflict in budgeting is a choice over how to use scarce resources. Most disagreements aren't between good and bad, but competing goods. That means valid points can be made for many arguments.

■ Look for regional themes. Showing how one city's problems relate to another's helps people understand how their community fits in with larger social and political forces.

■ Show impact. The budget process is ultimately about how government uses tax dollars. Find ways to describe these choices in concrete terms, by demonstrating decisions' affects on individual people.

Adapted from a memo resulting from a March 29, 1999, Virginian-Pilot *public life reporting team meeting.*

volunteers, a tenants' town hall meeting to organize against crime, and a cycling enthusiast who developed a history trail for bike riders in his town.

Getting down to the neighborhood level is one of the best ways to scoop public officials on what's important to a community. The *Savannah Morning News* sponsored a series of background barbeques at the start of its 1998 election coverage and discovered that, while local candidates had been focusing on city housing issues, they had overlooked a problem many residents were most concerned with: the city's drainage system. Listening to neighbors in small, informal settings helped the paper spot an election issue the politicians hadn't noticed.[5]

Some papers have taken on projects to systematically search their communities for the people and places where civic news originates and spreads, well below the official level. In these "civic mapping" exercises, journalists document places such as churches, mosques, barber shops, and diners where residents share ideas and information. By visiting these places and listening — not for quotes, but for patterns of discourse and repeated names — journalists discover citizen "catalysts" and "connectors," unofficial leaders whose social connections link neighborhoods and groups, and who can mobilize their communities to solve local problems. The "mapping" part happens when journalists build a profile of the neighborhood, expanding their source lists to include these grass-roots activists and diagramming how extremely local concerns bubble up into community consciousness. A how-to manual and case studies of civic mapping projects can be found in the "Tapping Civic Life" report on the Pew Center for Civic Journalism's Web site, at **www.pewcenter.org/doingcj/pubs/tcl.**

Building this kind of knowledge takes time and effort beyond the daily work of getting the paper out. It requires visiting places and talking to people without having a particular story in mind — and often holding conversations without ever pulling out a notebook. But the knowledge and relationships that come from this exercise can lead to great tips, more sources to tap on deadline, and a broader and more engaged readership.

Clark, of Poynter, calls the places reporters look for news "sentry posts." Watchdogs of public affairs have to be smart about where they're sniffing around. "If your reporting is limited to meetings, then your story vision will become more myopic," he says. "If in fact you're in the neighborhoods, if in fact you're talking to people who are out on the streets, police and others, neighborhood watch folks, if you get down to sort of a level of folks who are beneficiaries or victims of certain kinds of public policies, you're much more likely to tell more interesting stories."

Focus on people

If you follow Clark's advice and Knepler's philosophy, your local reporting will naturally revolve around how local policies and politics affect the people in your community. This reflects the first principle of public affairs reporting, that people are in charge of their government and their community's quality of life. This frame focuses journalism not on a new ordinance but on the residents it governs, not on high school graduation requirements but on the students who must meet them, not on city policies but on the public servants who see them through. Viewing the news through this lens makes public affairs personal, as in this story from Denver, after residents responded to a City Council ordinance that took away an unofficial community center:

> Jan Schorr reminisced Monday about how a tiny West Washington Park coffeehouse that opened last summer quickly became a neighborhood gathering place where residents shared their lives and the day's events.
>
> She and a handful of her neighbors recalled a feeling of sadness that overcame them when the coffee shop was forced to remove its 15-seat patio last fall, sending the shop into a tailspin.
>
> Schorr and nearly 40 other West Washington Park residents applauded the Denver City Council on Monday when it cleared a measure that could help put the Perk & Pub's once robust business on the road to recovery.
>
> "The Perk & Pub has enhanced the feeling and sense of community," Schorr said during a one-hour public hearing.
>
> Council voted 12-0 to approve changes to an ordinance that would allow the

Perk & Pub at East Ohio Avenue and Emerson Street and other neighborhood eateries in heavily residential areas to set up outdoor eating areas.

The council's vote reversed an amendment passed last summer that made it illegal for coffee shops and restaurants in neighborhoods such as West Washington Park to have an outdoor patio area.

The move prompted Councilman Charlie Brown to dub the measure the "boomerang bill."

"This has been a battle," he said. "It has not been as easy as we've seen and heard tonight. I've seen more correspondence on this issue than . . . pit bulls."

The measure allows the Perk & Pub and other neighborhood eateries to seek an exception from the Board of Adjustment for an outdoor seating area. The changes also allow for such businesses to seek a liquor license.

The board would be allowed to take into consideration the wishes and desires of neighborhood residents before granting a request...

The board also has the authority to restrict — or deny — the sale and consumption of alcoholic beverages and the hours in which alcohol could be consumed in outdoor eating areas.

The coffee shop has been at the center of a neighborhood dispute that led to a 40-pound rock being tossed through its front window and allegations that supporters of the shop placed a bag of dog feces on the front porch of a board member of the West Washington Park Neighborhood Association, which has opposed outdoor seating areas in the neighborhood.

It could be weeks before the Perk & Pub sees the return of its patio. The Board of Adjustment will consider its request for a variance on May 17.

Representatives from the West Washington Park Association did not attend Monday's meeting.[6]

This story makes sure to include important details about the council's decision — how the city could manage and restrict alcohol sales, for instance. But if those details had been at the top, the story would be less readable, and fewer readers might be intrigued to go deeper. Here, the details make sense after the impact is described. The story is also missing some important stakeholders: members of the civic league that had opposed outdoor seating. Tracking down one of those folks would have balanced the story better, but this is also a reminder that democracy, in large part, is dominated by the people who show up.

REMEMBER THAT FOCUSING on people requires acknowledging not only ordinary citizens' power, but also official people's humanity. The partnership between people and their government requires both awareness that ultimate authority rests with voters *and* a better understanding of the people who represent us.

To that end, the *St. Petersburg Times* decided readers would benefit from a detailed profile of a new school board chairwoman, a conservative Republican whose politics differed from most of the board but whose working relationship with other members had earned their respect. The story described how the chairwoman, Nancy N. Bostock, and her husband, who are white, had adopted minority children and moved to an integrated neighborhood so they could grow up in a diverse setting. The story let Bostock explain how her lifestyle fit into her conservative philosophy:

> "On the surface it may not," she said. "But if you step back, conservatives say we as individual people ought to step up and take care of each other — not government programs, not tax and spend.
>
> "I can be up there in Tallahassee lobbying to take more money out of everybody's pockets to have a program to help kids like Marquish. Or I could actually step up and help a kid like Marquish. And so I think it's very Republican, very conservative, to do something like that."[7]

Other parts of the story describe how Bostock gravitated to the Republican Party after being disillusioned by the taxes taken from her first paycheck, demonstrating how personal experiences drive policy perspectives, and how her civil and reserved style allowed her to work with a board majority with very different views. The story humanizes a school board member who's probably been just a caricature in the minds of many community members — especially those who disagree with her politics. In examining how her background and personal life informed her public decisions, the story pushed readers to look beyond stereotypes and reflect on human complexities.

Explain and monitor

Here's what happens if you don't focus on people, impact, or clarity — if your concern is purely technical:

> Upon the immediate approach of an authorized emergency vehicle making use of an audible signal meeting the requirements of this code and visual signals meeting the requirements of this code, or of a police vehicle, properly and lawfully making use of an audible signal only, every pedestrian shall yield the right-of-way to the authorized emergency vehicle.[8]

The translation of that St. Louis city ordinance: Don't step in front of a speeding police car, fire truck, or ambulance.

Government and the laws that support it are naturally awash in precise, detailed, verbose, and convoluted language — language that the average person would never use and that many people don't understand. As we discussed in Chapter 4, it's easy for a reporter to adopt this language: You're around it all the time and its patterns seep into your brain and shimmy down through your fingers as you bang out a story.

But it's neither wise nor fair to expect most of your readers to sit through this stuff. People whose daily lives don't revolve around the relationship between the planning commission and the City Council, or how superintendents are hired, or how state revenue sharing affects the number of cops on the street, don't have the patience to digest news written as though they were experts on it all.

Writing in language that would put an insomniac to sleep places you and your work in an elite club of policy wonks that isn't big enough to sustain a newspaper *or* a democracy. If the community is going to get any use out of your exhaustive reporting on a zoning change that could double the amount of hog waste in a local pond, or an end-run attempt by a school board member to fire a popular principal, you need to explain what's going on.

You can do this through proper tone and pacing, as in the St. Petersburg budget story at the beginning of this chapter. Write as though you were talking to another person in the room, not dumping facts from high above a vast, faceless crowd. As you do, make sure your translations from jargon to common language are accurate; it's not a bad idea to run your interpretation by your sources to ensure your simple version is a correct one.

Here's an in-your-face lead from a city council meeting shortly after a 7-year-old girl was hit and killed by a car. She had been walking in the street because a city sidewalk wasn't plowed from under several inches of snow, and officials were being called to account. Look how the use of questions, echoing what City Council members wanted to know, clarify the point of the story.

> How many sidewalk plows does Lansing have?
> How many vacancies are in the Public Service Department?
> When did the city last buy snow-clearing equipment for sidewalks?
> The head of Lansing's snowplow operation doesn't know.
> But Public Service Director David Berridge said he will get the answers to those questions and more before he meets again with City Council members next week.
> "It appears without any further information that we have a problem," Councilman Brian Jeffries said after a council meeting with Berridge on Thursday.
> "And we have a responsibility to provide residents with a safe environment. We are not able to do that without complete information."[9]

AS WE'VE SEEN in Chapters 5 and 6, there are a lot of ways beyond writing a traditional story to explain complicated issues, describe legalistic processes, and provide valuable context for the day's news. A variety of visual tools can make this kind of education easier on the reader — who can learn new concepts in simplified formats — and the writer — who can focus the story more on ideas and images, less on tangled bureaucracy or swamps of numbers.

Here are a few ways to break out, break up, and repackage information to help people make sense of the news.

The "double edit": All newspaper stories are summarized for the reader in some way, typically through headlines. A good headline captures the story's essence in a few words and entices people to read — but it can't itemize and explain the story's key points.

That's what a "double edit" does: For people who don't have time or inclination to read a whole story — or for the many people who process information better if major themes are repeated — the double edit presents the main ideas in type that's smaller than a headline but larger than body copy, in a few digestible chunks. Staffers at *The Virginian-Pilot* call this a double edit because, after editing the story once to make sure it's fair, accurate, clear, and complete, you edit it again to mine and organize important material in a different way. Other editors call the same process "content layering." Working down from the main headline, each layer reveals more details than the last.

People interested in the story will find it easier to digest after getting a preview from layered content. People with only passing interest may get all the information they need from the double edit — or they may be intrigued enough to read onward. Either way, readers end up better informed than if the content were presented in only one way.

There are a number of ways to break down information through double editing and content layering. A very simple construction that can work for almost any story answers three questions: What happened? What does it mean? What's next?

Information boxes: We ran through a number of these in Chapters 5 and 6. Anything you can do to share background, historical or geographical context, insight into process, biographies of key players, or summaries of pros and cons and what's at stake — do it. As one example, *The Patriot-News* of Harrisburg, Pa., runs a "Your taxes" box with every city and school budget story. The box explains any tax increases and gives numbers that homeowners can use to calculate their own tax bill. "The story can then focus on why a school district or municipality is spending more money," said City Editor Mike Feeley.[10]

Delays deprive troops of better body armor

Tens of thousands lack improved plating

BY MICHAEL MOSS
THE NEW YORK TIMES

For the second time since the Iraq war began, the Pentagon is struggling to replace body armor that is failing to protect U.S. troops from the most lethal attacks by insurgents.

The ceramic plates in vests worn by most personnel cannot withstand certain munitions the insurgents use. But more than a year after military officials initiated an

WHAT'S THE HOLDUP?

Only a few, small manufacturers – with limited production capability – make the enhanced armor.

A raw material needed to make the better armor is in short supply.

Upgrading plates for U.S. troops in Iraq will cost at least $160 million, and it will be months before a substantial number have it.

armor began in May 2004, just months after the Pentagon

A "double edit" provides a quick summary of a story's main points. (Reprinted with permission of *The Virginian-Pilot*.)

The update: One of the trickiest parts of covering the news as a journalist, or staying on top of it as a citizen, is following a developing story over days, weeks, or months. Journalists, watching every intricate twist and turn, can lose sight of the big picture and forget about educating readers on the story's importance. Readers, meanwhile, find it increasingly difficult to pinpoint what's new; every story features the same people, same problems, same background. Why do they keep writing about it?

Recognizing when a story has reached this stage requires good journalistic judgment. Doing something about it requires innovation. You don't ignore an important story simply because you've been covering it a lot. But you don't have to write 15 to 20 inches every day when there's been only a minor development or two. Finding graphical ways to report incremental news can maintain readers' awareness without putting them to sleep.

MAKING IMPORTANT NEWS INTERESTING

NewsTracker
Following Issues Important To YOU

The issue	Last we knew	The latest	What's next?
Moving Racine Heritage Museum into Memorial Hall	Officials are considering whether to move the Racine Heritage Museum into Memorial Hall, potentially replacing weddings and veterans' group meetings with artifacts of history.	Museum officials are still studying the idea, said Executive Director Chris Paulson. They are waiting for signals from the city on whether it wants to keep Memorial Hall as is for a new effort to attract conventions to the area. If the city will needs Memorial Hall for conventions, it may not be available for the Racine Heritage Museum.	A private firm is writing a feasibility study on the potential construction of a convention hotel along with more conventions for Racine County. The study is expected to hit City Hall in a private draft form by Wednesday. Museum officials and many in local government are eagerly awaiting the release of the study. — Rob Golub
Racine First	Racine City Council approved an ordinance last April that would require public works contractors doing projects valued at more than $200,000 to hire a certain percentage of workers from Racine's central city neighborhoods. The city estimates unemployment in those areas at 18 to 22 percent.	Six workers from the area have been hired through the construction companies involved in program. The workers were found by the companies, said Jerry Scott, Racine's affirmative action officer. Scott said city officials will need to work more closely with contractors to make the program successful. Officials predict that Racine First will create as many as 25 jobs for central city residents this year.	The city is waiting for a report from one the construction companies involved before issuing a final report, Scott said. Community activist Roberto Garza said Racine First backers plan to ask the Racine County Board to consider a similar program. The county's economic development plan calls for such a presentation to be made to the board. — Phyllis Sides
New medical clinic	A community group is trying to open a medical clinic to serve low-income, uninsured people.	Officials are still waiting to hear from the federal government. That should happen by the end of the month.	If the grant is approved, the clinic would open this summer. Efforts are under way to find private funds in case the federal grant isn't approved. — David Steinkrau
Festival and Memorial halls	The city owns Festival and Memorial halls and it rents out the space.	The two buildings fill up on the weekends but have plenty of availability on weekdays. The city would like to better market the space.	City officials are hiring a marketing company to come up with ways to promote Festival and Memorial halls. — Rob Golub
City bus service	The Belle Urban System has seen its ridership cut in half since 1981. On Feb. 1, Professional Transit Management of Racine began managing the Belle Urban System under contract with the city. PTM hopes to reverse the downward spiral of the city bus system.	PTM has written an operational plan that says several variables have contributed to the decline in ridership. These include perpetual system changes, decreasing local population, rising unemployment, the current transfer system and system ineffectiveness.	The PTM plan emphasizes customer service, consistency in service and a desire to become a national model transit system. — Rob Golub
Metal buildings	Wisconsin has switched from its own statewide building code to an international building code, which is similar, but which allows metal siding.	Some buildings with metal siding are of poorer quality or appearance, said City Development Director Brian O'Connell. Local city officials recently had no choice but to allow the construc-	"It will be our first and only building, I hope, with metal siding," O'Connell said. The Racine Plan Commission will consider an ordinance that would ban metal siding on Wednesday at 4 p.m.,

The Journal Times' NewsTracker updates readers on important news stories. Some of these items refer to full stories; others tell the story on their own. (Reprinted with permission of The Journal Times.)

150

The Journal Times of Racine, Wis., began its "NewsTracker" feature in response to readership research on the value of update-style information. The system works in both double-edit and grid formats to get readers up to speed on three ideas: where the story's been, what happened today, and what's happening next. "NewsTracker signals clearly that there's a new development," *Journal Times* Editor Randolph Brandt said.[11] "It also readily orients new readers to an ongoing story when perhaps they haven't seen the initial story. They can get a quick guide … so the full story makes more sense to them." NewsTracker graphics can run with a story if the news warrants, or they can stand alone. The paper also runs a daily grid tracking up to 10 ongoing stories in one place. Here's an example from a restaurant opening:

> LAST WE KNEW: A Downtown building at 306 Sixth St. had been a series of taverns, then vacant, before Mark Thomas bought it last year.
> THE LATEST: After extensive remodeling, Thomas, formerly part-owner of Cackle Jack's, opens the new Blue Rock Lounge today.
> WHAT'S NEXT: The restaurant part of Blue Rock Lounge should start in about two weeks. Thomas will try a no-smoking policy on the first floor during restaurant hours.[12]

Assessment: A corollary to the update process is the systematic assessment of how public affairs are going in your community: how effectively government is working, whether officials are keeping their promises, and how predictions from months and years ago square with reality today. You can monitor these things by noting projects and proposals your community embarks upon and then reporting the results, long after citizens have forgotten what the fuss was about. Here are some examples of assessment stories and graphics — culled from pages *The Virginian-Pilot* used to set aside specifically for this type of journalism:

■ Six months after the Virginia Beach City Council named its top priorities, a centerpiece graphic checked in on the city's progress. Instead of trying to smush updates of unrelated projects into a narrative story, the package used capsule descriptions of a dozen projects, complete with icons to illustrate and break up the copy. Each item gave the project's status, then explained it, like this:

> **Project**: Neighborhood Lighting, reduce backlog of requests.
> **Status**: Almost done.
> **Explanation**: The council spent $450,000 of its latest budget surplus to reduce the backlog of streetlight requests. All the work has been designed and should be completed by May.

> **Project**: Redevelopment Authority.
> **Status**: Dead.
> **Explanation**: Voters rejected the creation of an authority that would have the power to demolish declining houses and neighborhoods and replace them with new development. The council discussed but has not decided whether to put the question on the ballot again in an upcoming election.[13]

■ To keep track of time city councils and school boards spent in executive session, the paper launched a "Behind Closed Doors" feature. Beat reporters timed the non-public portions of each meeting and reported the totals. This helped keep city officials, and their constituents, conscious of how much public business was taking place in secret.

■ To monitor the progress of public building projects, like road widenings and school expansions, the *Pilot* ran a weekly "Status Report" graphic. The feature included a picture of the project; a few words on what it was for, how much it cost, who was paying for it, and who was building it; an estimated completion date; and a status bar showing how close it was to being finished.

These are just a few ways to educate and inform readers about important public processes and monitor the progress of officials' promises, in formats that are engaging, easy to read, and ultimately less demanding on newsroom resources.

One of the best things about boxes, grids, and graphics is that — contrary to skeptics' fears that visual elements must supplant good writing — they allow writers and editors to focus their creative energies on finding and telling great stories. Telling stories well is the last, and best, way to make important local news interesting.

Tell a story

Many reporters became journalists because they love to write and want to make a living at it. For beginning reporters thrust into local beats, the clash of their romantic literary ambitions and the reality of mundane bureaucratic procedures can be disillusioning. Reporters aren't encouraged by the conventions of news journalism, which call for studied detachment and bland, uninspired formulations. But a convention is not a law, and it's time for convention to bow to fact: The better a news story is written, the more likely it is to be read.

Roy Peter Clark distinguishes between two kinds of writing: strictly informational writing, intended to *point* readers in a specific direction, and narrative or descriptive writing, intended to *put* readers somewhere. A news story warning readers of a coming hurricane, explaining where and when it's expected to strike, and describing evacuation routes, he says, is a story that points people toward information they need to protect themselves. A hurricane aftermath story, evoking readers' senses to share a community's physical and emotional devastation, is an example of writing that puts readers somewhere.[14]

Each type of story calls for different techniques, Clark argues, but both require good, clear writing to be effective. The *St. Petersburg Times* budget story at the beginning of this chapter doesn't use many literary devices, but it is nonetheless a piece of writing — the author directs the tone and pacing of his material not just to put facts on the record but to arrest attention and call readers to action.

Clark also acknowledges that a writer can point a reader someplace and put her there at the same time, a more complex effort that comes closer to what some aspiring writers imagine when embarking on a journalism career. Sports writers do it all the time, writing vividly of a last-second three-pointer or a bloody, bruising goal-line stand while also reporting the score, the team's win-loss record and the quarterback's passing stats, and explaining what the game means in the context of the season. There is room both to point and to put, and readers leave a good game story with more knowledge plus an accelerated heart rate.

Most civic stories don't have the built-in excitement of an athletic contest, but that's no excuse to produce lethargic writing that lulls readers to sleep. If you're a writer stuck on the city hall beat, by God, find a way to *write* from your beat. Use your literary skills to put people places, and when you've got them there, use your journalism skills to point them toward civic involvement.

John-Henry Doucette, who reported on Santa Claus visiting the mayor of Suffolk in Chapter 7, is hard at work combining the elements of informational writing with the aesthetic pleasures of narration and description. Here he is showing how the vast city of Suffolk gets the word out about its budget:

SUFFOLK — Now and then the government here has a proposal it needs to get into the people's hands — a neat trick in a city so geographically huge.

On Wednesday, it was a $277.3 million operating budget proposal the City Council will soon consider. It needed to be delivered, as near as it can be, to tens of thousands of taxpayers scattered throughout this 430-square-mile city.

Veronica G. Thomas, the city's general services supervisor for public works, loaded a white city Jeep Cherokee with copies of the 160-page proposal. The retired Navy petty officer hit the road before lunchtime.

She buckled her seat belt, turned down the radio and, while she drove, ate a few mints. It was her first time on the route. She worked from directions, missing only a few turns.

One of Thomas' first stops was Driver Variety Store, a hardware, sporting goods and convenience store — and a village meeting spot run for generations by the Parker family.

"I need to drop off this budget," Thomas told three men sitting in the parking lot.

"Come back and see us," said one of the men, Red Parker. "I'll tell you what's in here."

The budget went on display on the counter, among the crackers and potato chips, about two feet from the cash register.

By mid-afternoon Wednesday, Thomas had logged nearly 90 miles on a 10-stop trek through a landscape that ranges from urban to farmland, from suburb to swamp.

A Georgia native, she has been stationed in San Diego and Japan, traveled the Atlantic by ship and settled here with her husband, a native New Yorker, and son. On weekends, she said she drives her own car around the city. "To see where things are," she said. "What new developments look like."

On Wednesday, she continued a city tradition that has been carried on quietly for years.

Though public display of government matters is not unusual, the lengths to which this city goes to accomplish it clearly are. Because of the city's size, budgets are not just dropped off at City Hall and libraries, or posted on the city Web site (www.suffolk.va.us). They are also left for public review at the airport, banks, markets and gas stations from Whaleyville to Chuckatuck. Other government materials, such as capital spending plans, are distributed this way, too.

"The original intent was, No. 1, we didn't have public facilities like we do now, and these are meeting places," said city Finance Director M. Christine Ledford.

"And Suffolk's really big. We wanted to make sure they're where people can get to them."

At Bennett's Creek Farm Market in the city's north, the budget is left out front, but workers said they let customers sit in the back to digest a tome that — including supporting sections — contains more pages than "The Bridges of Madison County."

At Crittenden Mobil, the budget can be found atop a refrigerated case well-stocked with sandwiches — an arm's length from a lottery machine.

"So everybody can be informed," assistant manager Tiffany C. Turner said.

"We do have people who stand there and look at it," manager Jane Williams said.

"We have people come in and ask to take it home and read it," Turner said. That's against the rules.

City budgets aren't exactly exciting reads. A casual perusal reveals zero sex or gunplay. The laughs are few, the numbers many. And there is, when it comes to government, plenty of apathy. At some stops Wednesday — particularly the city fire stations — people said few, if any, citizens are likely to seek out the budget.

Ledford, the finance director, has wondered whether people actually read the thing. She got her answer a year or so back when one man called regarding the whereabouts of a city document delivered a little late.

"People actually look at it, which I find amazing and encouraging," Ledford said.

This is not to imply those citizens are smiling over what they see in there.

One of Thomas' final stops Wednesday was Butler's Self Service, which has been the host of public documents for years.

"She's bringing the bad news," A.G. Butler said.

"No," Thomas said, laughing. "I hope not."

She handed it over.

"People do come in and look at them," John R. Butler said.

"You hear a lot of remarks, too," A.G. Butler added.

John Butler said the store has long had a spot for the city to post its documents.

"Even though I think it's a bunch of bull, at least it's here for people to see," he said.

T. Michael Butler, the latest in a line of Butlers to run the business, hasn't read the budget yet.

"I know they're spending too much," he said.[15]

In addition to getting a nice story from this ride-along, Doucette said he probably learned more about the city he covered that day than he had from his previous year on the beat. Note the homage this story pays to those unofficial civic gathering places we talked about earlier in the chapter — a general store, a gas station — where people meet to talk and engage in public life. Note the number of citizen voices included in the story, people chiming in with observations and one-liners. Note the development of a main character, Veronica G. Thomas, the city official who ticked off 90 miles delivering the budget from stop to stop. She's a Navy veteran, important to *The Virginian-Pilot*'s heavy military readership, and a Georgia native who likes to drive around the city on her own time to see how it's growing. Before she makes her stops, she eats her mints.

The detail, the playfulness, and the down-home tone of this story turn what could have been a brief into both a civics lesson and a reading experience.

"Our job is to make government stories not suck," Doucette said. "I hope."[16]

How to cover local news

■ Remember that most readers aren't experts in government and civic life. Your job is to report, write, and present news that helps people understand why government actions are important to them, and what they can do about it.

■ Look beyond board rooms and meeting agendas for news in your community. Probe networks of civic groups and religious leaders, and visit informal gathering places where people discuss common problems. Get to know the non-official players who connect people, groups, and government. Tap these citizen resources to discover the news before officials do.

■ Put people in charge by showing how they can drive what happens at the local level. Write about leaders as complex individuals, not single-minded politicians or mindless bureaucrats. Everyone has a role to play in making a community work, and everyone is motivated by a litany of thoughts, hopes, and experiences.

■ Creatively explain how local government works and monitor official promises. Report on your city's priorities, then check in to see how they're going. Municipal government is about making people's daily lives run smoothly; journalism is about making sure government works.

■ Use a variety of tools to explain complicated processes. "Layer" content by pulling key information out of the story and displaying it to supplement headlines. Use grids and graphics to break down numbers and tell complex stories. Present incremental news in an "update" format that doesn't require a new 12-inch story for every minor development. Let creativity, news judgment, and empathy for your audience — not convention — determine how you tell the story.

■ Write like a writer, not a stenographer. Find details, dialogue, characters, and scenes that interest you; they might interest readers, too. Get over the idea that the best writing in the paper has to come from features and sports; put your energy into city and school stories.

For thought and action...

1 Get a list of every citizen board and commission appointed by your city council. There will likely be a recreation board, a senior citizens committee, a youth commission, and perhaps a dozen others. Pick one of these boards and write a story about what it's for, what it does. How much influence do these anonymous citizens have over public policy?

2 Attend a meeting of a local civic league and find out what problems it's working on. Write a story about the most interesting problem, talking with civic league members, other people in the neighborhood, and city officials. How seriously are city leaders taking the problem? What could be done to get it solved?

3 Spend several hours in a neighborhood institution like a large church, a recreation center, or a popular diner. Eavesdrop on some conversations to get a sense of what public issues people are talking about. Then talk to as many people as you can. Write a report detailing what you learned about the community from your visit.

4 Find a story in a local paper that could be told better in some kind of graphic form, with information presented visually or broken down into smaller chunks. Suggest how the information could be divided up and the visuals you would use.

5 Find a local news story and write a double-edit answering the questions: What happened? What does it mean? What's next?

6 Attend a full city council or school board meeting and collect all of these things: At least three sentences of dialogue, one amusing thing that happened, a description of the most interestingly dressed board member, an anecdote describing a moment of tension, three sentences describing the smells in the room, a quote from somebody who fell asleep during the meeting, and a quote from a non-official citizen who stayed for the whole thing. Write a lead about the most interesting thing you observed at the meeting, regardless of its news value.

Chapter 10

State and National News

Many political reporters write stories designed to make them look very smart, clever and tuned-in. ... Rather than make ourselves look smart, I would vastly prefer that we make our readers feel smart.

— Holly A. Heyser, *The Orange County Register*[1]

Gov. Arnold Schwarzenegger was out to terminate taxes when he introduced his proposed budget for California in January 2005. His suggested spending increases did not keep up with the rising cost of providing services, and he planned to spend less money on schools, roads, and health care than funding guarantees called for. To ensure that taxes would hold steady, he was willing to sacrifice state programs.

The bold proposal came from one of the most prominent and fascinating politicians in the United States — an action hero turned chief executive who called opposing legislators "girly men" and attracted flocks of followers to his public appearances. But *Orange County Register* reporter Jim Hinch decided that Schwarzenegger's perspective wasn't the most important way to help readers make sense of the budget, its historical context, or its impact. Instead, Hinch found two Orange County residents with starkly different views about the role of government in people's lives. He let them tell the story, building in some history along the way:

> They wanted to send his kids to school in Watts. So Roland Boucher got out of Los Angeles.
>
> It was 1975, and L.A. schools were desegregating. Boucher moved to Irvine, where the houses were cheap and nobody tried to put his kids on a bus. He started a toy company. The IRS kept pestering him, so he became a tax-reform activist. He watched California take more of his money and spend it, in his opinion, unwisely.
>
> Then Arnold Schwarzenegger came along.
>
> "He wants government to be less involved in people's lives," Boucher said. "We have a crazy system where we try to give welfare to people who don't need it. We need to make sure everybody pays a little bit. ... Everything he's proposed (is) a very good start."

Gov. Arnold Schwarzenegger this month unveiled a no-holds-barred reform agenda and austere budget, single-handedly plunging California down one road of its complex and often contradictory history — the road taken by low-tax, small-government activists like Boucher.

Californians have always oscillated between reveling in the fruits of government largesse and rising in revolt against a tax-hungry bureaucracy. They clamored for federal highway funds and military contracts in the 1950s and 1960s. They took their property taxes back in the 1970s. Then they voted themselves guaranteed school spending in the 1980s.

Now Schwarzenegger is telling his people once and for all: "We have to live within our means."

[...]

Such words sound lovely to people like Boucher, who said he finally feels like there is a grown-up minding the state store.

But they strike fear into others.

Amber Toliver of Anaheim wears a button on her white pharmacy technician's lab coat. "There's no place like home," it reads.

Home is where she spends half of each day and most of each night tending her 24-year-old son, Ian, who was born deaf and lost the use of his arms and legs in a bicycle accident five years ago.

Lying in the hospital, Ian told doctors not to put him on a respirator to save his life. His family pleaded with him.

"Then he said, 'Mom, are you going to take care of me?'" Amber Toliver recalled. "I said, 'I'll take care of you as long as I can.'" Ian agreed to live.

A state program pays Toliver $8 an hour for each half day that she spends waking Ian and dressing and feeding him. The money, combined with her salary and her husband's, is all that keeps Ian out of a nursing home. A professional home nurse would cost $30 an hour, Toliver said.

Schwarzenegger wants to cut payment to Toliver — and the rest of California's home health workers — to $6.75, the minimum wage.

"It makes me sick. I don't know what we'll do," Tolliver said. "Am I going to have to let them put him in a home?"

Before Ian's accident, Toliver said she might have felt differently about people who collect state aid. [...][2]

That story takes abstract news about numbers — how the state of California will spend billions and billions of dollars — and makes very concrete points about how each line item can affect individuals. Every number in a budget is money taken from taxpayers and delivered to citizens, in the form of aid, employment, infrastructure, or services ranging from education to food safety. Match people with the numbers and you transport readers from an esoteric debate in Washington or the state capital to the neighbor who cares for her disabled son at home, and the neighbor who moved to keep his kid from being bused across town.

For Holly Heyser, state editor at *The Orange County Register*, this is the essence of reporting news from a capital city: Take the issues that are important to the politicians, and trans-

Focus | **IN DEPTH**

Cutting some services

Gov. Arnold Schwarzenegger proposed a $112 billion budget Monday – a plan to erase a $9 billion gap between revenues and spending without raising taxes.

His solution: Curb spending growth in schools and social services – in many cases resulting in service cuts – and borrowing more from Wall Street and state transportation funds. He also proposed a plan to prevent the deficit from resurfacing in future years.

RELATED STORY ON PAGE 1

Lawmakers now get their turn to review and change the plan. Legislative Democrats already have decried cuts to social services. Advocates for education, the poor and disabled also are protesting.

Meanwhile, Republicans largely support Schwarzenegger's measures as a necessary step to return the state's financial health.

MORE ⬤ **ONLINE**
The budget is online at **http://govbud.dof.ca.gov.**

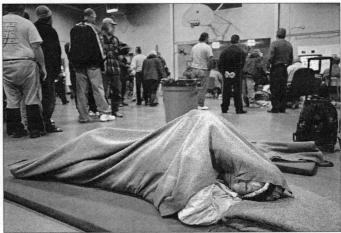

DANIEL A. ANDERSON, THE REGISTER

HOMELESS SHELTERS: Funding would fall by $864,000, or 22 percent of their $3.1 million budget, under the governor's proposed budget. Winter shelters at armories in Santa Ana and Fullerton could be open fewer nights as a result.

**Budget:
Start to finish**

Governor proposes the budget. It is a starting point for negotiations with the Legislature and a myriad of interest groups, ranging from educators to taxpayers.

YOU ARE HERE
▼

Interest groups file into the Capitol to plead for more money, or at least for more money than the governor wants to give them. Those whose funding isn't threatened or wholly inadequate tend to keep pretty quiet to avoid notice.

Legislative process to deliberate the budget formally begins in March, but lawmakers, including the governor, start working behind the scenes to develop strategies, alternatives and deals.

Senate and Assembly pass separate budgets and begin working to reconcile the differences in their budget bills.

The Big Five - the governor and the Senate and Assembly majority and minority leaders - begin backroom negotiations to hash out compromises on the most controversial items in the budget.

Deadline for the Legislature to pass budget is June 15, and for the governor to sign it, July 1 - the beginning of the fiscal year. However, the deadline has been met just six times in the previous two decades. There are no consequences for the Legislature for missing this deadline, although some payments to community colleges, all payments to vendors, some K-12 education programs and paychecks to the legislative staff are stopped until there is a new budget. Legislators still get paid, although they usually forgo their paychecks until the budget is passed.

Agreement is reached, and the Legislature passes the budget.

Closing the gap

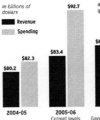

in billions of dollars

■ Revenue
▨ Spending

$80.2 / $82.3 — 2004-05
$83.4 / $92.7 — 2005-06 Current levels
$85.5 / $85.7 — 2005-06 Governor's proposed

If the state keeps funding all of its programs at current levels, there would be a $9 billion gap between revenue and spending - the so-called structural deficit. The governor's budget would close that gap.

Revenue comes up with $1.7 billion in new economic-recovery bonds and $400 million in other increases, such as higher gas-tax revenue, tobacco-settlement money and crackdowns on tax evasion.

Spending still increases, but only by $3.4 billion, not by $10.4 billion, which is what it would take to maintain current budget commitments.

Source: The governor's office
The Register

General-fund expenditures

in millions of dollars:	2005-06	Change	% change from last year
K-12 Education	$35,884	$1,449	4%
Health and Human Services	$26,708	$1,165	5%
Higher Education	$10,042	$679	7%
Youth and Adult Correctional	$7,014	$81	1%
Legislative, Judicial, Executive	$3,016	$143	5%
Resources	$1,270	$203	19%
State and Consumer Services	$563	$28	5%
General Government	$705	($303)	-43%
Business, Transportation & Housing	$380	$3	1%
Labor and Workforce Development	$87	$0	0
Environmental Protection	$69	($5)	-7%
TOTAL	**$85,738**	**$3,443**	**4%**

Highlights of proposed budget

The governor proposes balancing the budget without raising taxes, which means the state would have to scale back various programs and services. In many cases, programs would get more money, but not enough to keep up with current levels of service. Here are some of the proposed cuts:

PROPOSAL	EFFECTS	THE STORY
SCHOOLS: Get $1.4 billion more. That's $1.1 billion less per year than under a deal Schwarzenegger struck with educators last year.	Some school districts unable to keep up with rising costs would become fiscally insolvent. Orange County districts could cut class-size-reduction efforts, share principals between schools, raise the cost of busing and sell surplus land.	Last year, Schwarzenegger persuaded educators to give up $2 billion in exchange for future funding security. Now he is taking $1.1 billion more owed under Proposition 98. Schwarzenegger says the cuts are needed to spare other state programs.
POOR: Place most Medi-Cal recipients in HMOs. Cap dental benefits. Require $324 annual co-payment for health care.	816,000 beneficiaries would have to change doctors and could lose care in HMOs. 125,000 would lose dental benefits. 550,000 would be subject to co-payments. Recipients unable to afford co-payment wouldn't get treated.	Proposals are part of a broader overhaul of Medi-Cal, California's health-insurance program for the poor. Schwarzenegger proposed most of these changes last year but backed down on some and made little progress implementing others.
DISABLED: Reduce wages of in-home caregivers to minimum wage - $6.75 per hour.	Quadriplegics and other disabled people who rely on in-home caregivers to remain independent would have a harder time finding care. Some could be forced into nursing homes. State would save $217 million per year.	Schwarzenegger proposed similar cuts last year but backed down after protests from the disabled.

FILE PHOTO: THE ASSOCIATED PRESS
THE LAST STEP: Gov. Arnold Schwarzenegger's signs last year's state budget. His signature

In introducing and explaining California Gov. Arnold Schwarzenegger's proposed budget, *The Orange County Register* used a variety of tools, including a flow chart showing the process from "start to finish," graphics summarizing revenues and expenses, and a chart outlining six key proposals and their potential effects. (Reprinted with permission of *The Orange County Register*.)

late them into issues that are important to citizens. Bring the news home to your readers.

"What happens in any state is hugely important," Heyser said.[3] "We have to work harder to show how state government relates to people's lives at home."

The challenges of reporting and presenting state and national news are similar to those of covering local public affairs. But the distance of most readers from their capitals — both physically and psychologically — complicates every level of citizen-based reporting. Political rhetoric tends to escalate, often at the expense of thoughtful discourse. The connection between decisions in Washington, Springfield, or Sacramento and people at home is thinner and more fragile than the links between City Hall and its surrounding neighborhoods.

State and national decisions are more sweeping, and often more complex, than those at the local level. The work of representatives, senators, governors, and presidents is diffuse and hard to track. And citizens face even more barriers to participation than they do in their own towns. Journalists reporting and presenting state and national news must help readers understand the substance of debates, the relevance of the issues, and the connections between big problems.

Substance over style

As Gov. Schwarzenegger pursued an aggressive fiscal agenda on the West Coast, New Jersey acting Gov. Richard Codey was in a less certain position. With just two months on the job after a sexually charged political scandal drove his predecessor from office, Codey was preparing in January 2005 for his State of the State address to the legislature, which would be televised statewide. Papers across New Jersey wrote stories in anticipation of the speech, taking different approaches.

Here's the top of one story:

> When Richard Codey goes before a joint session of the Legislature tomorrow to present his ideas for the year ahead for New Jersey, he will have a chance to deliver his message with a minimum of static.
>
> Just two months into his stint as acting governor, Codey has done little so far to get critics sniping at him. Not (as yet) a candidate in November's election, his words won't necessarily be viewed as campaign rhetoric. And he can save any bitter medicine for his budget address next month.
>
> After 31 years as a Democratic legislator from Essex County, Codey will go before the other 199 members of the Legislature and a statewide television audience for the first time. He has never run a statewide campaign and never gave an inaugural address when he was sworn in after Gov. James E. McGreevey's resignation.
>
> "He's poised to step up," said Assemblyman John McKeon (D-Essex), a Codey adviser. "This will put an exclamation point on the first 45 days of his term and will be the beginning of the next chapter. He's going to show himself as a leader. [...]"[4]

Notice anything missing from those first four paragraphs? How about what Codey plans to *say* in his speech — his major themes, his priorities for the state? Lest we forget, the reason government exists is to use common resources to solve common problems, not simply to project an impression or create an image. Five more paragraphs lapse in this story before the substance of his speech is mentioned:

> Codey is expected to call for investing hundreds of millions of dollars in stem cell research, borrowing $200 million to build affordable housing for the mentally ill and developmentally disabled, and increasing the minimum wage to $7 per hour.
> In addition, he is also expected to push for tougher security at schools and recommend further ethics reforms.

That's about it for the meat of the speech, before we turn back to the table dressing: a political opponent's claim that the State of the State address is "smoke and mirrors," a description of Codey's rehearsal regimen and his introduction to a TelePrompTer, and a characterization of his state of mind as "focused but relaxed."

In contrast, here's the lead from another paper:

> TRENTON — Acting Gov. Richard Codey is set to face a joint session of the Legislature on Tuesday and deliver the sole State of the State address of his 14-month tenure. Among the topics Codey is expected to address: a proposal for $500 million to fund stem cell research; a $2.35 increase in the state's minimum wage; and plans to improve care for the mentally ill.
> But most in state government will be straining to hear whether Codey heralds his intentions for a potential gubernatorial bid in November.[5]

This story gets quickly into the politically intriguing question of whether Codey planned to run for a full term as governor. (He decided against a run just weeks later.) But what we learn about first is what this governor plans to do with his job, now. Instead of waiting until the 10th paragraph for stem cell research, a minimum wage increase, and more services for mentally ill citizens, readers of this story get it in the second sentence.

As in the first story, interested readers can move on to a discussion of what the speech means strategically for Codey. Unlike the first story, they can also learn more about his proposals and lawmakers' initial reactions to them. The first story is mostly style; the second story is mostly substance.

This might seem like splitting hairs: There's not enough in either story to help citizens decide where they stand on the minimum wage, and neither story is a thrilling read. So who cares if the one emphasizes the governor's TelePrompTer skills and the other emphasizes how he thinks the state should focus its energies in the coming year?

If that question hasn't answered itself, think back to the values of public affairs coverage: People would ultimately decide, if Codey chose to run, whether he should remain governor of New Jersey. The first story lets citizens know that Codey is working on the image that might make him electable. The second story lets citizens know what problems Codey intends to solve and how. The issues focus builds knowledge that will help citizens make a good decision about Codey. The image focus puts citizens on the sidelines — helpless targets of political manipulation.

Style is about putting people on; substance is about giving people choices.

REPORTING FOR SUBSTANCE takes extra effort, especially in state and national politics, where people thrive on appearances and spend their days crafting sound bites for broadcast and a quick quote for the newspaper. A desire to emphasize what matters is one reason *The Orange County Register's* state staff does little reporting on the day-to-day superficialities of government — the shows political pros put on. "We rarely write straight press conference stories," *Register* state editor Heyser said. "Where everyone else zigs, we zag."

The paper focuses on enterprise stories like the one at the beginning of this chapter, seeking out stakeholders in state issues and letting them speak; putting policies into historical and contextual perspective; closely tracking the efforts of Orange County's state legislators; helping make sense of complicated issues. The idea, Heyser said, is to focus journalists' brainpower on what's really going on, instead of what people are saying about it. The emphasis doesn't mean reporters avoid the staged news events and long meetings; it just means they look for something different when they get there. The approach isn't popular with attention-starved politicians in Sacramento, who want consistent exposure and control over the news agenda. But Heyser says the flak is worth it for the sake of Orange County citizens.

It's important to note that this strategy only works if the paper has access to wire coverage of day-to-day events. As in election coverage, while substance trumps style, there's still room for both. The mixture is a matter of priority and degree, not either-or.

For instance, President George W. Bush's second inaugural address, a mixture of style and substance, got a great deal of coverage. Papers quoted extensively from the speech and in many cases ran lengthy excerpts. But the address, as many major speeches tend to be, was long on mood and symbolism, short on background and specifics. In an attempt to provide context for the rhetoric in Bush's address, one story "translated" some of the major themes — adding background and commentary both on what the president said and what he didn't say:

> **Theme**: "The survival of liberty in our land increasingly depends on the success of liberty in other lands."
>
> **Translation**: Bush believes that fostering democracy abroad is necessary to protect America from its enemies, as he has attempted to do in Afghanistan and Iraq. This raises large questions about how he intends to spread democracy to other tyrannies, including such nations as Iran and North Korea and, conceivably, China, Egypt, Russia, and Saudi Arabia.
>
> **Theme**: "America will not impose our own style of government on the unwilling. Our goal instead is to help others find their own voice."
>
> **Translation**: Bush took pains here to reassure the world that he doesn't intend to implant freedom in other nations by military means, but rather will encourage human rights by standing up for them. His pre-emptive war in Iraq alarmed much of the world that his America was a bully, and he was trying to ease those anxieties.[6]

There is some risk in this kind of interpretation. Perhaps the writer correctly captured what the president intended, and perhaps he didn't. But the feature does fill in some of the gaps between the lines of the speech, and it helps advance the discussion. It layers some flesh of substance onto the rhetorical bones of style. And notice that the "translations" don't critique the speech or the message; they merely attempt to explain it.

Local relevance

Unearthing the meaningful developments in state and national government is one part of the battle; conveying the meaning to readers at home is another. The trick is displayed in the multifunctional story at the top of the chapter: Describe the impact of faraway decisions on the people next door.

Finding the right people for the right story can be a challenge, which is why Heyser says, "When people call you reacting to your stories, my god, save their name and phone number and call them back." Just as important for reporters in capital bureaus, Heyser says, is to make as much direct contact with the people and places in their readership area as possible, to get a deep understanding of the problems and perspectives of the community. From this knowledge flows the kind of writing that speaks to the citizens back home rather than the political sources in the suite of offices across from the Capitol.

Some of this work is as simple as the old-school notion of localizing the big story down to the community level: a sidebar detailing the budget's impact on local institutions, or a "local girl makes good" story when a hometown star takes a national stage.

While one journalist was translating George W. Bush's speech on inauguration day, a *Minneapolis Star Tribune* reporter was focusing on visitors from back home. He caught up with two very different Minnesota groups who had traveled to Washington for the event, and the contrast made for a compelling story:

> WASHINGTON, D.C. — Two organized groups of Minnesotans went to President Bush's inauguration Thursday. One was there to keep order. The other was there to dissent.
>
> The first group was a 70-member contingent from the Minneapolis Police Department and the Hennepin County Sheriff's Office, standing at attention among more than 3,000 out-of-town officers invited to protect the Pennsylvania Avenue parade route.
>
> On the other side of the barricades were 37 protesters from across Minnesota, about a dozen of whom made the 1,200-mile bus trip for a chance to turn their backs on the presidential motorcade.
>
> "I've seen enough of Bush," said Philip Goyette, 19, a University of Minnesota student and state organizer of Turn Your Back on Bush, one of several Twin Cities protest groups that chartered an overnight bus from Minneapolis. "Every time I see him, he makes me angry."
>
> By coincidence, Goyette's group and the 43-member Minneapolis police contingent stationed themselves on the same block of Pennsylvania Avenue.
>
> But in what proved to be a largely peaceful day, neither group had much reason to notice the other, although both were there for some semblance of

national exposure.

"Everybody knows what an honor it was to come here," said Minneapolis Police Lt. Jeff Rugel, who helped coordinate the law enforcement trip. ...[7]

MAKING BIG AND DISTANT stories relevant goes beyond just finding the local angle. Relevance can also be a personal revelation, a jolt of direct impact between policy and people. *The Detroit News* produced a three-part series explaining the impact of federal tax cuts, noting that the increased costs of child care, housing, and college tuition were outpacing many working families' tax savings. In doing so, the series took an idea presented as simple and abstract — lower taxes — and showed how it is both complex and concrete.[8]

USA Today took a similar approach with the headline presentation on a story about the magnitude of the federal government's financial obligations. In big type, the paper says:

$84,454 is the average household's personal debt.

$473,456 is the average household's share of government debt, including Medicare and Social Security.

The government isn't asking you to pay it. Yet.[9]

The introduction of the second-person "you" brings the issue even closer to home. This treatment confronts readers with the idea that their share of the nation's debt is nearly half a million dollars that someday will need to be collected. The approach is not only personal, but also more tangible than the multi-trillion-dollar figure that represents total U.S. debt. In this case the smaller number creates the greater impact, because it's on a scale people deal with every day.

Making connections

There's a cliché that a butterfly flapping its wings in Asia can influence the weather in California. It's a way of acknowledging that virtually everything connects to and influences everything else — sometimes obviously, sometimes more subtly.

But reading a newspaper often creates the opposite impression — a sense that isolated events occur randomly with no apparent connection to a larger cause or broader pattern. Citizens often think about problems as occurring in silos, separate towers of challenges that can only be addressed individually: Health care is one concern, education is another, and the availability of good-paying jobs is a third. Journalists, who break down the world into discrete beats and stories, can get even more hopelessly stuck in this myopic pattern. But in reality, many of the most important issues are linked. A lot of children struggle in school because they are underfed or sick — sometimes because parents are too busy to care for them properly, sometimes because the family has no health insurance. On the flip side, healthy children learn better, become more productive, and create more demand for products and services as adults, which creates a good employment atmosphere, which expands access to health care. Some programs like Head Start, which provides a variety of services to help prepare low-income children for school, try to attack these problems holistically. Good journalism does too.

If you're not thinking about connections, you might put a story about your university's alcohol policy on your front page, a story about another campus' alcohol-related death on an inside page, and a story about a new study of alcohol's effects on the brain on a third page. The events and information seem isolated, and readers might not pick up on the patterns, causes, and effects suggested by considering the stories together. If you're sensitive to connections, you might package all three stories on your front page, or jump one story to a page where the other two are packaged. You might use headlines and design tools to tie the stories' themes together. A little extra thought on your part can make readers more thoughtful, too.

THE ORANGE COUNTY REGISTER puts a lot of thought into helping readers see relationships among people, places and events. In another example from George W. Bush's 2005 inauguration, the *Register* ran a six-column *New York Times* photo of the inaugural platform while Bush was being sworn in. Graphical arrows pointed out a dozen people and groups from the scores visible in the picture as "Faces to watch" in the inaugural crowd and described the role each might play in national politics over the next four years. Among those identified was Massachusetts Sen. John Kerry, watching from a remote corner of the platform and described as a former and potentially future Democratic presidential candidate. Also selected was Chief Justice William H. Rehnquist, whose recently disclosed illness made him the center of speculation about possible vacancies on the Supreme Court. Other figures included Bill and Hillary Clinton, Florida Gov. Jeb Bush, controversial cabinet nominees Alberto Gonzales and Condoleezza Rice, and several legislative leaders.[10]

The graphic isolates, from a sea of potentially unfamiliar faces, islands of influence whose names and mug shots will appear in the news again and again in the coming years. It shows individuals who will be playing very different roles, often at cross purposes with one another, all sharing the national stage in a historic moment. It connects the three branches of government, the major political parties and the big personalities of the day, while also identifying their distinct challenges and motivations. It's a great blend of a news photo, journalism's explanatory function, and the "Where's Waldo" thrill of spotting a familiar face.

In the same paper, editors and designers found a way to help readers see connections among U.S. efforts around the world by creatively presenting a wire story. The story, maybe 15 inches total across three columns on an ad-dominated inside page, had a conventional summary lead about the White House seeking up to $100 billion for military operations and disaster relief in several countries.

To help tell this story, the paper pulled three wire photographs from affected countries and ran them side-by-side, one column each, between the main headline and the text. Each photo was labeled and captioned to show its role in the story:

AFGHANISTAN: The picture was of men picking poppies, the source of heroin; the caption was, "At least $780 million: To help combat drug trade."

TSUNAMI RELIEF: The photo showed a lone girl surrounded by rubble, with the caption, "Up to $1 billion: For Asian nations hardest hit."

IRAQ: The photo showed a soldier on alert in front of a burning building, and was captioned, "$1 billion to $2 billion: for new U.S. embassy."[11]

These three small photos accomplish many things at once:

■ They help draw readers into a story that the headline, "Emergency-spending package in the works," simply couldn't capture.

■ They sum up with great clarity the point of the story — that the United States was on the brink of sending billions more dollars to serve its ends overseas.

■ They bring into sharp relief how vast and challenging the country's political, moral, and security obligations are.

This kind of storytelling — playing to the strengths of text, photos, captions, and headlines to layer and coordinate complex information, can make a huge difference in how a story is received.

One of the easiest ways to make connections for readers is simply to put related stories next to each other. When Minnesota's state legislature is meeting, the St. Paul *Pioneer Press* runs a page called "In Session," which rounds up the state government's news of the day in stand-alone stories and a package of briefs. A screened bar across the top of the page lets readers know what's going on at the Capitol that day — the governor's radio show, legislators attending a symposium on elections — and points them with refers to legislative news elsewhere in the paper.[12] Simply knowing there's a regular place to find a certain type of news, and seeing it presented coherently, can improve readers' understanding.

COVERING THE IMPORTANT parts of political debate — digging for the impact on people instead of on politicians, then showing how economic, social and moral problems intersect with one another — sets the stage for informed citizens to monitor state and national deliberations.

Then, systematically following the actions of local representatives can help readers stay on top of events. *The Orange County Register* keeps track of its local legislators' activities by rounding up their work each week. The paper also reports what committees local legislators are assigned to at the beginning of each session, so readers know who specializes in what.

Summarizing major issues at the beginning, middle, and end of a legislative session is a good way of keeping readers informed without overwhelming them. When Michigan's legislative session ended in December 2004, the *Lansing State Journal* produced a roundup of the major laws that had passed. A story on the front page, headlined "500 state laws pass despite budget woes," listed major legislation in a few bullet points and referred inside to capsule summaries of laws ranging from cigarette taxes to mourning dove hunting. The page also highlighted major legislative pushes that failed. The brief review was a great catch-up tool for readers who hadn't been following these issues all year.[13]

Finally, being creative in how you present important issues can help your readers act on what they learn. *The Arizona Republic* created a "You Slash the Budget" board game so readers could play the governor making tough fiscal choices. *The Orange County Register* ran a column called "Red Ink," devoted to getting reader input and tackling budget issues, one at a time.[14] *The Capital Times* of Madison, Wis., covered a "People's Legislature," composed of disaffected citizens who wanted state lawmakers to focus on important problems.[15]

What all these efforts have in common is a commitment to the first principle of public affairs reporting — putting people in charge of public life. Washington and the state capital may be hundreds or thousands of miles away, but state and national government are a part of our daily lives. If you constantly remind your readers of this, you keep them in control.

How to cover state and national news

■ Emphasize the substance of political and government activities, not the superficial grandstanding and sniping. Report what public officials say, but focus on what they do. In policy debates, report and present the real choices and consequences involved, not just the strategies each side is using to get its way.

■ Show local readers how events in Washington and their state capital affect them every day. Localize budget issues to the money flowing in and out of your community. Find local residents affected by policy decisions and tell their stories. Follow the activities of lawmakers representing your readers.

■ Make connections between related people, places, and events. Collect and package related stories. Explain how a new federal program will affect your state and, ultimately, your community.

■ Provide basic information about the officials serving your readers. Introduce new lawmakers. List biographical, resume, and contact information. Get their plans and priorities on the record. Then keep track of what they do, and how they do it.

■ Systematically monitor developments over the course of legislative sessions. Find ways to briefly and graphically update key proposals and legislation. Point readers to sources of more information.

■ Help readers get involved with the issues and events in their capitals. Offer interactive features in the paper and on the Web that help them work through problems. Remind readers constantly that while they've hired public officials to do the heavy lifting, they're still in charge of what their governments do.

For thought and action...

1 Find a story about an important issue being discussed in Congress or your state legislature. Identify the paragraphs that focus primarily on the substance of the issue — defining the problem, giving examples, offering choices, explaining consequences. Then identify the paragraphs that focus primarily on style — politicians talking about what an important issue it is, politicians accusing other politicians of downplaying or overplaying its importance, speculation about the *political* consequences of various choices and their impact on the next election. Now calculate the percentage of substance vs. style. If less than 50 percent of the story is substantive, do enough independent reporting to add paragraphs until the story emphasizes what matters.

2 Find two local people who are affected differently by an important state or national debate and interview them. Write a single story contrasting these individuals' points of view while explaining the issue and its political status. Your local legislators' offices might be able to help you find sources for this story; so might local agencies that deal with the issue you're writing about.

3 Make a list of all the state and federal legislators who represent your region. Get their name, age, hometown, occupation, party, political resume, and contact information. Call each legislator's office and ask for the top three things the official hopes to accomplish this term. Now design a graphic that presents this information as interestingly and efficiently as possible.

4 Devise a weekly feature to help citizens keep up with the activities of their congressional delegation — the two senators who represent the state, and the representative who serves your local district. The feature should at least report how each legislator voted, what they did on their committees, and any visits they made to their home state or district during the week. Adding a funny or character-revealing anecdote would be even better.

5 Look through an entire newspaper — news, sports, features, and business — and see if editors missed any opportunities to make connections between related stories by packaging them or referring among them. Write a one-page critique examining how the paper could do a better job connecting news and events for readers.

Chapter 11

World News

We cover the world the way we cover the Olympics: If no Americans are involved, we are not interested. ... Ask publishers about this and you hear the same weary refrain: "Americans just don't care about foreign news." To which the reply should be: "Which Americans?" Followed by "How the hell do you know?"

— Pete Hamill, *News is a Verb*[1]

In an interconnected world, all news is also local. ... When you talk about the world as your backyard, "provincial" takes on a new meaning.

— Raman Narayanan, *The Atlanta Journal-Constitution*[2]

One of the biggest international stories of the past half-century broke very late on Christmas day, 2004. As most American editors were putting their newspapers to bed, or putting themselves to bed after getting the paper out, a bulletin moved that an undersea earthquake had created a huge wave that ravaged shorelines across the Indian Ocean. The earliest reports included small death counts, but in less than 24 hours it was clear that thousands of people had been broken apart by water and debris, or swept mercilessly to sea. Not long after, death estimates rose to tens of thousands, and finally to around 200,000 people.

The scope of the disaster dwarfed the toll of Sept. 11, 2001, and the tsunami received significant play in most American papers. Yet on the whole, western governments and media were sluggish in reacting. The United States and other nations offered paltry initial aid packages, until political pressure and mounting deaths pushed the dollar figures higher. And at least one editor acknowledged a misjudgment in his paper's early approach to the story. Dennis Ryerson, editor of *The Indianapolis Star*, told readers that he had signed off on a front page devoting more space to a passing record set by Indianapolis Colts quarterback Peyton Manning than to the first full day of reporting from the tsunami. Ryerson's explanation is honest and instructive as we examine the role of world news in American journalism:

...I confess to having been caught up in the Indy moment that was

Manning's record. I reasoned that this was the big story of the day in Indianapolis, and that readers would appreciate the major presence of the story and related photos on Page One.

We had considered stripping the disaster story across the top of the page, with the football story running below. But I ultimately went along with a plan that placed the Manning story in the dominant space on the left side [of] the page, with the quake story occupying secondary, right-side space.

Looking back on it, I was wrong.

The play of international stories has long been an issue for the American news media. Living in a country separated by vast oceans from so much of the rest of the world, Americans tend not to be as interested in international events as are people in some other countries. That lack of interest is reflected in news coverage.

It wasn't that many years ago when journalists were strongly advised against "Afghanistanism," a term that referred to our reporting long features about far-off countries at the expense of local news.

As trade and communications have expanded, and with breaking international events, the world has gotten smaller. Things changed further after Sept. 11, 2001, when U.S. troops invaded Afghanistan to oust a repressive regime that had harbored terrorists. "Afghanistanism" now has an entirely new meaning.[3]

The reference to Afghanistanism takes us full circle to this book's introduction and its central premise that important news is intrinsically interesting if we have the skill and leadership to show it. Before Sept. 11, Afghanistan was a breeding ground for terrorists hell-bent on wounding the United States, and yet journalists across the country avoided Afghanistan stories by name, because they represented a far-away place no one cared about. After Sept. 11, Afghanistan hadn't changed, but our attention to it certainly did.

The major challenge for journalists is to find the next Afghanistan and make citizens aware before it blows up in our faces. Citizens can only focus their government's attention on what they know and care about, and it's easy enough to ignore important matters for those that are more immediate. Already our nation's attention has moved on from Afghanistan, which has made great strides but is still dangerous (and was growing more unruly by mid-2005), woefully lacking in infrastructure and resources, and a huge contributor to the world's illicit drug market.

In early 2005, the *American Journalism Review* reported that only two news organizations, *The Washington Post* and *Newsweek*, had full-time reporters based in the capital city of Kabul, with other outlets relying on stringers or correspondents based in other regional capitals. The number of dedicated reporters was down substantially from May 2003, a year and half earlier. Most journalists *AJR* talked to for the story seemed OK with the level of coverage, but *Newsday* foreign editor Roy Gutman was critical, saying, "it's very important to keep a spotlight on Afghanistan to see whether the U.S. government is able to manage it and able to succeed."[4]

For most news organizations, reporting on world news is a matter of packaging and adding value to others' reporting. But the fact that you don't have the people or money to send a reporter to Beijing or Baghdad does not diminish the significance of events in those cities, and it doesn't reduce your obligation to make international news relevant to your local audience. Here are some things to consider as you explain the world to your readers.

Give world news its due

Proximity — the distance between a news event and your audience — is an important news value, but growing less so every day. Naturally a murder in your own city will take precedence over a murder in Istanbul. But this doesn't excuse American editors' refusal to take note of political and cultural forces abroad that help shape our own lives. *Washington Post* media critic Howard Kurtz interviewed former CBS foreign correspondent Tom Fenton about this problem in early 2005. Fenton, who wrote a book, *Bad News*, on the subject, claimed that lack of foresight and poor judgment on the part of network executives resulted in the scuttling of Fenton's plan to interview Osama bin Laden in 1996. Kurtz quotes the book as saying that "Foreign correspondents like myself came to be regarded as alarmists, waving our arms from remote places like Rwanda or Yugoslavia, trying in vain to get attention."[5]

It was this failure of proportion that led *The Indianapolis Star* to favor the triumph of a local athlete over the destruction of thousands of foreign lives after the 2004 tsunami, and it's that failure repeated in daily news decisions across the country that results in Americans' general ignorance of and apathy toward nations whose citizens share different cultures or skin colors than the U.S. majority. The quaint notion that events on the other side of the world don't touch American lives was shattered on Sept. 11, and yet there has been little change in our strategic approach to portraying and explaining world affairs.

It's worth noting, for instance, that world response to the 2004 tsunami was not purely a humanitarian concern. The *Los Angeles Times* adeptly pointed out that institutions friendly to democracy weren't the only ones helping victims. One story reported that militants favoring Islamic rule had entered an Indonesian province by the hundreds to provide their own disaster relief, leading to implications that a competition might ensue for the loyalty of desperate tsunami victims. Although the story suggested a tense peace among groups working in the region, it shed light on the possibility that U.S. attention to developing nations' problems has political and security ramifications, as well as moral ones.[6]

Meanwhile, a decade after media and international governments largely ignored a genocide in Rwanda, news organizations were once again reticent about an unfolding crisis in Africa — this time the Sudanese province of Darfur, where government-supported militants were slaughtering people by the thousands. In a column, *San Francisco Chronicle* readers' representative Dick Rogers noted that United Nations officials had declared Darfur the worst humanitarian crisis in the world. And yet, Rogers noted, "[t]he words and images that would convey the drama, the sadness, the horror, the futility, the politics and the infrequent signs of hope have been insufficient." Only three Sudan stories had made the *Chronicle* front page by late November 2004, compared with 14 front-page stories on San Francisco Giants' outfielder Barry Bonds' steroid scandal and 36 on the Scott Peterson murder case. Rogers concluded:

There may be more to this than resources and the difficulties of reporting from a distant land. To Americans, and thus the U.S. press, the story is largely an abstraction. Our men and women aren't on the firing line. We have no great strategic interest in the country. There are no strong cultural, historical or traditional bonds that tie us to the outcome. It is, simply, a humanitarian tragedy of vast proportions.

One lesson of Rwanda, site of another African genocide, is that much of the world was allowed to look away. Newspapers, this one included, should apply that lesson in Sudan. ...[7]

In *The Elements of Journalism*, Bill Kovach and Tom Rosenstiel develop the analogy that the journalism of today is like the old art of cartography, back in the age when geography was as much guesswork as science. The old mapmakers would fill in uncharted regions with imaginative representations of dragons and gold mines to impress their audiences. "Sensation made for popular maps," the authors write, "though they were poor guides for exploration and understanding." Like maps, they say, journalism must be complete and proportional to be useful:

Journalists who devote far more time and space to a sensational trial or celebrity scandal than they know it deserves — because they think it will sell — are like the cartographers who drew England or Spain the size of Greenland because it was popular. It may make short-term economic sense but it misleads the traveler and eventually destroys the credibility of the mapmaker. ... A journalism that leaves out so much of the other news in the process is like the map that fails to tell the traveler of all the other roads along the way.[8]

This mapmaking analogy applies particularly well to coverage of the world in proportion to national and local events, sports, and celebrity news. In an increasingly interdependent world, when your neighbor's job might be transferred to another country any day, when your other neighbor might have been born on another continent, and when disaffected people across the globe are plotting our destruction, a map of reality that focuses narrowly on events from New York to California is as deceptive as telling a lie. Americans have to understand the world better, and journalists are about the only people who can help them.

Begin at home

In 2002, *The Atlanta Journal-Constitution*, recognizing that its population was changing at home and increasingly affected by world events, launched a weekly section to help connect its readers to cultures and capitals around the globe. To spearhead the section, the paper rehired Raman Narayanan, a former staffer who had most recently been working with the Atlanta-based CNN International. "The '90s saw a huge influx of immigrants into the Atlanta area, adding to the diversity of what had been traditionally a black and white city," Narayanan said.[9] "It was thought there had to be a way of telling the story of how Atlanta has grown as an international city. ... The idea was to explain the issues about globalization but tell it through the voices and eyes of people living here."

The *Journal-Constitution* was capitalizing on an important tenet of journalism: The closer you get to what people know, what they do, and where they live, the better you can explain anything. In a world that had become an increasingly complex, confusing, and — after Sept. 11 — frightening place, the paper's six-page "Atlanta & the World" section aimed, in Narayanan's words, "to clear up some of this confusion, explain some of the complexities and alleviate some of those fears."

The section has three diverse target audiences: The *Journal-Constitution's* core readership, including people who have never left Atlanta or the state of Georgia; well-educated middle-class immigrants who subscribed to national papers and saw the Atlanta paper as too provincial; and middle and high school students who will enter the 21st century workforce as global citizens. It's quite a challenge to produce a section that can engage all three of these groups, but Narayanan, who later became the *Journal-Constitution's* international editor, said the section has managed to do just that.

In one edition, the section carried a story of an Atlanta Muslim family embarking on a hajj — a pilgrimage to Mecca. The story addressed the family's dual worries about returning to the United States through immigration and customs officials in a post-9-11 atmosphere, and traveling as Americans among Middle Eastern Muslims who see the United States as the great Satan. The story's framing and its headline, "Hajj beckons Atlantans," demonstrated that even within a southern city where most citizens are drawn weekly to church a few blocks away, your neighbors' religious obligations might carry them halfway around the world, Narayanan said.

With a story about dual citizenship, the section printed short essays from people whose hearts belong both to their birth nation and their adopted home, and it ran sample questions from the government knowledge test immigrants must take to become U.S. citizens.[10] Another issue featured a profile of the green card, including the fact that the immigrant ID is no longer green.[11] A centerpiece on increasing homeownership rates among Latinos and Asians led to an inside page with stories on the home-buying process in China, Russia, and Mexico.[12]

Narayanan recognizes that most newspapers don't have the people, money, or space to create their own freestanding section. But that shouldn't stop anyone from improving their international coverage, he says: "For me the issue is not whether you have the space or the section or the resources; for me the issue is your mindset. And if you approach the news with the global-is-local mindset, then the way you approach stories and the way you play stories is going to be different."

Doug McGill, an independent online journalist, calls the idea of beginning international stories at home "globalizing local news." At a conference hosted by The Poynter Institute, which Narayanan also participated in, McGill cleverly turned the idea of localization on its head. By conceiving world news as simply an extension of what happens at home, journalists can reconstruct their whole conception of what it means to report internationally.

"The practice of globalized journalism doesn't generate new kinds of stories so much as it changes how traditional kinds of stories are written," McGill told his Poynter audience. "Globalized journalism is a way of writing the news that describes and explains a community in the widest possible useful context, which is very often — I am tempted to say most often — a global context."

McGill offered these examples:

> A story on a loosening of state gun control laws would ideally contain not only a comparison to gun control laws in other states but also in other countries, so readers can see how loosening the law correlates elsewhere to gun-related violence. A story on the annual spring flu season would contain a sentence explaining that the flu originates in southern China each year and spreads from there around the world. A story about a local medal-winning weightlifter would explain that the world record for weightlifting is held by an Iranian, Hossein Rezazadeh, who lifted 472.5 kilograms, or 1,266 pounds, in Warsaw in 2002. The overall impact of these accreted details will be to situate your community more firmly, for your readers, into the matrix of the world as it is actually situated. It opens readers to a world of useful knowledge and fact from which they can pick and choose best practices, by comparing their own lives to those of others living in this world.[13]

In other words, it creates a more accurate map.

One simple representation of globalizing local news comes from a *Kansas City Star* feature called "Come Into My Kitchen," in which a reporter is invited into a resident's home and treated to a house recipe. In the spirit of the "Atlanta & the World" section, one such visit was to the home of an immigrant:

> Assyia Madit has lots of help and observers as she prepares a traditional Sudanese dish. Her daughter, Anok Riak, 15, and niece, Ashan Acouth, 17, lend a hand with chopping and stirring, and they lead Madit and her visitor past any language obstacles. Three other daughters, a son-in-law and a sister-in-law stop in, too. The kitchen is lively with fragrant food and multilingual chatter.
>
> **Home**: Northeast neighborhood, Kansas City, but soon to be moving to a house she helped build through Habitat for Humanity in eastern Kansas City.
>
> **Work**: Dishwasher at a riverboat casino.
>
> **Special cooking interest**: Cooking in the style of the Sudan, her native country.
>
> **The dish**: It's called Mouchacal, or mixed vegetables with lamb. It is for a regular meal, not a celebration especially. It is eaten with rice or bread. It serves many people. The ingredients are very common in Africa.
>
> **Can you get the ingredients you need for your Sudanese dishes in Kansas City?** Oh, yes, but here we have to get them all at the store. In Africa, we raised many of the ingredients ourselves. We grew cantaloupe, watermelon, pumpkin and squash. If we have a party, we kill the lamb at home.
>
> In Kansas City, we find many of our foods in the Vietnamese store. They cook okra like us.
>
> **What would you serve for a party?** We might make Sambousa (a sort of turnover or egg roll) or fried chicken. In Kansas City, we have African gatherings every so often, and everyone brings their favorite food, and we all share

them. It's nice.

What else is typical in a Sudanese kitchen? We always serve good African tea. We boil our water first with cinnamon stick and cardamom seeds because in Africa the water doesn't always taste so good. The spices make it taste nicer and add flavor to the tea.

How did you learn to cook? In our culture, mothers cook with their daughters. I learned it at home from my mother, and I teach my daughters everything. My daughter Nora already knows it all. Anok is still learning. I have seven daughters and three sons in all.

How long have you been in the United States? I've been here 6 1/2 years. We came because of the war. (Sudan was involved in a bitter civil war for more than 21 years; a peace accord was signed in early January.)

Are there American foods you have learned about that you have come to enjoy? I see many different kinds of food on the buffet at the casino. I like cookies and cake![14]

At first glance, this might seem like an innocuous example of bringing the world home to a typical reader. It's a food story — not about policy or diplomacy, war or peace, economics or development. And yet this little feature serves many important purposes. It introduces readers to a person and culture they otherwise might not see. It moves readers past the stereotypical images of people from developing countries as helpless victims of nature or oppressors — here we see a woman in her warm home, surrounded by family, making good things to eat. And it might well change the way Kansas City residents think about the Darfur crisis in Sudan, which continued even after the separate civil war between northern and southern regions of the country subsided. The faraway, abstract conflict described earlier by the *San Francisco Chronicle's* Dick Rogers becomes less anonymous when we know of someone in our community who used to live there.

In short, it makes the country and people of Sudan real for Americans in a way that many stories (remember the lead from the beginning of Chapter 5?) could never do.

In a newsier example, journalists across the country made international news local in early 2005 by finding Iraqi immigrants in their communities who planned to vote in the country's post-Saddam elections through polling places in the United States. *The State News* found people from two generations who planned to take part — a college student and a man in his 70s. The older resident was Sam Hindi, a retired accountant who had moved to the United States after finishing high school in Iraq and had last visited in 1980. The student was Faisal Hamadi, a 20-year-old Iraqi citizen and Michigan State finance sophomore — someone the paper's readers may have seen in class, the library, or a coffee shop across from campus. Through the paper, he told his fellow students about the challenges of choosing his country's leaders for the first time:

…As a student at MSU during the 2004 U.S. presidential election, he witnessed the abundance of political information firsthand. For the Iraqi election, information on the candidates is not easy to come by, he said.

Iraqis will vote for candidates from more than 100 political parties to form a 275-member national assembly. There are thousands of candidates vying for the spots.

"Right now I have a list of people I know nothing about," Hamadi said. "I'm scared to make the wrong choice."[15]

In an increasingly globalized world, there's a decreasing distance between important events anywhere and the people in your community. Starting at home, globalizing local news, can help your readers begin to see how their lives, their jobs, and their hopes are interconnected with those of people everywhere.

Make it personal

As we saw with the Sudanese immigrant above, an individual can do more to make abstract events relevant than a whole chart full of numbers or a page of meaningful statements from institutional leaders. A 2002 study of reader interest in international news found stories about ordinary people to be most popular, trumping political, economic and disaster stories. "Important news is made by ordinary people, and it is people, not institutions, ultimately that matter," the study says.[16]

Yet the biggest thing missing from most international stories is the emotional component that allows readers to connect with people whose background, culture, religion or skin color is different from their own. The universal things that make us all human are the only practical bridge across oceans, cultures, and languages.

So while *The State News* used its resources to find local people who had a chance to vote in Iraq's elections, *The Christian Science Monitor* turned to a Baghdad family — a family the paper had been following since before the war began:

> Sitting in her dark, cramped apartment during another seemingly interminable power failure, Karima Selman Methboub promises to cast aside her family's fears of violence and doubts about the new Iraq to vote in landmark elections on Sunday.
>
> "We are under the mercy of Allah — I will take all my family with me," says the matriarch, nodding at some of her eight children. "If something will happen, we will all die together."
>
> "We will go directly, suddenly, do our job there, and come back," says Mrs. Methboub, making clear that no car bombs will stop her from a process that, she says, could hardly make things worse.
>
> "Up to now, I don't know who we will vote for," she explains, as one daughter brings sweet tea for guests. "We think after the election, the situation will change for the better — we will have a new government."[17]

This kind of reporting makes the election personal not just for the family, but for readers who have gotten to know them over two years of coverage. "While Americans may not be able to relate to some of the issues that are going on in Iraq, they can relate to the cares and concerns of individuals," *Christian Science Monitor* International Editor David Clark Scott said.[18] "It's just a matter of helping our readers connect to the story on a more down-to-earth, people-to-people basis. Once they're there, they can begin to relate to the larger issues, too."

Provide context

Oregonian Public Editor Michael Arrieta-Walden wanted to know how readers were responding to his paper's coverage of the 2004 tsunami, and how they were using the paper compared to other media. From a group of loyal readers, he learned that the newspaper wasn't their primary source for tsunami news, that TV and radio were beating the paper on rapidly developing information such as the disaster's death toll. Arrieta-Walden took the responses as a wake-up call that *The Oregonian* had to add value beyond standard reporting:

> …That means finding local connections, selecting wire pieces with moving human stories and using enterprising approaches that don't seem repetitive. That means filling gaps in wire stories with the history and backgrounds of countries and cultures affected, choosing photographs that offer a new view, and developing graphics that give readers unique understanding of a region or a development. …
>
> Perhaps the newspaper should have … asked readers what questions they want addressed; given teachers specially designed tear-out pages on the region and tsunamis that would be easy for students to understand; and helped readers early on identify the most effective charities as well as the best Web sites and reference materials.[19]

Arrieta-Walden was suggesting a number of ways for newspapers to provide context to an international story — to fill in details that make the facts make sense. There are many ways to do this, and a lot of them harken back to the principles of teaching people about the world and helping them act on what they learn. The most significant context for most international stories is a base of knowledge that helps readers understand what's going on. Here are some categories of context you can provide:

Historical context: Explain how we got to this point — the political, cultural, and geological forces that helped shape current events. Maps of the countries involved, complemented by bio boxes of key countries and people, build literacy about the "what" and "where." A timeline, or chronology of the events leading up to this news, fills in the gaps.

A story about a civil war in Africa can include a timeline showing when and how the war began and other key moments in the conflict. A story about a new government in Eastern Europe can capsulize the country's political history over the past couple of decades or centuries. A story about new diplomatic efforts between Israel and Palestinians, or India and Pakistan, can identify the origins of the conflict and key moments leading up to this new outreach. In the case of the tsunami, the geological history of the region is relevant — how and when the affected continents were believed to have formed, other large earthquakes measured in the region, the history of other tsunamis to strike the area.

Relational context: Show and tell how events in the affected country will change the rest of the world. Escalating tensions between nations in the Eastern Hemisphere can lead to weapons proliferation that might endanger the West. A famine in a developing country can destabilize its government, creating a potential haven for terrorists. A change in one government's priorities or ambitions can shift the balance of trade, jobs and investment opportunities for people all over the world.

New York Times columnist Thomas Friedman put it this way:

> [M]ore than ever, the traditional boundaries between politics, culture, technology, finance, national security and ecology are disappearing. You often cannot explain one without referring to the others, and you cannot explain the whole without reference to them all.[20]

Tools for making these connections include editing the wires for stories with meaning, not just hard facts; asking local experts' opinions about the impact of world events; "double editing" stories to answer the questions "What does it mean?" and "Why should I care?"; packaging related stories from a particular region or a particular topic (if Mexico, Zimbabwe and Tunisia are all struggling with similar population, health, or political problems, link those stories through editing and design); using the Q&A format to explain complex ideas; and inviting readers to submit questions that reporters and editors can research and answer in a day or two.

The day before Iraq's 2005 national elections, for instance, the *Lansing State Journal* compiled a sidebar headlined "How to understand the election." The short piece answered questions about who was overseeing the election, how votes would be counted, and the roles different ethnic groups would play in the results.[21]

Moral context: Billions of people are suffering outside of Americans' consciousness for a variety of reasons — disease, starvation, political oppression — many of which have been solved or eradicated in the developed world but are allowed to fester through the ignorance and apathy of wealthy nations or the greed of the poorer nations' own governments. People can choose whether to heed to these problems, but journalists have an obligation to make them plain, not simply keep them out of sight because no tangible impact is obvious. Americans made clear in the 2004 election that values of right and wrong are important to them; it follows, then, that the moral plight of people who have fewer resources than we fits snugly into mainstream news judgment.

A glimpse of the future. Looking ahead is important in any public affairs reporting, but global patterns are so sweeping that many aspects of the future are predictable. Climatologists studying yesterday's and today's data are extrapolating how average temperatures may change around the globe. Population experts recording births and deaths can predict nations' growth rates out for decades. *Lansing State Journal* Editor Mickey Hirten, after a weeklong visit to India, brought home perspective on how that developing nation had increased its appetite for oil, presaging gas prices even higher than the record-setting prices the United States was already experiencing.[22] Pointing out global trends that affect every one of us can raise the kind of awareness that leads to good policy.

A big part of helping readers control the future is giving them information they can act on — where and how they can help people, how to reach organizations that monitor and influence international events, contact information for U.S. legislators who weigh in on foreign policy. This kind of context makes readers a part of the global future, once again in charge at least of their own response to important news. Cover the world in a way that empowers your readers to make their own difference.

How to cover world news

■ Give readers important world news that is interesting, relevant, and meaningful. Remember that reporting on Afghanistan was considered a bad idea right up until people living there launched one of the worst domestic attacks in American history. You owe it to your audience to keep them informed about important world news — not to the exclusion of more immediately appealing information, but to the extent that they have an accurate view of reality.

■ Show readers the international connections right at home. Introduce neighbors from other countries. Show how local businesses are finding opportunities overseas. Talk to local organizations that participate in relief and research efforts around the globe. To paraphrase a cliché: Think globally, report locally.

■ Tell big stories through small stories. Roundups and explainers give readers what they need to understand world events, but if the information lacks an emotional connection, it may fall flat. Find international stories with universal themes: love, hope, heroism, entrepreneurship. Show that most people of different places and cultures ultimately hold the same priorities: They love their families and want to live happy, productive lives. Then explain the obstacles they and their fellow citizens face.

■ Put world events in context. Show how the situation has developed over time — politically, culturally, geologically. Explain the impact of events in one country on countries and people around the world. Show what trends suggest for the future, and help readers participate in that future. Use maps, graphics, pullout boxes, and other non-narrative tools to show and tell readers about the world.

For thought and action...

1 Count the number of full stories (not briefs) carrying datelines from foreign cities in a weekday edition of your local newspaper. Unless you're reading a big metro paper, there aren't very many, are there? Think about whether people in small cities and towns across the country should know less about the world than their fellow citizens who read major metropolitan newspapers. Brainstorm five ways your local paper could get more meaningful world news into its daily editions.

2 Pick one international story from the local paper. Write a local sidebar, drawing on experts from your school, resident immigrants from the affected country or region, relief or political agencies with an interest in the issue, military officials or families, and other local residents who may be affected or have an opinion.

3 Pick another international story from the local paper. List and describe five non-narrative elements — maps, breakout boxes, chronologies, etc. — that could help readers understand the story better.

4 Write a profile of an immigrant in your community. Focus on how this person has adjusted to living in the United States, what he or she misses about his or her homeland, what motivates him or her to stay here. Among other questions, ask: If you had the power to change one thing about the United States, what would it be? If you could explain one thing about yourself to your neighbors, what would you explain?

Chapter 12

Business News

These days, if you don't speak any business and economics, you can't get by — or you get by without understanding the forces that are buffeting you.

—Jim Russell, creator of *Marketplace*[1]

In China today, Bill Gates is Britney Spears. In America today, Britney Spears is Britney Spears — and that is our problem.

— Thomas Friedman, *The World is Flat*[2]

When Chinese restaurant owner Yuen-Ming Lim wanted to begin serving alcohol in 2005, there was only one place to turn: the East Lansing Planning Commission. The restaurant was a private business, entertaining people who just wanted a meal and maybe a drink. But the decision of whether the restaurant could get a license to sell alcohol was ultimately a public one.[3]

As the U.S. military continued efforts to bring order to war-torn Iraq — the ultimate act of public will — it relied heavily on private contractors to feed and supply soldiers, build and repair infrastructure, even to guard enemy prisoners. A U.S. government audit reported in January 2005 that at least 232 civilians had been killed doing U.S. government work in Iraq.[4]

Also in 2005, President Bush crisscrossed the country, calling for an overhaul of the Social Security system. The fate of a program that taxes businesses and workers to support retired and disabled Americans rested not with private enterprise, but with the elected and publicly paid president and Congress.

Government and business, business and community life, intersect at infinite points along society's continuum. Business journalism is certainly a distinct discipline from public affairs reporting, requiring heaps of specialized knowledge we won't dwell on in this book. But business' influence on public life is pervasive, and public affairs journalism must reflect this.

Businesses don't vote, but they contribute millions of dollars to political campaigns, arguably influencing public policy as much as or more than private citizens. Government agencies regulate virtually every aspect of business, from hiring practices to the width of doorways to the sale of stock to the temperature of restaurant refrigerators. Businesses' successes and failures can have huge effects on the health of communities, which is why many governments offer taxpayer-funded subsidies as incentives for companies to locate or remain in a particular place. Local business leaders serve on charitable and government advisory boards, shaping more than simply the economic climate of the community. And most people spend the majority of their time working for a business, running one, or buying and consuming goods and services provided by private industry.

If building readers' understanding requires making connections, smart journalists will routinely weave business angles through their public affairs coverage. This chapter explores a few ways to bring business stories into the fold of important news made interesting.

Make it accessible

Nowhere are the principles of clarity and education more pertinent than in business reporting. The complexity of economic matters, the sheer length of corporate names and titles, and the detail involved in financial regulation require, first, a commitment from journalists to keep asking questions until they understand the story; and, second, the care to write and present the information so readers can understand it, too.

One of the best examples of people-friendly business journalism is the radio program "Marketplace," produced by American Public Media. The show's tone is so chummy, its reporting so suited to the everyman, that any subject it tackles comes across as fresh, interesting, and inevitably relevant. *Marketplace* host David Brown once introduced a story on a CEO's fraud trial testimony by likening it to "the Bart Simpson defense," quoting the TV character's famous disclaimer: "I didn't do it, nobody saw me do it, you can't prove anything."[5]

Look at the tone in the show's Web-based teases from its morning report:

What's with the mergers?
What's fueling all of the big corporate mergers we've been hearing about recently? Host Kai Ryssdal gets some answers from Marketplace's money expert Chris Farrell and explores whether these big deals are really all they're cracked up to be.

Can responsible also be profitable?
We hear a lot of talk about the need for businesses to be socially responsible. But is it profitable? Reporter Ashley Milne-Tyte examines some of the latest research. Then, the Economist's Clive Crook explains why you should be wary when you hear businesses boast about the good things they've done for society.

Do we work and consume too much...
America's free-market system of capitalism offers us [...] a wealth of riches, but some argue it also locks us into a world of overwork and over-consumption. UCLA researcher Peter Whybrow's new book, American Mania, explores the topic. [...][6]

Marketplace sounds like non-businesspeople talking about business because that's what it is. Marketplace creator Jim Russell boasts of earning a D in Economics 101 and says public radio honchos approached him to launch a business show precisely because they were trying to reach a broader audience.

"It just seemed to me that people like myself needed to have access," Russell said.[7] Approaching a public radio audience, most of whom were highly educated but many of whom knew little about economics and finance, "meant we had the privilege of defining business anyway we wanted. It turned out that we could, under the umbrella of business, cover any damn thing we wanted to." That meant covering the business of sports, the business of entertainment, and the business of religion, right alongside the more typical economic news.

Marketplace combines this expansive definition of business news with a cheerful, irreverent approach to storytelling. The driving force is curiosity, a search to describe not just what happened, but *how* it happened, like "a great detective story." Russell had read a book about how stupid mistakes nearly ruined many major companies, which gave him the perspective that "error and folly and stupidity and vanity and all those things are part of business." So covering business well requires "just being willing to be honest, just taking business off some kind of pedestal. ...Frankly, being a little bit smartass — not in a nasty sort of way, because the audience doesn't want that — but they do like it when we kind of poke each other in the ribs."

One of Russell's favorite stories in 16 years of doing *Marketplace* was a mock game show the staff produced on the day America Online announced its merger with Time Warner. The game went on for over a minute, with the host repeatedly asking "Who owns..." one company after another. The answer, every time, was AOL-Time Warner. The only exception was the International House of Pancakes.

The skit used hyperbole and humor to illustrate just how pervasive the new merged company had become. "The fact of the matter is that people remember those stories," long after they've forgotten routine reporting, Russell said.

Here are some ways to make business coverage clear, educational, and accessible:

Avoid alphabet soup. Business news is just dripping with proper names, acronyms, abbreviations, and initials. Putting the who and what together in a business story can sometimes feel like filling in a crossword puzzle with random letters. For a reader not familiar with the institutions involved, the prose can be impenetrable.

This is what happens when you stick all the proper names into a lead:

> American Community Bancshares Inc. has filed an application with the
> Federal Deposit Insurance Corp. and the N.C. Commissioner of Banks to merge
> First National Bank of the Carolinas into American Community Bank.[8]

Of the 32 words in that sentence, 21 are part of proper names — three banks and two regulatory agencies. This lead appeared in a business journal, so the audience has a business orientation, but it's not unusual to see this approach in a newspaper. If the names mean something to you, perhaps there's a story here. If not, good luck.

One remedy for alphabet soup is to:

Slow the pace. Roy Peter Clark talks about the pacing of information as one of the most powerful tools writers have to preserve clarity. The more complex a subject, the more deliberately you should roll out the facts in soft, low waves, rather than dumping a bucket of information over the reader's head. So instead of trying to pack as many bits of data as possible into a business lead, bring them out one at a time, explaining as you go, and help the reader along.

Here's a lead that does too much too fast:

> UnumProvident earned $134.5 million during the final three months of 2004 despite having to write off $127 million to cover a fine and the cost of changes in its business practices to settle a multistate investigation of claims-handling processes.
>
> On a per-share basis, the company reported Wednesday that it earned 45 cents for the three months ending Dec. 31, beating the average estimate of stock analysts by 2 cents a share, according to First Call/Thomson Financial.[9]

Here's a lead, on the same subject of company earnings, that's a little slower paced:

> How much should Amazon.com spend to run its business?
>
> The online retailer yesterday reported $2.5 billion in fourth-quarter sales, a 30.6 percent surge compared with the year-earlier period.
>
> Amazon's fourth-quarter profit was $346.7 million, or 85 cents a share. Excluding a $244 million tax benefit and certain expenses, it earned $149 million, or 35 cents a share, 5 cents below Wall Street expectations.
>
> That missed target — coupled with news that it would shrink profits further this year by investing more in technology and marketing — sent the company's stock tumbling 17.6 percent in after-hours trading.[10]

The average sentence length for the two paragraphs in the first example is 38 words. The story's first sentence, in explaining how much the company UnumProvident made and why it didn't make even more, uses three numbers and, by my count, nine prepositions.

The average length in the four paragraphs of the second story is about 19 words — half as long. The first sentence in the Amazon story doesn't have any numbers, but rather a question raised by the numbers. The second sentence has only two numbers. Things don't start getting hairy until the end of the third paragraph.

The effect of the first story is to bombard the reader with information, leaving him (me, anyway) dazed and puzzled and requiring him to read it again. The effect of the second story is to raise an idea in the reader's mind, reveal the background behind the idea a few bites at a time, and then begin pursuing the idea.

The first story is about numbers; the second is about business.

Build a glossary. Compile a list of business terms — revenue, profit, earnings, limit order, the Federal Reserve — and have their definitions ready to drop into an info box when they appear in a story. The box doesn't get in the way of people who know the terminology, and it can be a big help for people who don't.

The Minneapolis *Star Tribune* offers a feature like this on a page called "Ka-Ching," which I'll describe in more detail below. As the paper defines the jargony phrase "diluted earnings," notice how the tone resembles those *Marketplace* teases:

> Dilution is not something we want in our cocktails. Nor do shareholders like to see their holdings diluted when a company issues more shares.
>
> But when it comes to earnings per share (EPS), investors should insist on seeing "diluted earnings per share."
>
> Diluted earnings account for the EPS if all stock options, convertible bonds and warrants were traded in for stock. This would increase the shares outstanding — and lower the earnings per share. Thus diluted EPS is a more accurate reflection of a company's earnings.
>
> So, next time you order up earnings per share, tell the chief financial officer: "Make mine diluted."[11]

This little piece assumes the reader knows some business concepts, like what earnings per share are and why they're important. There's a little of the alphabet soup syndrome with the acronym EPS. But this feature represents a good attempt to pull the reader aside and say, "Hey, here's something that will help you understand the business world better." And that's what a lot of readers need.

Show the big picture. As with other reporting of value, context is king in business journalism. Awash in the sea of names and numbers, it's easy to forget how the story fits into the bigger picture — how the business you're writing about factors into its industry and the economy at large; how a store opening or closing will affect traffic and spending in your city's downtown; how factory layoffs will hurt the lunch counter across the street and the real estate agent down the block. Nothing happens in isolation, so the reporting can't stop with the press release and a few quotes from a corporate spokesperson. The why, the how, the impact and the what-next have to be top questions in your mind.

"When you see something going on, ask what it represents," *Philadelphia Inquirer* economy columnist Andrew Cassel said in a story for BusinessJournalism.org.[12] "Are you seeing a one-time event? Are you seeing something that always happens? Is this a change from a historical pattern? Is this something that's statistically significant?"

Go for the pocketbook

There are three overlapping audiences for business news: business professionals, who have the most knowledge and interest; curious citizens who understand, or can be shown, the relationships between business, public policy, and the community's health; and people concerned for their own financial future, who want to learn more about saving, investing, and building wealth.

Business journalism traditionally targeted people in the first category, so jargon and limited context weren't a problem. In recent years, newspapers have been working harder to attract the other two groups to business coverage — partly as a piece of broader efforts to build readership, and partly out of the realization that a growing number of people invest in businesses through Individual Retirement Accounts, 401K plans, and other savings. Business is personally relevant to an increasing share of the population.

So one aspect of business coverage that can help draw people into the subject, make them smarter about finance and economics, and ultimately make them better decision-makers, is the realm of personal finance. Many business sections are now devoting at least some space each day to columns advising people on real estate investing, retirement accounts, and career moves. Some have gone even further.

The Minneapolis *Star Tribune* devotes the back page of its business section every Friday to "Ka-Ching," a collection of personal finance features targeting the 35-and-under crowd. In addition to explaining financial terms — like "diluted earnings" above — the page includes a column that answers readers' financial questions, a centerpiece focusing on one aspect of household finances (like the unexpected costs of a baby), and a feature about regular people's financial decisions.

This feature, called "Cash Check" and modeled on a *Wall Street Journal* online item, does a nice job helping young people see how their peers approach financial matters and getting them to think about their own cash-management issues. Here's a profile of Sarah Anderson, 22, of Minneapolis, who's pictured in a cutout photo with her boyfriend:

> **Job:** Administrative assistant in the Private Client Service group at Wells Fargo & Co.
>
> **Annual earnings:** $32,000 to $42,000
>
> **Education:** Bachelor's degree in finance and marketing from Bethel College
>
> **Last major purchase:** 2004 Honda Accord, $25,000
>
> **Next major purchase:** A townhouse or condominium in the Twin Cities
>
> **Smart money:** After graduating from college in December 2003, Anderson created a computer spreadsheet listing all her monthly expenses, from rent to food to health care insurance. She allocates almost all of the money left over — about 20 percent of her gross income — to a personal savings account and 401(k) retirement plan.
>
> Anderson figures she saves about $100 a month by having a friend cut her hair at home instead of going to a beauty salon. About a year ago, she stopped buying music CDs and started listening to the radio instead. "You can drop $20 every couple of weeks on CDs," she said. "It's a dangerous habit that can turn into a disaster before you know it. I've seen it first-hand with friends."
>
> **Stupid money**: Buying the new car. Anderson lives in Uptown Minneapolis and takes the bus every day to work, so she rarely uses the car except on weekends. By waiting another year or two, Anderson figures she would have saved more money for a down payment and qualified for a lower interest rate. Besides, her previous car, a 1993 Geo Prizm, had no engine troubles.[13]

Once someone begins thinking and learning about her own financial situation, she'll start absorbing larger principles of business and the economy by osmosis. Teaching people about their own credit, buying habits, and stake in the financial markets puts them on the road to learning about corporations and the role of business in our society.

The Grand Rapids Press used personal finance to establish a broader trend in a business centerpiece story about the growth of home equity loans. The story led with the tale of a couple in their 30s who had just moved into a 3,000-square-foot house and, in addition to their mortgage, borrowed against the value of their home to pay for appliances and other improvements. The story's personal focus, complete with photographs of the family unpacking boxes in their new home, set up readers for the story's deeper theme — the trend of home equity borrowing across the country.[14]

Combine the economic knowledge such stories build with the skills of citizenship we're developing through the rest of this book, and your journalism is helping people become better-informed, more productive, and more confident participants in their community, in democracy, and in the economy that drives both.

Be creative

When *Journal Times* reporter Michael Burke noticed a lot of small businesses launching around Racine, Wis., he wanted to get into the heads of hopeful entrepreneurs and show readers what starting up a business was like. He could have taken the usual route: Visit a couple of new businesses; interview some owners, customers, and experts; and write up a good weekender summarizing his reporting.

But Burke wanted to do more. So he enrolled in a 12-week course for would-be entrepreneurs, offered by the county's Small Business Development Center. He picked out three members of the class and followed them through conceiving and writing a business plan. After introducing the entrepreneurs to open the series, Burke checked in with them individually at various stages of their business-building. A standing graphic with the subjects' mug shots pointed readers to the stories, which were usually paired with a tip provided by the business center's director.

Here's how Burke introduced one entrepreneur on the first day of the series:

> TOWN OF BURLINGTON — The "friendly skies" of United Airlines are looking more and more like fair-weather friends these days to Bill Kreuder.
>
> Fortunately for the Burlington-area resident, he has other skills that may allow him to earn a living on his own, he believes.
>
> Kreuder, 48, and his wife both work on the "ramp" for United Airlines at O'Hare [I]nternational Airport. That job includes loading, fueling, de-icing the aircraft, and similar duties.
>
> He's been at it for 16 years and makes a good wage, but United is in Chapter 11 bankruptcy reorganization. The Kreuders' United stock, as employee-owners, is at an all-time low. And the airline continues to reel from both internal and external forces.
>
> Kreuder thinks now is the time to strike out on his own, by opening a metal restoration shop. He's handy with a welder; in fact Kreuder already runs a small side business out of the back of his truck. He earns extra money by rescuing boaters with broken boat trailers, or fixing farm equipment in the field.
>
> If Kreuder turns that skill into a full-time business, he'll also offer services such as plating (chrome, gold, etc.), powder finishing, glass beading and sand

blasting. Potential customers include stock car owners, the aviation industry, farmers, boaters and dealers of those types of craft.

Kreuder already has a business name in mind, Restoration Engineering Services, and a logo. He knows how large a building he'll need.

Currently, he's about 80 percent sure he'll be able to start that business, and he'd like to do it this fall. At first, his wife will keep her job with United Airlines, but that could change if the restoration business does well.

"We'd both kind of like the freedom," Kreuder said.

The freedom to fly solo.[15]

As *Journal Times* Editor Randolph Brandt says, the series "made for a terrific ongoing package on new business formation and the promise and disappointments of entrepreneurship, told from a compelling, real-people perspective."[16]

WHEN *THE VIRGINIAN-PILOT* decided to spotlight a shortage of consumer advocacy in the state and call attention to new legislation that could further weaken consumers' rights, it published a long story on its business front exploring the issue. It also published a clip-and-save "Consumer Lifesaver" — a list of consumer protection agencies, what they do, and how to reach them that readers could cut out and fold into the size of a business card.

With the jump of the package, the paper ran tips on avoiding identity theft and dealing with financial institutions. It also ran detailed summaries of consumer-related legislation being considered by the General Assembly, complete with bill numbers and sponsors. The intersection of government, business, and personal finance was clear.

So in addition to traditional, in-depth reporting, the package was full of educational and utility information — plus some attitude with the consumer protection cutout, which was illustrated with a little life preserver. The headline, picking up on the lifesaving theme and asserting that consumers weren't being heard, was "Drowned out."[17]

WHEN THE NEWARK *STAR-LEDGER* decided it was time for a story about the business of comic books, the paper also decided it was time to break the mold of newspaper storytelling. The result was a six-page, full-color comic that was also business journalism. Discarding the rules, *The Star-Ledger* chose what it decided was the best way to tell this particular story. The only traditional text in the package was a few inches of type under a centerpiece-sized drawing on the BusinessSunday front and the headline "ACTION FIGURE$":

Comics are big business. Again.

After a decade long drought during which one company filed for bankruptcy-court protection, 1,000 comic-book shops went out of business and 11 of the 12 major comic-book distributors dropped by the wayside, superheroes are once again performing herculean financial feats.

Stalwarts such as Spider-Man, Batman and the Hulk, and relative newcomers such as the X-Men and the Ultimates, are helping to extend the comic-book industry's reach into mainstream America in the form of movies, toys, games and graphic novels.

And New Jersey is playing a part. Red Bank's Kevin Smith, an award-winning writer, director and comic-book shop owner, will bring the Green Hornet to the screen next year, and famed comic-book artist Joe Kubert runs a one-of-its-kind school in Dover for aspiring cartoon and graphic artists.

With the comics industry going multimedia, worldwide sales from licensing and publishing make it a multibillion-dollar business.

Beginning on Page 5, The Star-Ledger offers an experiment in explanatory financial journalism: a meticulously reported account of the ups and downs of the modern comic-book industry — presented as a comic.[18]

The cartoon opens with the theft of a valued comic book, then takes readers into *The Star-Ledger* newsroom, where an intrepid staff member persuades his editor to let him pursue the story. "Chief," the reporter says, "comics aren't just for geeks like me anymore. It's a multi-million-dollar biz, and there's a super villain chipping away at it in our back yard…" A note at the bottom of the page acknowledges that the storyline is "clearly fictional" but says the statistics and trends are accurate and that the interviews depicted in the comic were conducted by cartoonist Drew Sheneman and reporter Amy Nutt.

THE WILLINGNESS OF THESE packages to break convention to tell a story, and the creativity to produce useful journalism that also creates a buzz, is the kind of attitude "Marketplace's" Jim Russell says can sustain newspapers. "It's funny that we journalists have to keep learning the same lesson over and over again, and that is: A good story sells, period," Russell said.[19] "It's never the subject, it's always the treatment."

Russell recommends assigning people with less business expertise to cover more business stories — people willing and able "to report it as you would any good feature story and not try to be taken so seriously or to hide the blemishes or to make the story black and white, either good guys or bad guys."

Reporting with an eye beyond the bottom line can lead journalists to ask more personal questions of business leaders, to get a better understanding of the people whose financial decisions affect the lives of thousands of employees and millions of shareholders and consumers. "You can learn a tremendous amount by just listening to people talk about what they're passionate about," Russell said.

Examining how personalities affect business doesn't mean ignoring the numbers. Often the nuts and bolts of financial statements reveal truths about businesses that executives are unwilling or unable to share. The challenge is to understand the interactions between the personalities and the numbers, and to tell the full story behind both. Reporting deeper, and approaching the subject with less reverence, can lead to the fascinating stories behind business decisions, which Russell says are often nothing more than "a roll of the dice, a giant bingo game." Challenging conventional wisdom, asking how and why questions, can lead to better, more interesting stories.

Even the routine stories — or perhaps *especially* the routine stories — need a burst of creativity to make them worthwhile. Vandana Sinha, associate Web editor of BusinessJournalism.org, urges business writers to bring a fresh perspective to annual assignments like holiday sales stories. Her tips include:

To tell the story of comic books as big business, *The Star-Ledger* made its own journey into the comic-book genre. (Reprinted with permission of *The Star-Ledger*.)

■ Going through your archives and other publications to gauge what's been done and what hasn't with your story, and to search for angles you can borrow from other papers.

■ Taking the historical perspective and tracing an annual event back to its roots. How did it start? What made it a hit?

■ Focusing on an individual whose example can tell the big story.

■ Following the money: Who puts up the funding for an event, and where does it go?

■ Visiting new people and places to tell the old story. If you're seeing how retailers did with holiday sales, go to neighborhoods you've never been; talk to businesses you've never heard of. The goal is to "Make sure you're covering how a story affects everybody, not just readers who think, shop and deal like you do."

■ Pay attention to reader feedback, Internet blogs and other sources that can tip you off to trends and ideas you may otherwise miss.[20]

THE MORE WE EXPLORE specific realms of reporting, the clearer it should be that the fundamental principles in the first part of this book apply universally in good journalism. As Jim Russell says, it's not the subject that counts, it's the treatment. Whether it's business, elections, local government, national news, or the state of the world itself, journalism that focuses on people, their problems, and their ideas; that tells stories with honesty, clarity, and compassion; that helps teach readers and shows them how to act on what they've learned; and that breaks tradition when necessary to engage an audience — that's the journalism that will survive in the 21st century.

How to cover business news

■ Look for the intersections between private industry and public interests. Examine how public policy affects business, and vice versa.

■ Make business news accessible to non-experts, by:

● Avoiding overuse of initials, abbreviations, and collections of proper names and titles. They tend to stack up in sentences, creating dense prose that looks less like a story than a series of phone book entries. Aim for no acronyms, a minimum of abbreviations, and the use of only one or two names and titles per sentence.

● Slowing the pace of information to make it easier to digest. Don't try to answer the five W's in the first sentence. Tackle the story one major fact, one key element, at a time. Arrange these elements in a logical way that the reader can follow, idea by idea.

● Building a glossary of business and financial terms that you can define for readers when they arise in stories.

● Reporting, writing, and presenting the big picture. Show how the financial piece you're covering fits into the larger economic puzzle — historically, politically, and culturally.

■ Pursue business coverage through the lens of readers' pocketbooks. Show the impact that economic news will have on individual consumers, investors, and employees. Make personal finance and workplace issues integral parts of your coverage strategy.

■ Find creative ways to tell business stories. Approach economic reporting as an outsider instead of a boardroom buddy. Apply your curiosity to get past the episodic, press-release nature of most business reports — quarterly earnings, personnel changes, economic indicators — and dig into the "why" and "how" of financial affairs. Find the people behind the decisions, and figure out what drives them. When you get a good story, tell it in a way that's true to the story, not true to convention.

For thought and action...

1 Make a list of every business you interact with in a given day. Include products you use, the services you buy, the company you work for, advertisements you see and hear, spam e-mail you receive, and everything else you can think of. Now make a case that business news doesn't directly affect your life.

2 Find a business story with too many names, numbers, and acronyms in the first few paragraphs. Rewrite those paragraphs to slow the pace of the story and spread out the proper nouns. Figure out what story the reporter is trying to tell, and see if you can tell it better.

3 Go through a business section, identify five terms you're not familiar with, and find out what they mean. Now write plain-English definitions for them. Check with experts to see if your interpretations are accurate.

4 With your class, brainstorm the five most important things college students need to know about personal finance. Report and write up answers to those questions in the form of a personal finance column.

5 Select any three business stories from a week's worth of newspapers. Imagine and describe a more interesting way to tell each of the stories. Think about different angles, different sources, different emphases, different writing and presentation techniques. Make sure your creative suggestion is not only interesting, but also an effective way of getting across the important information.

Chapter 13

Opinion Pages

If an editorial page does nothing else, it ought to make people think.
— Kay Semion, *Daytona Beach News-Journal*[1]

The whole question is the personality the newspaper has chosen for itself. Alas, most have chosen the personality of the boring guy everybody avoids at the Rotary Club.
–Richard Aregood, former Newark *Star-Ledger* editorial page editor[2]

On a trip to Southern California in early 2005, I discovered the *Los Angeles Times'* Sunday Opinion section on my aunt's kitchen table. The opinion pages had recently been taken over by Michael Kinsley, a liberal magazine editor and online pioneer whose hire by the button-down *L.A. Times* had raised some eyebrows. I surveyed the section, and was rewarded immediately.

The front page was a big cartoon, even more intriguing than *The Star-Ledger's* graphic story on the comic book business mentioned in the last chapter. It was an installment of a comic-book-style diary of the Los Angeles mayoral primary by political cartoonist Mark Alan Stamaty, who'd been commissioned to provide "an outsider view" of the race.

The cartoon is funny at first glance; it's got candidates in capes and hang gliders, candidates using themselves as chess pieces, and airplanes soaring over crowded, palm-studded freeways entwined like spaghetti. But even as these images entertain, the text enlightens through incisive summaries of the candidates' personalities and political postures. Stamaty's drawings are cheerful and amusing, but his text draws heavily on direct quotes from the candidates and people he interviewed. It's part news story, part editorial, part comic book.

Page 2 of the six-page section had a lengthy commentary on local crime, an op-ed on the mayor's race, and — another innovation — a quiz inviting readers to match 15 goofy or politically incorrect quotes with the mayoral candidate who had uttered them.

On Page 3 was a roundup of Iraq-focused political cartoons, introduced by Pulitzer Prize-winning cartoonist Joel Pett. There was a personal essay about religion, culture, and child-rearing — not so much an opinion column as a meditation on responsibility and the discoveries of parenting. And a new feature, "Outside the tent," which invited people to critique the *Times*, took the paper to task on its terrorism coverage.

Pages 4 and 5 featured a pair of tightly written editorials on national and business issues; a healthy helping of letters from readers; and a variety of opinion pieces, including a defense by Kinsley of shows like *Crossfire*, the political shout-fest that CNN had just canceled in favor of less vitriolic programming.

Then on the back page, a final treat: Under the headline "Look Who's Buying the Mayor's Race" was a big map of the Los Angeles area, dotted with color-coded circles showing which candidate was getting how much money from which ZIP code. Numbers on the map corresponded with neighborhoods such as Downtown and East L.A., each of which got a few sentences of description illustrated by a cutout head shot of the candidate picking up the most cash there.

The section's creativity, its tone, its playful examination of important matters, and its parade of surprises from page to page won me over. I was an instant fan.

Interestingly, I learned a couple of weeks later that this very edition had enraged many *Los Angeles Times* readers, who accused the paper of running "inane" and "useless" columns, giving too much space to cartoons, and "dumbing down" the section.[3] The backlash was to be expected, because Kinsley had been hired to reinvent the section. A profile of Kinsley in *Los Angeles Magazine* noted that, in a shift from the *Times'* historical editorial posture, Kinsley "doesn't view his pages as a place to hand down the Word but to start tongues flapping."[4]

Can there be a better objective for editorial pages than to start tongues flapping — when the alternative is fostering civic indifference? Opinion pages, even more than news sections, have traditionally been the grayest repositories for the most ponderous prose in the newspaper. And, yet, at their heart, they may be the purest embodiment of the First Amendment principles that embrace and protect the press. Democracy lives on the opinion pages, where a night-shift janitor with a beef can go toe-to-toe with a senator, where an angry taxpayer can call out the mayor, where ideas wrestle for supremacy. The opinion pages should be the liveliest place in the paper, and Kinsley's were making a run at it.

Ultimately, it didn't work out for Kinsley, who was pushed from the *L.A. Times* in September 2005. Many of his continuing innovations had been criticized on a number of fronts, from neglecting local issues to going overboard in encouraging reader contributions (one experiment with letting readers collectively edit the paper's editorials online was shut down when it was inundated with pornographic posts).[5]

But effective innovation doesn't require a wholesale sacking of tradition, just a willingness to fulfill vital democratic responsibilities in new and intriguing ways. In this chapter we'll look at some of the obligations of meaningful opinion pages.

Be transparent

Readers don't understand newspapers as well as they used to, and the opinion pages are a particularly dense thicket for people unfamiliar with the landscape. Reared on the idea that newspapers are to be entirely neutral, they get confused or angry on discovering the paper's institutional voice. You'll see letters to the editor complaining about "biased" editorials — when all good editorials take a side. Political endorsements are the ultimate offense: How can journalists cover a campaign fairly on the news pages when "the paper" backs a particular candidate?

It's for these reasons that educating readers about the paper is more important on the opinion pages than anywhere else. Most opinion pages don't regularly explain how their role is distinct from the newsgathering process, identify the editorial board, and demonstrate how editorial positions are reached — but they should. Most opinion pages that endorse candidates don't explain why — but they should, just as Ed Ronco of *The State News* did in the column highlighted in Chapter 5.

Most opinion pages do encourage readers to express their views through letters to the editor and guest columns, but they don't offer guidance on how to get a point across, cite sources, conduct basic research, and double-check assertions — lessons that could be presented in detail through the Web. Maybe this is a step beyond what we should expect from a newspaper, but who else is going to educate the public on how best to communicate an opinion? *The Post-Crescent* of Appleton, Wis., for instance, published an editorial explaining why it doesn't run form letters to the editor that people can cut and paste from political parties or advocacy Web sites. "We suspect that, in most cases, people aren't aware that there's something wrong with sending a form letter," the editorial says. "That's why we include it in our contact information at the bottom of this page every day, and we write about the issue a couple of times a year."[6]

The better readers understand what the opinion pages are all about, the more respect those pages will earn, and the more powerful a voice the institution will have in the community.

Be inviting

Once you've explained how the opinion page works, you have to bring as many voices to it as possible. This means not only accepting letters to the editor and op-ed columns, but also *soliciting* them from a variety of community stakeholders. If there's a debate about whether to close an aging school, invite a half-dozen people to write about the issue. Include a parent, a student, an administrator, a teacher, a homeowner, a school board member. Give your readers a full range of opinions and ideas to choose from.

When Kay Semion became associate editorial page editor of *The Daytona Beach News-Journal*, she had to learn the area and cultivate sources just as a beat reporter would. Going to meetings and getting to know the community's experts meant she knew whom to tap when seeking opinions on important issues. When the paper was putting together a package on slavery for Black History Month, instead of turning to a wire story, Semion called an area museum director who helped her find a local commentator. "If you know the community and you know who's in the community, then you know who to call," she said.[7]

As an editorial staff member at papers in Tallahassee and Dayton, Semion put together panels of reader-columnists who wrote local commentary from a variety of perspectives. In Dayton, after soliciting applicants, she had more than 160 people from which to choose 10 columnists. In an article for the editorial writers' publication *The Masthead*, she wrote of her winners:

> Our choices looked good: A talented high-school sophomore; a former psychiatric nurse and foster parent; an urban planner and native Daytonian; a blue-collar worker with natural writing talent; a former mayor and lieutenant governor; a divorce lawyer; a conservative, pro-growth suburbanite; an independent grant writer with interests in the arts; a university educator on history and race relations; a farm wife, stay-at-home mom and self-described reactionary. [...]

Their topics? When a post-Columbine bomb went off in her high school (no injuries), the sophomore told us about the students' reactions. When the new Star Wars movie came out, the blue-collar worker wrote about how he couldn't go see it in his largely black community because there were no longer any first-run theaters. The ex-mayor weighed in with well-grounded insight about the city [schools'] $20 million deficit.[8]

Think of the range of perspectives this panel added to the editorial board's own expertise. By cultivating a diverse pool of commentators whose lives revolved around something other than the newspaper, Semion shared authentic viewpoints that people from across the community could relate to in different ways. She expanded the breadth and reach of the opinion pages, by inviting people in.

One of the greatest tools of invitation and inclusion nowadays is the Internet. Newspapers, many of them limited by space to a half-dozen or so letters a day, can run as many as they get on their Web sites. Some papers offer comment buttons and forums with every story that they run. Others host online journals, or blogs, by their editors and opinion writers. Readers can respond to these editors and to one another; some even get their own blog space. We'll explore more opportunities and realities of Web-based journalism in the next chapter.

ELECTION SEASON IS a golden opportunity to expose a variety of ideas, including those out of the mainstream. You can run a series of op-ed pieces from third-party and independent candidates. Give them space to make the case for their world view that they might not be getting in the news pages.

The *Detroit Free Press* presented a collection of viewpoints on the Sunday before the 2004 election, compiling endorsement excerpts from 32 papers around the country, including the *Boston Globe, Houston Chronicle, Orlando Sentinel,* and *Denver Post.* The blurbs, which ran about 50 to 100 words each, alternated between papers supporting George Bush and those supporting John Kerry. By rounding up and extracting arguments from various papers, the *Free Press* was able to pull out each endorsement's strongest points, leading to a diverse array of bite-sized arguments for readers to chew on.[9]

Invitation also means finding different ways to keep readers involved with news and events. Recognizing that not everybody reads the opinion pages every day, *The Orange County Register* publishes an "Opinion week in review" on Saturdays, reprising in a few words the editorial positions the paper has taken in the previous six days. A note at the top of the column explains that the editorials are the opinions of the newspaper's owners. At the bottom, letters are solicited under the headline "Join the debate."[10]

The *Lansing State Journal,* tired of crummy driving conditions, invited readers to weigh in on the region's worst roads. Under the headline "Driven to distraction," and a close-up photo of a tire rutted in a pothole, was a form readers could use to nominate their least favorite roads, accompanied by a witty editorial:

> Ah, the sounds of spring. Birds chirping, the crack of the bat … that awful *ka-thunk* as your front tire plunges into a pothole.
> Yep, it's spring all right. …[11]

On a more serious note, after crowds of students were teargassed by police following Michigan State's loss in the 2005 NCAA basketball semifinals, *The State News* invited witnesses to share their stories through letters to the editor. Many students, store owners, and bystanders believed the police were overaggressive, and the paper opened a second opinion page for more than a week to capture dozens of accounts and opinions condemning, and supporting, officials' actions. The volume of letters, and their tales of students being gassed in groups of twos and threes, helped prompt the city of East Lansing to formally investigate what had happened that night.

Inviting readers to participate in public deliberations embodies many principles of good public affairs journalism: It makes citizens the focus of public debate, it gives stakeholders a voice in decisions, and it helps people act on what they see and hear in the news. The opinion pages are your community's town square, a gathering place for the exchange of ideas. Enrich the conversation by finding as many unique voices, and as many opportunities for readers to participate, as you can.

Be skeptical, not cynical

The best opinion writers are neither cheerleaders nor naysayers. They don't carry water for any party or interest group, but they don't dismiss anyone out of hand, either. They will consider any idea, regardless of its origin, and reason through its merits. When they see something good, they'll trumpet it; when they see something bad, they'll attack it. They may be loyal to their community, but not to an ideology. This is what makes them credible arbiters of public debate — they are honest brokers.

"If our craft is going to survive and play more than a decorative role in our respective institutions — as well as bring some order and precision to the public marketplace of ideas — we must have the intellectual wherewithal to get beyond the façade of propaganda and grasp the essence of the issues," *Omaha World-Herald* Editorial Page Editor Francis L. Partsch wrote in the preface to *Beyond Argument: A Handbook for Editorial Writers.*

"Wrapping ourselves in unexamined ideology, whether that of the left or the right or the greens or the libertarians, is not going to cut it."[12]

To be an asset to a community, editorial writers have to look critically at every proposal, plan, and program that will affect their audience. But poking holes is only half the job; finding ways to plug them is the other half. Good editorial writers don't just heckle from the sidelines, they suit up and put their own ideas in play.

Be bold

Democracy is a raucous, energetic creature, and the opportunity to engage in it should be celebrated. Free and open debate should be not just a right but a source of joy. We have to take serious matters seriously, but we also must take pleasure in the intellectual challenge of the argument, the versatility of the language, the crispness of a logical train, and the lyricism of an eloquent appeal. Opinion pages should be robust, bold, blunt, amusing, and infuriating. A successful page is one the reader hurls across the room in anger, then rushes to reclaim in anticipation. As Kay Semion says, "The biggest delight I ever get is when people get mad at me."[13]

There are a lot of ways to produce bold opinion pages:

Do your own reporting. Semion, who served as president of the National Conference of Editorial Writers, says there was a shift in the 1980s from editorial writers simply opining on regurgitated facts to aggressively reporting material on their own. Editorials whose authors make their own phone calls and dig up their own details add value to the news reporting and lend authority to their advocacy. An opinion pulled from the top of one's head (what *The Elements of Journalism* would call the "journalism of assertion") has little credibility or staying power compared to an opinion based on a thorough knowledge of the facts (*Elements'* "journalism of verification"). "You have to know your subject extremely well," Semion said. "I couldn't emphasize enough that understanding who you're talking to and understanding your topic are the two key things in my mind to writing a good editorial."

Take a firm position. It's hard to stir anyone up with equivocating language that tries to make everyone happy. Opinion writers, to be fair and complete, are obliged to recognize multiple points of view, but — unlike news writers — they are equally obliged to make a case for the best position. The quest for a strong voice has led some papers to eschew editorial boards, to avoid drafting milquetoast opinions by committee. But editorial boards don't have to produce bland opinions and boring copy. Consensus, after all, is a goal of public policy, and conclusions reached through deliberation are often more powerful than those reached by individuals. The challenge is for the editorial writer to deliver conclusions through a single, strong voice, rather than create a patchwork argument that tries to acknowledge every viewpoint equally.

The Examiner of Washington, D.C., gets in your face with this critique of a *Washington Post* story calling attention to Metamucil and Pepto-Bismol ads in *Ebony* magazine. The ads invoked Black History Month as part of their sales pitch — which some people in the *Post* story called exploitative. *The Examiner* disagreed:

> …Perhaps, rather than lament the racial division sowed by Procter & Gamble, we might celebrate the fact that black history has become such a big deal and that blacks have become such an important market that advertisers treat African-Americans with the same shabby disdain they used to reserve for everybody else.
>
> Christians have to put up with the fact that Jesus' birthday is more important as an economic indicator than a religious holiday. Jews have to deal with the fact Noah is used to sell everything from rain gear to bagels. Italians (and Native Americans) have to put up with the fact that Columbus Day is now known more for lively white sales than the discovery of America. The lines on Memorial Day are longer at the mall than at veterans' cemeteries.
>
> The fact that Martin Luther King Jr. is being used to sell cars and Buffalo Soldiers are used to promote Wal-Mart doesn't mean blacks are getting the shaft; it means they're part of the club. Welcome to the mainstream, where everything you love and revere will be turned into dollar signs and smarmy schlock. […]

As each day passes, race is less of an issue. If Secretary of State Condi Rice is oppressed by anything, it is a horde of bloggers and activists desperately trying to draft her for a 2008 presidential run. Sen. Barack Obama, D-Ill., went from nobody to superstar in nothing flat.

Black homeownership and household wealth are at record highs. The black middle class is larger than ever before. Racists groups have dwindled from the heights of power to such irrelevance that they have to go to court to get the right to pick up trash on Missouri highways.

Of course, too many problems remain and racism is not entirely dead. But it is dying. And stupid Pepto ads are just more proof.[14]

You may or may not agree with the premise and tone of this editorial, but you can't ignore it. It gets your hackles up. It makes you think. And it probably makes you want to join the discussion.

The Examiner, a tabloid launched in 2005 whose opinion pages have given it a distinctive personality, was willing to take tough talk as well as dish it. A couple of letters from the same day's opinion section share the headline: "Readers to Examiner: You're jerks."[15]

Pick the right tone. Editorial topics vary from intense policy debates to reverent appreciations to scoldings of misbehaving officials. Good editorial writers modulate the tone of their rhetoric to match the gravity of their subject. They think about the problem, the stakeholders, and ways to mold their argument to the circumstances. This creates a sense of variety and surprise on the opinion page. Here's how one paper handled a dispute over a high school test:

Teenagers like to say it's adults who foul things up. This time the teens are right, at least the ones at Newton High School who through no fault of their own ended up taking the wrong version of the PSAT, a test required for a shot at a national scholarship program.

Just which adults messed up is a matter of much finger-pointing between high school administrators and the folks who oversee, write and distribute the tests. But the result is that 91 Newton High students now will have to take a different, longer test this spring to be eligible for prestigious $2,500 National Merit Scholarships.

A retest of some type will be needed, no way around it. But the adults should make the process easier for the students instead of giving the kids an unwanted lesson in bureaucratic bickering.

The trouble arose because Newton kids took a version of the PSAT on Oct. 16 that should not have been used after Oct. 13. There is a different version for each date to prevent later test-takers from learning questions from earlier examinees.

School district officials say they ordered the proper test. Exam distributors ETS of Princeton says it sent what was ordered, and anyway, the problem could easily have been avoided if the district had examined the shipment when it arrived, as protocol requires.

Nyah, nyah, nyah. So far, the only certainty is that Newton students must take a tougher test this spring to have a scholarship chance. That's not right, even though the high school will help them prepare.

The fairest solution would be for the testing folks to fire up the computers and spit out another PSAT for the Newton students. But the organization that issues the scholarship won't hear of that. It doesn't fit National Merit procedures.

Education aims to help students prepare for the real world. It's too bad this particular preparation will be useful only when the Newton students find themselves dealing with the frustrations of the DMV, health insurers and others of unhelpful ilk.[16]

The editorial is about a serious subject, but the problem is primarily a matter of inconvenience requiring a remedy of fairness. This, rather than a question of life and death or other grave circumstances, gives the writer some leeway to strike a playful note. The editorial establishes the theme of grown-up incompetence causing trouble for guiltless teenagers. It uses idioms like "messed up" rather than the more formal "erred." It invokes the schoolyard taunt "Nyah, nyah, nyah" to characterize the finger-pointing between the school system and the testing company. In other words, it places the dispute linguistically in its proper setting.

Even creative use of punctuation can help set a tone. This lead, from an editorial in the

"Write essays, not editorials"

John McCormick, deputy editorial page editor of the Chicago Tribune *and a 2002 editorial writing winner from the American Society of Newspaper Editors, got this advice from his boss,* Tribune *Editorial Page Editor Bruce Dold: "Write essays, not editorials." As part of a series for* Poynter Online, *McCormick shared seven questions opinion writers can ask themselves to produce good work.*

1. To whom would this be written? Are we writing for power elites? Average readers? Or are we just writing to ourselves?

2. What's our attitude? Are we angry? Pleased? Perplexed? Befuddled? What tone will we project?

3. What, exactly, are we trying to accomplish? An official response? A public change of attitude? An explanation? Entertainment?

4. What are we contributing to the debate? What's the added value here? Just our opinion? New facts? New arguments, contexts, or dimensions to consider? The best opinion is reported opinion. The power of your voice comes not from your job description, but from the strength of your facts and the reasoning that drives your arguments. When you feel queasy about stating an opinion, it's often because one of these elements has come up short.

5. Do we have something new to say about this? Are we advancing the conversation or just dishing up warmed-over wisdom from the editorial board? Yes, we have a topic and an opinion. But do we have a solution in mind?

6. Have we fiercely attacked our own premise? Does our position survive the scrutiny? What would be our opponents' most compelling arguments against our position? Are we right or just rote?

7. Are we stirring up a "three-bowler?" That borrowed phrase refers to the possibility a reader will be so bored by the unrelenting earnestness of a newspaper article as he sits at breakfast that his face flops into his cereal bowl once, twice or, if the article is especially boring, three times.

Ashland, Wis., *Daily Press*, makes its point with a series of periods:

> "There. Are. Many. New. Stop. Signs. In. The. City. Of. Washburn."[17]

Daily Press Editor Claire Duquette, who wrote that line, recalls feeling a sense of frustration while driving her daughter to school. "I sometimes think (and speak) in sound effects," Duquette said, "and was thinking it felt like: hhhmMMPh. clunk. hhhmmpHH. clunk. to drive through the city. That feeling morphed into putting a period after each word."[18] Reading Duquette's sentence creates almost the same visceral feeling of frustration that she encountered on her start-and-stop tour through Washburn. It's a nice example of the infinite possibilities the language affords us, if we stretch our minds to discover them. Duquette also notes that many of the stop signs came down after her editorial ran.

Outright humor is another way to get attention and make a point at the same time. Editors at *The State News* knew that getting on their high horse and moralizing wouldn't persuade students to vote on Nov. 2, 2004. So instead of lecturing from the editorial page, the paper created a special box that ran every day for weeks, right by the letters to the editor. The box counted down the days to the election, offered an impossibly goofy reason people had better vote, and provided Web addresses for the presidential campaigns. Here's one installment, a sendup of the Jimmy Stewart film *It's a Wonderful Life*:

> **Today's reason to vote:** If you don't vote on Nov. 2, there is a very good chance that you will be visited by a man named Clarence who insists that he can show you what the world would be like had you voted. You will become increasingly skeptical of Clarence after you notice him breathing deeply into a plastic shopping bag that appears to contain gold spray paint.[19]

Don't try to follow the logic of that argument; instead, put it in the context of a campaign to keep the elections front and center without preaching — and maybe by getting a chuckle or at least a puzzled look out of readers each day. When readers were being saturated with logical arguments and historical references, said former *State News* Opinion Editor Patrick Walters, "why not save a little corner of the page for some sarcasm and obscure pop-culture references?"[20]

Keep the pressure on. The reason-to-vote box is an example of using repetition to keep an issue on the forefront of readers' minds. Here's another:

In 2001, aghast at what students were paying to take public buses to their public schools each day, *The Sacramento Bee* launched a crusade to have bus fares lowered for student riders. In addition to writing more than 20 editorials over a couple of months, the editorial page ran a picture every day of a family of three children who rode the bus to school, tallying how much they had spent to date on transportation that year. The fare was eventually lowered, Editorial Pages Editor David Holwerk told *Editor & Publisher*.

"If you look at newspaper advertising people, what do they say is the key?" Holwerk asked in the *E&P* story. "Frequency. One of the biggest tools we have to be effective is repetition. It works for ads, it works for advocacy."[21] Holwerk said the repeated message was especially powerful because it confronted readers daily with "the human faces" of the children involved. "Without that, I don't think it would have been as effective, or at least not as quickly."[22]

In the spirit of repetition, I've pushed several times in this book for recycling information to ensure that readers understand important issues — whether the redundancy is used to attack inaccurate conventional wisdom, remind readers of an opportunity or obligation, or beat relentlessly against the doors of power until they open or break.

The power of a repeated message is a tool newspapers can use to much greater effect than they do now, as is the power of a robust and aggressive opinion page.

How to produce compelling opinion pages

■ Let readers know what you're doing. Make room to explain the distinct role of the opinion pages and the value of the newspaper's institutional voice. Also use the page to take the mystery out of the institutions you write about. Show how things work, and how readers can be involved.

■ Invite diverse voices into your paper. Represent as broad a swath of the community and its viewpoints as possible. Present opinions that don't get a hearing anywhere else. Find local commentators to weigh in on important issues. And find creative ways to include your readers in the search for solutions.

■ Use your paper's credibility and independence to cast a skeptical eye on politicians, policies, plans, and promises. Hold people accountable for their statements, for errors in logic, and for misplaced priorities. But never go out of your way to poke holes or degrade others. Use your credibility and independence also to point out successes, to support well-meaning people, and to suggest your own fixes.

■ Do your own research — both to double-check the published information you're drawing from and to advance and add value to the issue. Make your editorials a place where readers can learn something new, not just see old facts rehashed.

■ Take strong positions. Give readers an opportunity to agree or disagree with you. Choose topics of controversy, not general agreement. The goal of an editorial is to foster robust discussion, not summarize or dilute it. Taking a strong position does not require taking an extreme one — only stating what you believe is right.

■ Use tone, language, and humor to tai-

---

23 days left until the general election

Today's reason to vote:
If you do not vote on Nov. 2, there is a very good chance that you will plummet off a cliff in the middle of the desert. No amount of arm-flapping will help you, and you eventually will hit the ground, resulting in a small, circular puff of smoke and a hole shaped in the exact outline of your spread-eagle silhouette.

Learn more about who you're voting for at:
www.johnkerry.com
www.votenader.org
www.georgewbush.com
www.badnarik.org
www.votecobb.org

DECISION 2☑□4

The State News used a humorous countdown box to keep Election Day on readers' minds. (Reprinted with permission of The State News.)

lor your writing to the situation you're addressing. Write conversationally and provocatively — "an essay, not an editorial" — and take advantage of the great flexibility language gives you to be witty, biting, colorful, and compassionate. Write to be remembered.

■ If you opine once and are ignored, don't give up. Use the power of repetition to remind, goad, and shame people into action. If you see a problem, your work doesn't end when you've brought it to light. Your work ends when it's solved.

For thought and action...

1 Write an editorial explaining the purpose and value of opinion pages to newspaper readers. Take a position on whether it's a good idea to endorse candidates for office.

2 Monitor one newspaper's opinion pages for a week. Come up with three ways the paper could improve the quality and diversity of the viewpoints it offers.

3 Find an editorial that raises a question in your mind about how a policy or proposal should work. Research the question and write a new editorial based on what you learn.

4 Find a wishy-washy editorial — one that seems to take all views into account but does little to assert or defend a particular course of action. Research the subject and write your own editorial, taking a firm position.

PART 3: THE FUTURE OF PUBLIC AFFAIRS REPORTING

Chapter 14

The Online Revolution

[J]ournalism, as traditionally practiced, has been a lecture, almost completely one-way, from journalists to readers. But it's changing now to a conversation between and among journalists and readers, one that breaks down artificial barriers between us and readers and involves unprecedented levels of transparency in how we do our work.
— Lex Alexander, Greensboro *News & Record*[1]

There's writing on the wall for the newspaper industry, but it's in code, and the business' smartest thinkers haven't cracked it. Circulation trends have been negative for going on two decades; the average age of readers is increasing; fewer young people are picking up the habit (see the next chapter); and new technologies like the Internet have opened the publishing world to everyone with a computer and a modem — smashing the traditional press' unique role as the arbiter of what gets reported, and what doesn't.

These data and demographics have prompted concerned head-scratching among those who love newspapers: the journalists who produce them, the business people who profit from them, the academics who study them, and a smattering of loyal readers who cherish them. Will the Internet spell doom for newspapers? Will print cease to exist, or become an elite niche product for rich old subscribers? Will the phenomenon of bloggers — independent Web journal-keepers whose output ranges from ignorant opinion and idle gossip to meaningful, history-altering reporting — overtake traditional news organizations, rendering them obsolete?

Newspaper leaders are scurrying to answer these questions and stave off the most doom-invoking answers. Most have established Web sites but are still trying to figure out how to make money from them. Many simply use the Internet to dump out the contents of the daily paper in electronic form. Some require a subscription for access to Internet content; others offer content in exchange for users' personal information; and still others distribute their work for free, hoping to maintain a reputation and market share while groping for money-making ideas.

Meanwhile, papers across the country are examining readership research, experimenting with in-house blogs, eliminating newsroom jobs, and cutting back on newshole to save money — trying to get what they can from what may be a dying business model before the curtain comes down.

The Greensboro *News & Record's* Lex Alexander, assigned by his paper to decode the writing on the wall, came up with this:

> Our audience is moving from print to online, and some of the wealthier and better-educated people among our audience are leading the charge and taking ad revenue with them. If we are to survive as a business dedicated to producing quality local news, information and dialogue, we need to move, too — with people and resources.
>
> But that means more than just re-creating the print product online. It means understanding the culture of the Internet, and of blogging in particular, and understanding how we can work on and with the Internet (i.e., with users of that medium), to expand the quantity and quality of the local news, information and dialogue we provide.
>
> It also means understanding that the very definition of news, or journalism, is changing. Particularly with the growing popularity of blogs, online audiences expect to have a say — not total control, but a say — in what we cover, how, and why.[2]

The leadership at the *News & Record* bought this interpretation, and within weeks began transforming the paper's Web site to meet what it perceived to be the demands of the modern era — to create, in Editor John Robinson's words, "a virtual town square, a trusted place where people can get the news, share information, talk to each other and us, and engage in building community."[3]

To that end, the paper:

■ Increased its complement of staff-written blogs to about a dozen, including Alexander's, Robinson's, and blogs on education, local government, religion, business, traffic, and editorials.

■ Created an interactive feature for online letters to the editor, allowing readers to post their own comments in response to each letter.

■ Added reader forums on a variety of topics, including area colleges, sports, and local news.

■ Began "podcasting" — creating audio files of interviews or news events that people could download to review as they pleased.

■ Invited readers to report and write their own stories to be posted online, or rewrite published stories if the readers disagreed with the angle taken by the paper.

Alexander, whose memo prompted the changes and who was charged with making them work, says the motivation for such radical innovation, the move toward "some kind of Web-based, open-source journalism," was simple: survival. The changes were necessary, he says, because:

> 1) If we as an industry just keep doing what we're doing, we die within a generation.
> 2) It's what our readers want.
> 3) We really can make our news report broader, deeper, more authentic —

better overall — by going this route. We think the result also will be a health-ier community from a civic standpoint.[4]

In the third part of his answer, the Greensboro experiment intersects with the purpose of this book. By and large, the principles and practices outlined in the preceding pages are not diminished, but enhanced, by Web technology. The empowering, inclusive, honest, educational, and engaging journalism that can reinvigorate newspapers and their communities are complemented by the interactive approaches being pioneered on the Web. Public affairs as conversation, as a deliberative process that touches all citizens and not a privileged few, is one of the most promising aspects of Internet journalism.

The promises and pitfalls of this new interactivity between news people and their audiences is one of the hottest topics in journalism. Jay Rosen, a New York University associate professor and pioneering blogger on the subject of journalism and democracy, is a leader among those who believe the Internet can improve journalism by broadening the scope and transparency of newsgathering. Dan Gillmor, a 25-year newspaperman who left a reporting job at the *San Jose Mercury News* in 2004 to pursue Internet-based citizen journalism full time, and who wrote a book called *We the Media: Grassroots Journalism By the People, For the People*, summarized the collaborative nature of the new medium with the mantra "My readers know more than I do."

This revelation is the key to helping journalists tap the Internet to improve their work. Recognizing the value of immediate feedback from readers and experts across the globe who can point out the flaws, inaccuracies and omissions of a story, and provide tips for the next one, creates an unprecedented collaboration between journalist and audience that makes everyone smarter.

But there are still more questions than answers about this awkward new partnership — or turf war, depending on whom you ask — between reporters anointed by news organizations and the self-defined Web journalists who take pleasure in knocking the "mainstream media." As traditional journalism stands at a crossroads between serious, civic-oriented news and self-inflicted irrelevance, Internet journalists are working out whether they'll be a powerful new force for informing and empowering citizens or a conglomeration of mean-spirited egomaniacs who put mischief ahead of public service.

Blogging — the new reporting?

In early 2005, The Poynter Institute held a conference called "Web + 10: The Future of Online Journalism." Among the conclusions was that many news organizations had come to terms with the new, "two-way" relationship between journalists and their audiences.[5] A week later, Poynter Online Managing Editor Julie M. Moos wrote about the potential of weblogs to foster this relationship. If people with certain religious faiths or political priorities feel underrepresented in the paper, for instance, why not grant them blog space to share their views through your organization? And why not use that added wisdom, perspective, opinion, and source base to help round out future news coverage?[6]

Before posting the story, Poynter Online Editor Bill Mitchell shipped it to senior news leaders (and one news consumer) around the country, so their responses could run simultaneously with the piece. It was an experiment in the very kind of cross-communication Moos' article proposed, and it yielded some interesting results. Many of the commentators, like *Tampa Tribune* Executive Editor Janet Weaver, favored the development of blogs, with reservations:

> The issue of audience and diversity of voices is at the core of everything we are thinking about and talking about. We just had a forum last night with members of the Latino community. One of the real themes that emerged from that conversation was this: We are often pessimistic about the state of journalism. But I was most impressed with how much people do want to connect with the newspaper, and how they still believe newspapers can make a difference in the community. One way of tapping into that need for connection is by getting more members of the community to create content, to bring us closer to what people are thinking and talking about.
>
> I do think we'll have to work through some of the issues of editing and blogging. There are legal issues to consider, and I think we still have an ethical obligation to consider what kinds of messages are being communicated under our auspices. But I think working through those issues would be time well spent.[7]

For other respondents, the reservations outweighed the potential, at least for the moment. Gary Farrugia, editor and publisher of *The Day* of New London, Conn., wrote that his 40,000-circulation paper had made a major push in recent years to publish more readers' letters, and that the effort had been successful. Getting that participation in the daily paper made fragmenting the audience through blogs unnecessary and undesirable, Farrugia said:

> In one sense, blogs are the antithesis of what newspapers ought to be. The mission of any newspaper worth its salt is to be a cohesive force within the region it covers. Newspapers highlight a shared sense of community; a common bond that links people to their neighbors, their environment, their government and their merchants.
>
> Blogs feed the push toward fragmentation, toward the individual as a community of one. Conservative bloggers cloister themselves in liberal-media conspiracy theories. Liberal bloggers demonize Fox News. Boaters communicate only with boaters. Parents with school-aged kids hear only what they want to hear from like-minded people within their demographic slice.[8]

As Poynter's discussions were taking place, bloggers operating independent of traditional news organizations had already been credited with, or were in the process of, digging up information that:

■ Led to U.S. Sen. Trent Lott's resignation as Senate majority leader for racially charged comments he made at a party for an aging colleague.

■ Prompted Dan Rather's premature retirement as CBS Evening News anchor for airing unverified documents about President Bush's National Guard service.

■ Unmasked a White House "correspondent" who had been using an assumed name and reported for a Web site closely affiliated with the Republican Party.

■ Forced the resignation of a CNN executive who, during an off-the-record panel discussion at a global conference, reportedly accused the U.S. military of intentionally targeting journalists in Iraq.

These were all stories the big news organizations had either missed or downplayed until bloggers made them impossible to avoid. With each new incident, emboldened bloggers crowed that they were chipping away at the foundation supporting the mainstream media, the once all-powerful monolith that stood between the truth and the people. It was in this atmosphere that news executives were weighing the costs and benefits of incorporating blogging into their organizations.

In the introduction to *We the Media*, Dan Gillmor describes an example of blogging's power to influence events as they unfold. Covering a speech in Phoenix by a CEO of a telephone company, who was complaining about the challenges of leadership and raising capital, Gillmor posted a running diary of his reactions online, noting at one point that the CEO shouldn't fuss when he was making good money even as his company lost market value. A lawyer monitoring the posts from Florida promptly e-mailed Gillmor, pointing him to online documents showing the CEO had made more than $200 million selling his company's stock while its value slid. When Gillmor posted these details, observers in the room began to notice a "chill" toward the speaker, most likely prompted by audience members who had been following along with Gillmor and another blogger's posts. Even as the CEO spoke, Gillmor's reporting, aided by a reader two thousand miles away, had changed the nature of his speech.[9]

One of the pitfalls of embracing blogging is the highly personal, ideological, and reactionary nature of many blogs. Critics of mainstream media have been decrying what they perceive to be politically motivated hidden agendas evident in news coverage. For most bloggers, disclosure of bias is a major factor in building credibility and support. But allegiance with factions and ideologies also diminishes independence — a crucial factor in producing journalism that enlightens rather than manipulates its audience. One characteristic that sets legitimate journalists apart from partisans and hacks is a sense of moral obligation to seek out and fairly represent opinions that differ from their own. If this obligation disappears from public discourse, the discourse will suffer. A shift from lecture to conversation may be healthy, but not a shift from curious questioning to universal spinning. Traditional news organizations' continued insistence on employing open-minded journalists who apply professional newsgathering standards will help these institutions maintain their authority in this chaotic sorting-out period.

Blogging also creates pro and con arguments regarding stakeholders. On the plus side, instituting a series of community blogs gives more stakeholders a voice in public affairs. But on the other hand, as Farrugia fears, each category of stakeholders might only seek out people they agree with, thereby preventing the communication necessary to help people come to a decision. Does a cacophony of bloggers help build a community, or does it create a series of insulated sub-communities oblivious to, or antagonistic toward, one another?

Jan Schaffer, a Pulitzer Prize-winning former reporter and editor for *The Philadelphia Inquirer* who runs the non-profit J-Lab: The Institute for Interactive Journalism, believes the old mass-marketing model for news — a "one-size-fits-all journalism" — is in its latter days. Niche content and fragmented media are inevitable, she says, but that won't prohibit meaningful discourse.

"It's really nice to say you wish everybody in the community would be on the same page, but I'm not sure that's going to happen," Schaffer said. "It's more important to start a conversation about issues. ...If the conversation is open and it generates momentum, it will sweep up the niches."[10]

As this book was written, the buzz about blogging overshadowed bloggers' actual impact on the general public. A CNN/USA Today/Gallup poll from early 2005 found about a quarter of Americans claiming to be very or somewhat familiar with blogs. Only about 15 percent said they read blogs at least a few times a month.[11] But the impact on mainstream journalists and politicians was evident from the dramatic examples of blogger-inspired resignations above. And journalist-entrepreneurs were just beginning to test the blogging format as a business model for doing community journalism.

Debbie Galant, a former *New York Times* columnist, launched a local-news blog focusing on three New Jersey towns in 2004, and a year later was working with a second writer and a business manager to build a profitable business based on ad sales. The blog, Barista of Bloomington Ave., combines traditional reporting, wit, and reader contributions to create a virtual news community that Galant sees as a legitimate competitor to the region's weekly newspapers.

"The local small-town newspapers are boring. They're really, really boring," Galant said.[12] "We kind of inject a sense of humor into everything. ... It just sort of made sense that you could do what a local newspaper did, only it could be a lot more fun."

Take Barista's coverage of Montclair Township's new logo. In addition to its running commentary on the logo's cost and selection process, the site solicited reviews from marketing experts and offered a series of tongue-in-cheek runners-up to the winning design. (One featured a car in a circle with a line through it, with the motto "Montclair: Don't even think of parking here.") The blog was also a forum for dozens of residents to comment on the process, an interactive opportunity Galant says "creates a place where people can just kind of talk and debate things and feel like they have a say."

Interactive projects

The Web is a vast frontier of new ways to give people a say in public affairs. J-Lab, a spin-off of the Pew Center for Civic Journalism, recognizes innovative uses of new technology that involve people in public issues "by providing access to news and information that stirs their imagination and invites participation."[13]

At a 2004 awards symposium honoring the most innovative uses of new technologies, Schaffer moderated a panel of winners discussing their projects. Sean Polay, then news and operations manager of Projo.com, *The Providence Journal's* Web site, described how his paper had connected citizens with members of the military serving overseas. Called "Tribute to our troops," the Web site allowed people to set up a page for a service member, to which readers around the world could contribute greetings and messages of appreciation. The site was open to links and participation by military organizations, family sites, and other media.

"I am daily humbled and amazed at the quality and the heartfeltness of these messages," Polay said at the session. "I mean, it is absolutely mind-blowing. Mothers writing to their sons and daughters, wives writing to their husbands, particularly new mothers talking about how a baby has taken their first steps and posting that to her husband. It nearly brings you to tears at times when you're reading through some of these messages. It's extremely powerful content."[14]

Polay said the site reflects the organization's broader "recognition of the value of user content ... [F]rom a strategic standpoint it breeds loyalty. You turn a casual user into a devoted user and hopefully a devoted user into an evangelical user that goes out and says, 'Hey, go check out ProJo.com. It's a cool site. I had a lot of fun there. ...'"

In the same session, Sean Fagan, a senior producer at KQED, a public broadcasting station in San Francisco, described a project incorporating many of the values expressed in the first part of this book. The feature, called "You Decide," begins with the simplicity of any Internet poll: It asks a yes/no question about a hot-button issue — like, "Do Americans pay too much in federal income tax?"

The twist comes after someone clicks the "yes" or "no" button and is confronted with a new question: "Are you sure?" followed by some information that challenges the respondent's point of view. Participants get a chance to affirm or change their response, then get to see another argument testing their opinion. The challenges go both ways; the feature plays devil's advocate with people of either position. After they've read through the arguments, participants get a final chance to cast a vote that counts toward the survey totals.

So the project empowers participants as contributors to policy debates, it confronts them with the pros and cons of their choices, it educates them on impacts they might not have considered. It makes them think in ways they may not have thought before, but ultimately it stands back while they decide. Discussion forums branching from each issue allow people with different opinions to challenge each other. The result of the more constructive discussions, Fagan said, is that people who disagree begin to understand one another's feelings.

"[T]ake the gun issue," Fagan said. "If you live in West Oakland, guns to you mean gangs, and you just don't want them on your street because you want your kid to safely go to school. Well, if you live in North Carolina, guns to you might mean hunting, or even just target shooting, and your kids have never been threatened with a gun in school. But both of you are coming from this point of view that, 'Even though I'm sitting across from you and there's this enormous ideological divide between us, I recognize that you just want to protect your children and I just want to protect my children and you just want to have an education for them and you just want safety. ... So you share all these values, it's just the way you want to accomplish them, the way you believe we as a nation should accomplish them, that is polarized.'"[15]

Here are some other interactive public affairs projects:

■ *The Washington Post* in the 2004 election featured a "Comparing the Candidates" page that allowed readers to view George Bush's and John Kerry's positions on the issues, side by side. Clicking an issue such as abortion, the economy, or civil liberties would bring up information about each man's stance on several sub-topics. Readers interested in civil liberties, for instance, could scroll through positions on the Patriot Act, same-sex marriage, the death penalty, and faith-based initiatives, and determine, point by point, which candidate more closely mirrored their own thinking.[16]

■ As part of a series about its city's future, the *Democrat and Chronicle* of Rochester, N.Y., set up a calculator that let people compare what they paid in income, property, sales, and gasoline taxes with residents in 16 other U.S. cities. Other activities included quizzes on public safety and standardized testing, live Web chats with community leaders and opportunities for participants to register their preferred solutions to the city's problems.[17]

■ Grade the News, Stanford University's media criticism site monitoring print and broadcast news in the San Francisco Bay area, offered a feature called "Grade the news yourself." It invited audiences to download a news scorecard and assign a "quality score" to a newspaper edition or news broadcast based on the type and depth of stories reported and the number and diversity of sources.[18]

■ The St. Paul *Pioneer Press* maintained a database of state legislators so readers could look up how lawmakers had voted on major issues. Readers could click on any representative in state government, check off the bills they wanted to know about, and get a rundown on how — or whether — the lawmaker voted.[19]

These are just a few of dozens of projects that news and civic organizations have undertaken to make public affairs more meaningful in people's lives. The possibilities for interactive journalism that informs, engages, and encourages action are limitless. There are pitfalls, too. The anonymous nature of many Internet discussions invites coarse language and destructive commentary. One paper, the *Ventura County Star*, suspended its unmoderated discussions in May 2005 after too many forums veered off into ugly racial commentary and abusive posts.[20]

Citizen journalism

Another growing phenomenon in online journalism is soliciting news content from non-journalists — inviting readers to contribute their own photos, stories, and commentary to create deeply local and personalized news. Many mainstream news organizations and pioneering entrepreneurs are trying their hand at this "citizen" or "open-source" journalism. At the community level, these platforms offer a chance for even the smallest news items to find an audience. When one of the biggest criticisms of journalists is that they've lost touch with their communities, this is an opportunity to embrace everyone.

"At YourHub.com, we're not going to say no," *Rocky Mountain News* Editor John Temple promised in a column introducing his paper's new open-source offering, which features a Web site for each of the 40 communities in the paper's metro area. "Many of you know the frustration of not getting your letter in the paper. Or of not being able to convince us to tell the world enough about your organization or event. At YourHub.com, you can do the talking without any interference from us."[21]

When everyone's a journalist, everyone's a reader. And everyone's more invested in the public life of the community that professional journalists cover full time.

Here are some other citizen journalism projects introduced in recent years:

■ *The Bakersfield Californian* launched a community Web site, updated daily, along with a print newspaper delivered free to 24,000 homes in Bakersfield's Northwest neighborhoods every other Thursday. Stories and pictures in *The Northwest Voice* are almost entirely submitted by readers. Most revenue comes from ads in the print edition, which draws stories from the best Web offerings, with online advertising available.[22] Top online postings on a spring day in 2005 included a story about the community helping pay vet bills for a family whose colt was born with a ruptured bladder, a gardening column, a photo gallery from a Tot T-ball class, and an announcement of a free class from the Bakersfield Meditation Society. The Web site warns that contributors are responsible for the opinions and accuracy of their posts.[23]

■ A class project at Northwestern University's Medill School of Journalism had students running "goskokie," a resident-centered Web site covering Skokie, Ill., that, in addition to student-generated content, solicited news and commentary from its audience. The site's slogan was "news for the people, by the people."[24]

■ The *Missourian* built a site called MyMissourian.com, seeking stories from area residents to be posted "with editing help by student editors from the Missouri School of Journalism."[25]

■ Former *Washington Post* reporter Mark Potts created an independent hyperlocal news organization, built entirely on reader-supplied content, with Backfence.com. The site launched in two towns in Northern Virginia with hopes of going national.[26]

In the hyperlocal spirit, J-Lab in early 2005 called for proposals for a $1 million project called "New Voices," aiming to help start up 20 educational and nonprofit community-based news ventures over two years. "Our goal is to really solicit good ideas and give them a little seed capital," J-Lab's Jan Schaffer said.[27]

THE WAY NEWS and information is delivered — along with the kinds of people who are reporting, writing, and delivering it — is evolving almost too quickly to keep up. As journalists and citizens rewrite the definitions of news and journalism, it's important to stay focused on the principles of accuracy, fairness, and open-mindedness that form the bedrock of independent reporting. Platforms might change, but principles and values are portable. Be sure to bring the principles of good journalism with you across the new frontier.

How to make important news interesting online

■ Recognize the Internet as a permanent, though evolving, tool of reporting, commentary, and conversation. It is an immediate, vast, and accessible venue for sharing information, but that information is often disorganized and unreliable. News organizations have to figure out how to create a new journalism that incorporates the strengths of Internet communication while minimizing its weaknesses.

■ Exploit the parallels between the Internet's versatility and the principles of good public affairs journalism:

● Help people take charge of community affairs by providing forums for comment on the news and your news organization. Create direct pipelines from citizens to officials and to your own staff.

● Use the infinite space of the Internet to expand people's access to information about problems and solutions in your community. Link to official reports, expert essays, and other sources of data about choices and consequences. Host discussions on your Web site that help people exchange ideas. Consider requiring registration and forbidding anonymous posts, to keep the conversation civil.

● Invite stakeholders from across the community to participate in online chats, and consider linking to or publishing readers' weblogs on your site. Let your bloggers know you will hold them to the standards of fairness, taste, and honesty that you hold your staff to.

● Hold sources accountable for their words and actions by providing links to official records and past statements.

● Offer links to educational and historical sites; interactive tutorials explaining government processes; maps, charts, and other graphics; interactive quizzes; online glossaries; and other tools that improve readers' understanding of current events.

● Create online communities that help citizens share ideas, form organizations, and solve problems together. Explore ways to help readers generate their own content that broadens your coverage. Offer links and contact tools for decision makers cited in your stories.

● Find opportunities to incorporate audio and video to invigorate online reports. "Podcast" interviews and important events so audiences can download the sound and listen when and where they please. Create interactive games that simulate the work of budget writers, mayors, and legislators. Develop calculators readers can use to figure out how much a tax or fee increase will cost them personally. Use the potency of multimedia content and interactive features to draw readers' attention to important news.

● Develop and maintain a core of ethical principles to carry you across any medium or format that your journalism takes, now and in the future. Society is still coming to grips with the kinds of communication possible through developing technologies; do your part to make sure the new models serve the public good — not just a select few entrepreneurs and power brokers, and not just a teeming cesspool of unreliable, irreconcilable jabberers.

For thought and action...

1 Explore a news-oriented Web site. Write a critique of its strengths and weaknesses. How does the site engage people with the news? What could it do better?

2 Find two weblogs written by people with competing ideologies. Compare and contrast how the blogs portray a single issue in the news. What information do they leave out? What information do they emphasize? Does either blog offer enough information for readers to make up their own minds? How about the two blogs together?

3 Pick any newspaper front page. For each story, devise an interactive Web feature that would make it both more interesting and more educational.

4 Write a short paper imagining how people might get their news 10 years from now. What form will it come in? Who will select it? Will people read it, hear it, watch it, or all three? How will they interact with news organizations, newsmakers, and fellow citizens?

Chapter 15

Reinventing Journalism

What appears to be an earnest attempt at tailoring the news to multi-tasking readers often comes across as pandering. [...] Most aim for cute and conversational and — here's where the pandering comes in — instead come off snarky and air-headed. Why not try for literate and engaging?

— Brian Orloff, Northwestern University journalism student[1]

The college newspapers where many of you are now working don't need to look like the city newspaper in the nearest town. In fact, they shouldn't. They should be laboratories for cutting-edge journalism.

— Susan Goldberg, *San Jose Mercury News*[2]

Schoolhouse Rock *was cool, but the newspaper is not — at all.*

— Nicole Schilt, Michigan State University journalism student[3]

A favorite pastime of both educators and journalists is spotlighting the ignorance of the general public — especially today's students. Just as I did in Chapter 5, they revel in surveys demonstrating how few people can identify their representative in Congress or the attorney general of their state. They love commiserating over the results of public affairs polls contrasting young people's attentiveness to MTV celebrities with their apathy toward current events.

For these folks, young people's inattention to the nation's power elite and policy debates — juxtaposed with their capacity to identify an infinite number of entertainers and their love interests, hobbies, and favorite foods — is a signal that the country is going to hell in a handbasket, that democracy has run its course, that we're on the cusp of realizing the doomsday scenarios of happily ignorant masses blithely doing the bidding of tyrants as foreseen in *Fahrenheit 451* and *1984*. These educators peer down the bridge of their noses, these journalists pontificate from their isolated newsrooms, fearful that the coming generation won't have the knowledge or skills to keep the world turning when it takes over. A *Detroit News* columnist lamented in early 2005 that students in a college journalism class she visited couldn't name a single newspaper columnist. Even young people who wanted to work for newspapers didn't read them.[4]

It's easy for print people to be jealous when confronted with evidence that today's college students prefer not to get news from newspapers. But in a book called *Tuned Out*, David T. Z. Mindich presents an even bleaker picture. His conclusion is that most college students, and in fact most people under 40, prefer not to get news at all.

Mindich notes that seven in 10 older Americans read a newspaper each day, compared to less than one in five young Americans.[5] In 2002, he points out, 19 percent of people aged 23 to 27 were daily newspaper readers; 30 years earlier, nearly half of that age group read a paper daily.[6] Beyond this marked decline in newspaper reading among succeeding generations of young people, Mindich builds a case that, contrary to conventional wisdom, younger citizens don't make up the news deficit through television or the Internet. Across the board, he argues, younger generations are less interested in, and less knowledgeable about, public affairs than their elders are and than their own age group has ever been.[7]

So I'm one of these snobby Chicken Littles who shudder at both the statistical and anecdotal evidence that most college students today don't know squat about what's going on in the world of politics, policy, or diplomacy — and worse — that they don't seem to care. In the same week I was preparing this chapter, I saw characteristic blank looks arise on the faces of journalism seniors in my ethics class as I mentioned Seymour Hersh — a world-famous journalist whose investigative reporting spans five decades and who had just won a national award for reporting on the U.S. military's abuse of Iraqi detainees at the Abu Ghraib prison — and Oliver North, an iconic ex-Marine who was convicted of lying to Congress during the Iran-Contra affair in the 1980s, ran for the U.S. Senate from Virginia in the 1990s, and reported for the Fox News Channel in the 2000s. When I asked my class how many had seen the movie *All the President's Men*, which recounts the most famous act of journalism in history — Bob Woodward and Carl Bernstein's reporting on Watergate in the early 1970s — close to half raised their hands; but many others shook their heads or shrugged their shoulders to show they'd never even heard of it. (This was before the famous anonymous source Deep Throat unveiled himself as W. Mark Felt in mid-2005.)

I wasn't giving pop quizzes or asking ambush questions to try to make my students feel dumb; I was just bringing up these names in the course of discussing ethical issues and journalistic milestones. But every time I see that blank stare, I feel a mixture of condescension, frustration, and dread.

The problem is, none of these emotions is constructive, and blaming young people for adopting the priorities our culture has laid out for them is both unfair and unwise. Condescension, especially, helped create this mess, and frustration and dread won't get us out of it. Many, many people in the news industry have been banging their heads against the wall trying to think of what WILL get us out of it, but so far all they have to show for it are bruised and bloodied heads.

Reaching out

The highest-profile efforts to bring young readers into the news-consuming fold in recent years have been the introduction of free or cheap tabloid papers — most of them spun off from established dailies — generally targeting people aged 18 to 34.

The first problem with that strategy is that 34-year-olds don't have a lot in common with 18-year-olds. The younger crowd is still in college, single, staying up late, and trying to figure out what to do with their lives. People in their 30s are far more likely to have careers, be married, and own their own homes. If you've got a job, a spouse and a mortgage, you'll tend to spend your time and money differently from those who don't.

The second problem with the specialized publication strategy is the flawed assumptions many publishers bring to their tabloids — namely, that the only way to reach young people is to treat them like idiots. Drawing on research of young people's current events knowledge and leisure activities, these papers do the opposite of what journalism and democracy need: They try to make the interesting important. They've given up on the idea that smart, sincere, and helpful journalism can ever attract someone from Generations X or Y, and so they follow the demographic curve and hype entertainment and frivolous lifestyle news to the near exclusion of significant information.

In *Tuned Out*, David Mindich compares editions of the *Chicago Tribune* and its hip, young-person tab *RedEye* from the same day: Jan. 3, 2003. The *Tribune's* front page has stories about the economy, presidential politics, lower air fares, international events and *Lord of the Rings* author J. R. R. Tolkein's 111th birthday. The top stories teased on *RedEye* are only the airlines — "Fare Warning" — and new television shows. Mindich acknowledges that tabloids by their nature have a lower story count on their front pages, but he decries the tone of the youth-centric paper, saying it approaches readers not as "citizens but spoiled, selfish, insatiable consumers wanting TV, fun entertainment, food, and titillation."[8]

I tried a similar exercise on Dec. 22, 2004, the day after an attack at a military mess in Mosul, Iraq, killed almost 20 Americans, one of the highest single-day U.S. casualty counts of the war. Nearly every real newspaper led with the story.

The *Tribune's RedEye* cover headline was "New Rape Link," a serious story about a string of related attacks on women in Chicago. The Iraq attack was on page 12, without so much as a refer from the front page. The *Chicago Sun-Times'* competing tab, *Red Streak*, devoted its front page to the release of *Meet the Fockers*, the sequel to the Ben Stiller movie *Meet the Parents*. To its credit, *Red Streak* put the Iraq story on page 3 and promoted it in a little corner of page 1. Also to its credit, *Red Streak* had played an Iraq story on its cover the day before.

For the most part, it's hard to disagree with Mindich's conclusion that these papers approach young people as though they're incapable of monitoring important events and, instead, are myopically focused on gratifying personal and entertainment interests. ("I don't think 'nipple ring' is printed on paper enough," *RedEye* sports editor Michael Kellams told *The Ball State Daily News*. "[…]We try to give readers what they'll find interesting.")[9]

Efforts in other cities include the *St. Petersburg Times' tbt** (for *Tampa Bay Times*). It promises "zippy news for time-challenged adults" and, in the description of the *St. Petersburg Times'* story about the publication, delivers the news "in short chunks with colorful photos and no attempt at serious analysis."[10] The lead story on *tbt**'s tampabay.com site on Feb. 24, 2005, was a lengthy staff and wire mix on young entrepreneurs — a topical and relevant choice. If you were looking for news on the site, though, you'd be hard pressed to find it. The "Hot Topics" button at the top of the page, which seemed like it might be a trendy way of saying "current events," went to a feature headlined "So you want to be a porn star." Other content choices came under the Web headers "Planner," "Grub & Club," "Entertainment," "Living & Style," "Career & Money" and "Deals."[11]

In Denver, *Westword* reported that *The Denver Post* and *Rocky Mountain News* were teaming up to create *Bias*, a magazine targeting young adults with a prototype encouraging readers to tour sites of notorious Denver murders and toast the killers and victims. "Such prose is intended to be outrageous," Michael Roberts wrote in response to *Bias* promotional copy invoking serial cannibal Jeffrey Dahmer, "but for the most part, it's less startling than stale — an attempt to convey a post-modern sensibility that founders on its own desperation." Roberts reported that *Bias* was being promoted to potential advertisers as "the no-walls, interactive media & marketing experience that connects young, info-savvy communities with each other and with the advertisers who crave them."[12] The *Bias* Web site launched in June 2005, blending actually useful advice on home-buying and a humorous take on a state referendum with a page where reader-members contribute their "stupid little stories" about hiring hookers for pre-wedding celebrations and getting flashed by their spa clients.[13]

These projects may or may not succeed in attracting younger readers. At least one early study suggested that Chicago's *RedEye* and *Red Streak* were gaining ground with their target audiences,[14] but by the end of 2005 the *Chicago Tribune* stopped charging for *RedEye* and the *Sun-Times* had shut down *Red Streak*.[15] Overall, perhaps any inroads similar tabs make in getting young people to read newsprint are positive. But it's unlikely these publications are going to help young people be better-informed citizens, because they aren't really trying.

NOT EVERY ATTEMPT to woo younger readers appeals to their most banal instincts.

Many alternative weeklies in metropolitan markets such as New York's *Village Voice* and the *Chicago Reader* do try to engage readers with serious news and analysis (plus extensive local entertainment and event listings). Younger people make up larger proportions of these publications' readership than they do for mainstream newspapers, although recent studies have shown that alternative weeklies' audiences are growing older. Still, these papers demonstrate the potential for in-depth, thoughtful journalism to attract people who still have all their hair: As mainstream newspapers suffered circulation declines in the 1990s, alt weekly circulation and revenues soared on a national scale.[16]

In a serious attempt to reach even younger people — high school students — the *Quad-City Times* in Davenport, Iowa, launched a weekly publication called *Your Mom*, with the Web site **www.yourmomonline.com**. Yeah, the name's edgy, and so is the content, because the audience is young and looking for something different. But here's how the *Quad-City Times'* story describes the new venture, whose content is primarily generated by its high school-aged audience: "It has opinions. It has news. It has reviews. It has photos. It has polls."[17] The emphasis, at least in the telling, is on opinion and news. Real stuff.

Your Mom Online's home page on Feb. 24, 2005, was dominated by a banner graphic teasing to a high school student's story about drug use. Based on anonymous interviews, the story mixed first-person descriptions of students' first drug experiences with a list of the ways drugs can harm the body. A centerpiece feature focused on trendy colored wrist bands, but deeper on the page was an opinion piece on anti-discrimination laws and a news-oriented feature called "your mom's take," which offered short, formatted riffs on current events — two local, two national, and two international. Here's *Your Mom's* take on importing prescription drugs from Canada:

> **Last Your Mom checked:** Getting drugs from Canada was a big thing.
> **But then:** The Canadian government is considering banning the export of

prescription drugs to the United States.

    And so: It looks like some spam e-mailers might have to go back to supporting the porn industry.[18]

These are just news bits — a clever blend of the news brief and the "update" format we explored in Chapter 9 — but for teens it seems to have a good mix of detail and attitude to at least draw attention to a serious subject, which might make them more receptive to information when it's raised in another context. "A spoonful of sugar helps the medicine go down," said *Your Mom's* founding editor, Hillary Rhodes.[19] "They're inadvertently learning about six pretty hard news pieces that happened in the last week without even realizing it."

    Your Mom's philosophy is that, while teens' interest in news might be different from or less than adults', they still have an appetite for it and enough sophistication to process it. "We're operating on the assumption that teens are curious and intelligent and opinionated people, and interested and interesting," said Rhodes, a 2004 graduate of Northwestern University's master's in journalism program. She and her classmates created the *Your Mom* concept for the *Quad-City Times* through the program's management class. The paper was so impressed with the proposal that it hired Rhodes to see it through.

    By many measures, *Your Mom* had an impressive first year. Within its first few months, the magazine and Web site had explored such serious issues as abortion, drugs, politics and body image. One of the most controversial early editions talked about how trendy it had become to be Christian in the Quad-Cities area. The cover mimicked the "Buddy Jesus" conceit from the Kevin Smith movie *Dogma*, with a costumed Jesus being worshiped by a throng of admirers like a rock star. The issue included opinions from students who believed the teen years were meant for rebellion and mischief, which was being ruined by reverent goodness, and from others who talked about what a great experience their church youth group was. "We showed both sides, but everyone had strong opinions," Rhodes said.

    By the end of 2005, *Your Mom's* efforts had attracted plenty of industry attention. *Editor & Publisher* magazine named it one of its annual "10 That Do It Right" for its aggressive and edgy content. The Newspaper Association of America bestowed Rookie of the Year honors for *Your Mom* as a youth section. But the print version of the project succumbed to business pressures, publishing its last standalone edition in December after failing to earn enough ad revenue. The online content continued, along with a planned new print format in the pages of the *Quad-City Times*.[20]

What young people want

    There's some evidence that public-spirited content — packaged in the right way — can attract and hold younger readers. Northwestern's Readership Institute distilled reactions from young people into a series of newspaper "experiences" that can either turn readers on or turn them off. In a July 2004 report, the institute identified six key experiences that led to higher readership: If readers say the paper gives them "something to talk about," "makes me smarter," "looks out for my civic and personal interests," has useful ads, offers "value for my money," or provides good service, that makes them more likely to read the paper than those who don't have those experiences. The report also notes two experiences likely to drive young people away from the paper: a sense that it discriminates and stereotypes, and a feel-

In the *Star Tribune* experiment, a group of young readers was asked to evaluate three papers. The original front page (above left) used traditional news judgment. The "experience" front page (above right) aimed to create the reactions "gives me something to talk about," "looks out for my interests" and "turned on by surprise and humor." The experience paper, while maintaining its news focus, was by far the most popular. (Reprinted with permission of the *Star Tribune*.)

ing that the paper delivers too much content to digest.[21]

A couple of findings from this report seem to support the efforts of the young-people-oriented publications described above. The evidence that young readers are overwhelmed by bulky papers, high story counts and long stories is bolstered by the results of focus groups held by *The Washington Post* in 2004, which found many younger non-readers wouldn't even take the paper if it were delivered to their door for free, because they didn't want all that paper "piling up" in their homes.[22] So there's some sense to *RedEye* and its peers creating smaller publications with fewer, shorter stories. Likewise, these papers fall over themselves to give their young readers "something to talk about," by focusing on cultural issues like movie releases and sensational stories like local crime.

But the Readership Institute research also suggests that editors across the country are missing opportunities to attract younger readers by appealing to their intelligence and civic potential. The "makes me smarter" motivator validates the principle that journalism should educate: If you deliver the news in a way that lets readers in on the process instead of launching it over their heads, you're more likely to see those readers again. Those who had the "makes me smarter" experience made statements such as, "Even if I disagree with things in this newspaper, I feel like I have learned something valuable."[23]

Even more promising is the finding that young people prefer newspapers that they perceive to be looking out for their civic interests. The report says the meaning of this experience is that "[t]he newspaper helps people take part in the community and also acts as a watchdog for the community." One of the direct quotes from a news consumer in the study: "Reading this newspaper makes me feel like a better citizen."

That's the kind of stuff that doesn't seem to turn up in most publications targeting young people, and yet, it's the kind of stuff young readers say they want.

In 2005, the *Star Tribune* of Minneapolis tried its hand at delivering an "experience-based" paper to younger readers. The paper presented a targeted group with three front pages: an original page as it was published, a page that repackaged the original lineup with a new emphasis and tone, and a brand-new page reconstructed with new story choices. The overhauled paper, which aimed to create the experiences "gives me something to talk about," "looks out for my interests" and "turned on by surprise and humor," was a runaway hit.

The new page's lineup included a centerpiece on proposed legislation to legalize Texas Hold 'Em poker, presented in the "debatable" format we discussed in Chapter 6 (the headline: "Should poker be a crime?"), and a story about identity theft that had originally run in the business section, illustrated with a photo of Paris Hilton, whose cell phone directory had recently been hacked. The new page dumped stories about a woman whose goal was to walk every street in Minneapolis and about local civic officials setting up blogs.[24]

It's important to note that while the revised news judgment sought to make the prototype paper interesting, it also relied on stories of civic consequence. The poker issue wasn't just a lifestyle matter; it was state legislation. The identity theft story used Paris Hilton to get attention, but it addressed the broader problem and gave advice for how readers could protect themselves. Readers said the paper was "'real news' focused" and "covered topics that were relevant, current and important."[25] The results led Readership Institute staff to this heartening conclusion:

> It's commonly and, we think, erroneously assumed that the only way to engage younger adults is through so-called softer news such as entertainment, lifestyle and sports. To be sure, these topics are encompassed in their definition of "news." But it's a mistake to think they are uninterested in hard news.
>
> What doesn't engage them are process-focused or institutional stories, stories that seem to have no relevance to their lives, news that seems just a repetition of what they have already seen or heard, and presentation that doesn't allow them to easily access the main points.

The *Star Tribune* purposely chose the front page and inside pages of the front section for their experiments to test experience techniques on hard news. The results show it's a field ripe for innovation.[26]

THE QUEST FOR BLUNTER, more engaging, more intriguing news delivery has driven many young people to non-news sources. A study by The Pew Research Center found that one in five people under 30 learned regularly about early 2004 presidential campaigning from shows like Jon Stewart's *The Daily Show* on Comedy Central, putting humor shows roughly on par with newspapers, the Internet, and evening network news as places young people picked up campaign information. The Pew report said people who learned about the campaign from entertainment programs were among the least likely to be able to answer questions about the background of the candidates then running for the Democratic presidential nomination.[27]

But a study conducted a few months later — closer to Election Day — by the Annenberg Public Policy Center reached different conclusions. The Annenberg survey found that late-night comedy show viewers, and *Daily Show* fans in particular, were more likely to know campaign details than those who didn't watch those shows. Poll respondents took a six-question test, and those who didn't watch any late-night comedy scored an average of 2.62 correct answers. *Daily Show* viewers got 3.59 answers right — scoring better than national news viewers and newspaper readers even after the study adjusted for education, party identification, political interest and other factors. During the study period, *Daily Show* host Jon Stewart had interviewed John Kerry, Sen. John McCain, former President Bill Clinton, and senior Republican strategists.[28]

If you wanted evidence that public affairs news made interesting is worth the effort, there it is. Annenberg researchers concluded that the superior knowledge of *Daily Show* viewers was probably a combination of how much the audience knew going in and what they took away from the show. It's reasonable to conclude that something about the *Daily Show's* irreverent, satirical but ultimately informative formula helps build interest and knowledge in politics — even while the show's host protests, and serious journalists fret — that its prime purpose is entertainment. There must be something meat-and-potatoes journalists can draw from the show, without giving over their professional ethics or clowning up public affairs. One college student offered this suggestion in *The Daily Pennsylvanian*:

> Framing news in terms of two supposedly equal but opposing viewpoints ignores the reality that the facts are not always balanced between parties, and thus legitimizes factually inaccurate opinions. ...
> [T]hose like me who prefer factual journalism to balanced journalism have been abandoned by the networks. Instead, we watch the fake news of *The Daily Show*, which avoids the pitfalls of "balance" by using satire as its basic form.[29]

The reasons newspapers are missing out on young readers may be similar to the reasons they're losing readers in general: They aren't producing journalism that is relevant to their lives, that makes them smarter, that engages them as members of the community. Efforts to reach young readers seem to appeal to their baser and shallower instincts. But perhaps if we begin treating young people as citizens, as *Your Mom* does in its own way, they will start responding as citizens.

An election of hope

The 2004 elections offered a sign that young people can emerge from their apathetic cloaks when they see a stake for themselves in public decisions. About 47 percent of 18- to 24-year-olds voted in the 2004 national elections, according to U.S. Census Bureau data, up from about 36 percent in 2000. The turnout rate among 25- to 34-year-olds was up to 56 percent, a 5-percentage-point increase from 2000. Turnout increases among younger people outpaced every other age group.[30]

The higher participation had been predicted, based on effective voter registration drives organized by groups ranging from MTV to grass-roots local outlets. Jane Eisner, a columnist for *The Philadelphia Inquirer* and author of *Taking Back the Vote: Getting American Youth Involved in Our Democracy*, noted before the election that today's young people are engaged with their community, but in a different way from previous generations. Uninspired by the political process, many younger people participate in local volunteer activities, she wrote. But she added that some young people were coming to understand that individual actions without voter-inspired policy changes would be short-term fixes for long-term problems. And she noted that the most successful way of getting young people to vote is through direct exhortation by peers.[31]

A lot of newspapers, both commercial and collegiate, went out of their way to connect younger readers to the 2004 election. As discussed in Chapter 8, *State News* staffers made a special point of writing from young people's perspectives. They convened a panel of undergraduates to watch the presidential debates and reported on those students' reactions. They profiled students and recent graduates who were volunteering with campaigns and get-out-the-vote efforts. They repeatedly ran detailed information about how to register to vote, how to get an absentee ballot, how to contact the campaigns. On the Opinion page, they ran a daily graphic with a new goofy reason students should cast a ballot. On Election Day, they ran a giant map of campus-area voting precincts so students could find their polling places. The headline was "NO EXCUSES."

An online survey by MSU's Institute for Public Policy and Social Research concluded that about 90 percent of Michigan State students voted — well beyond the collegiate or general population totals.[32] Even if this number is high because nonvoters were less likely to respond to the survey, it's good news. And it's fair to speculate that *The State News'* coverage contributed to the turnout.

A second logical leap would suggest that, more broadly, when young people see other young people making a difference, they want a piece of the action. "The challenge now is to build upon those [turnout] numbers and get this new-found interest to stick," *The Inquirer's* Eisner said.[33]

Reinventing journalism

Our earlier look at the teen-focused *Your Mom* magazine is a good opportunity to talk more broadly about the kind of journalists and citizens we're preparing for the coming decades. Editor Hillary Rhodes described the goals of her publication this way: "One is to provide teens their own newspaper and their own forum for conversation and a place for them to exchange ideas and information. ... And another goal is to get them acclimated to the general idea of reading newspapers and keeping them up to date with public affairs and news so that eventually they're readers of a mainstream daily newspaper."[34] Embedded in those goals are first the citizen model, and then the business model, of a news product targeting young people. They're inextricably linked.

Your Mom, which has riled some parents with its edgy content, stands out in a culture that seems all too squeamish about the value of the First Amendment, especially as it applies to teens and young adults. In an era of constant warfare against what George W. Bush calls "the enemies of freedom," nearly a quarter of adults surveyed in 2005 believe the First Amendment goes too far in the freedoms it protects (this is down from almost half of respondents in 2002). An even higher proportion — 39 percent — believe the press is too free.[35]

Echoing this sentiment, nearly half of high school students in a mammoth Knight Foundation survey said newspapers should not be allowed to publish without government approval of stories, and more than 40 percent said high school students shouldn't be allowed to report controversial issues in their newspapers without school officials' OK. Overall, students were less likely than principals, teachers or adults in general to believe that people should be allowed to express unpopular opinions.[36]

Why do so many young people feel this way? Why are they so unsure of their own expressive rights, the foundation of liberty?

In 1988, the U.S. Supreme Court decided the case of Hazelwood School District *v.* Kuhlmeier, in which a majority of justices created the right of high school administrators to review and censor student publications. There were limitations on what could be censored — administrators must have a reasonable educational justification — but the ruling has been broadly interpreted by school officials as a right to butt in and kill any story, photo, or graphic that rubs them the wrong way.

In one of countless examples, a Florida principal in February 2005 pulled 3,000 printed copies of a student paper from circulation because it contained a column by a student about losing one's virginity. The column ultimately argued for care and caution in sexual situations, but that didn't satisfy the principal, who argued that most students wouldn't read to the end. Though acknowledging that she often overheard teens talking about sex in the halls, her conclusion was not the First Amendment-friendly idea that an opinion piece might help elevate the discussion, but rather that a story about something students constantly talked about might lead them to ... talk about it.[37]

The principal's last quote in *The Palm Beach Post* story, "You have to learn that you can't just write whatever you want," exemplifies the educational message of the Hazelwood decision — a message that has been instilled in young people for going on two decades. We can teach about freedom and the First Amendment in government classes forever, but in the battle between what adults say — that free expression is valuable — and what they do — stifle free expression — you can bet that the actions are more powerful than the words.

The same day the *Palm Beach Post* reported this censorship case, a columnist for the *Peoria Journal Star* wrote a tribute to Hunter S. Thompson, one of the culture's most notorious, freewheeling, innovative, and irresponsible journalists, who had shot himself to death earlier that week. Thompson's model of journalism and his reckless lifestyle are not what most people could or should emulate, and yet his talent and his relentless distaste for bullshit inspired a number of young people into the profession. The *Journal Star* columnist, Phil Luciano, lamented how much more boring journalism and journalists seemed to be in the modern era, and how unwilling newspaper people are to take chances today, for fear of offending an audience or distressing a corporate bean counter.[38]

I don't condone Hunter Thompson's lifestyle or hail him as a hero, but I sensed a powerful connection between Luciano's observation of journalistic blandness and the high school principal's admonishment that "You have to learn that you can't just write whatever you want." In fact, one of the censored students was quoted in the *Palm Beach Post* story saying, "We're very fluffy as a newspaper. ... That's what every person tells us: We don't write about real topics."

When today's student journalists and their news-consuming peers learn that topical, controversial, and sensitive subjects will be censored from newspapers, they carry those attitudes with them to college. The college newspaper students I've worked with in recent years — while talented, intelligent, and eager to do good journalism — are a little too willing to take an official's "no" for an answer. And while many college papers, including *The State News*, operate independently of their schools, many others are dependent on administrators and student groups for funding and support. There is growing pressure on many of these students, and their advisers and instructors, to toe the university line at the expense of good journalism, or risk their academic careers and their jobs. At Rutgers University, a part-time instructor whose fall 2004 investigative reporting class caused some discomfort among campus officials was told the course would only be continued in the spring if students confined their reporting to off-campus issues.[39] Administrators reversed their position about a week later, after the decision received national attention.[40] Meanwhile, a June 2005 ruling of the Seventh U.S. Circuit Court of Appeals began the judicial process of extending Hazelwood rules to public universities, implying higher education administrators could begin censoring student papers on campus.

Is it any wonder, then, between a stifling First Amendment education and the growing influence of corporate types in professional newsrooms, that a lot of journalism seems so safe, routine, and formulaic? That it doesn't intrigue or invite young people, who have been reared to expect irrelevance and timidity in news coverage? And that news "reporting" that is sharper, edgier, more independent, and more entertaining — like *The Daily Show* — ends up being a more frequented, more trusted news source among many young people than traditional journalism?

JOURNALISM IN GENERAL, and newspapers in particular, were in a crisis as this book went to press. Audiences are fleeing in droves. Credibility is diminishing. Interest in public affairs, especially among young people, is as low as it's ever been. When the older generation of loyal newspaper readers disappears, it's possible there will be no generation to replace them.

Into this maelstrom lurch today's young journalists — concerned about the fate of American democracy and the world's people, committed to reporting and presenting important news that can help citizens make sense of what's going on, live better lives, and contribute to the health of their communities.

Your understanding of how to produce public affairs journalism has been formed by what you've learned in class, what you've read in the newspaper and online, and maybe what you've seen for yourself in newsrooms. By following what you've heard, seen, and read, it's possible you've produced some pretty good journalism.

But there's a flaw in your apprenticeship:

The people teaching journalism classes, and the people running professional newspapers, don't know how to do serious journalism that reaches young citizens. There is no successful model for that kind of work.

And so your job today is to do some journalism from scratch. Twenty- and 30-something journalists are of a generation that, by and large, sees little relevance in public life. But if you're a part of this age group, you have something veteran journalists will never have: an inside understanding of what intrigues, inspires, motivates, and speaks to young people, and therefore the potential key to what will make important news interesting to them.

If you want to connect your peers to public life, for their sake and ultimately for the sake of democracy, you've got to take responsibility for how that gets done. The journalism required to do it hasn't been invented yet; you need to invent it. This book offers some ideas for bringing journalism closer to all citizens, but neither I nor your professors nor the latest round of Pulitzer winners has produced the answer for bringing today's young people into the fold.

Today's smart, committed, and engaged young journalists have an opportunity — no, a mandate — to develop public affairs journalism that is serious, relevant, and accessible to younger generations. This won't be done overnight; we're talking about realigning the culture here. But it can, and it must, be done. The fate of the nation literally depends on it.

And if you don't do it, who will?

How to reach young people

■ Take young people seriously. Treat them like citizens, not kids to be coddled or consumers to be targeted. Talk TO them, not AT them. Educate without lecturing. Make your efforts to reach them sincere; they'll see through attempts to pander or condescend.

■ Put young people in the paper, especially young people who are civically active. Show how these people are affecting their communities.

■ Focus on impact. Show what policies will do to and for young people, and how young people can affect policy.

■ Invite young people to share their priorities, concerns, and ideas with your staff and readers at large.

■ Hire young people and give them room to produce journalism that speaks to their peers.

Create and innovate

Susan Goldberg, executive editor of the San Jose Mercury News, spoke to the National College Newspaper Convention in February 2005. In these excerpts, she implores college students to create and innovate when delivering the news.

[T]oo often, the college journalists I meet want to be journalists in the mold of today's newspaper journalists. Often, the young people I meet have as traditional a view of our business as people 30 or 40 years older than they are! Sometimes, they are even more rigid, even more traditional, in their view of what the news is and how to present it. [...]

As young journalists, you have more freedom now, to experiment, than you ever may have again.

The college newspapers where many of you now are working don't need to look like the city newspaper in the nearest town. In fact, they shouldn't. They should be laboratories for cutting-edge journalism.

In addition to the late nights and pizza and camaraderie, make the most of every assignment. Do things that help make your college paper indispensable to readers. Don't be afraid to try new, unconventional approaches. [...]

[D]on't be narrow in your thinking about the world of the possible. After all, assuming you are not committing some kind of journalistic treason, what's the worst thing that can happen by trying out a new approach? [...]

I am not suggesting that the fundamentals of the craft of journalism are no longer important. In fact — in an age of information clutter and mis-information — they are more important than ever.

No whiz-bang computer graphic or navel-gazing blog is going to take the place of learning how to gather, package and disseminate information on the events of the day — information that is accurate, fair and revelatory. Information that can shine a light on injustice, explore a societal trend or simply get people to think about momentous and small occurrences in new ways.

More than ever, we need information that is honest, ethical and gathered transparently.

So learn your craft. Newspapers are the public trust. Be proud of that responsibility, and take it seriously.

But don't shy away from being bold about it. [...]

For thought and action...

1 Poll the class to find out who regularly reads a newspaper. For those who do, why? For those who don't, what would it take to get their attention?

2 Interview five students you don't know about how they get their news. Find out not only what sources they use but why they use them and ignore others. Ask what they do with the news they learn about.

3 Come up with five suggestions for how your local newspaper could better reach young readers. Consider how your ideas might make someone say the paper "makes me smarter" and "looks out for my civic interests."

4 As a class, brainstorm ways to engage college-aged people in public affairs. Come up with as many ideas as possible. Share them with your student and professional newspapers.

END NOTES

PREFACE

1. "State of the News Media 2004," the Project for Excellence in Journalism, http://www.journalism.org/resources/research/reports/definitions/differences.asp, accessed Nov. 9, 2004.
2. James Fallows, "Breaking the News: How the Media Undermine American Democracy." New York: Pantheon, 1996, p. 8.
3. Ibid, p. 243.
4. Bill Kovach and Tom Rosenstiel, "The Elements of Journalism: What Newspeople Should Know and the Public Should Expect." New York: Three Rivers Press, 2001, p. 17.
5. Ibid, p. 155.

INTRODUCTION

1. Davis Merritt and Maxwell McCombs, "The Two W's of Journalism: The Why and What of Public Affairs Reporting." Mahwah, N.J.: Lawrence Erlbaum Associates, 2004, p. 8.
2. Kovach and Rosenstiel, "The Elements of Journalism," p. 149.
3. Jim Drinkard, "Polls were busiest since Nixon-Humphrey in '68," *USA Today*, Nov. 4 2004, p. 3A.
4. Guy Gugliotta, "Politics Is In; Voter Apathy Is Out," *The Washington Post*, Nov. 3, 2004, p. A01.
5. Gary Hart, "Is Security Possible When War Becomes Crime?" speech at Yale University, Oct. 2, 2001, http://www.garyhartnews.com/hart/writings/speeches/yale2001.php, accessed March 3, 2005.
6. The search was for keywords hart, security and commission in major papers from Jan. 1, 2001, to March 1, 2001.
7. Arianna Huffington: "What if nation's corporate media had done their job?" *The San Diego Union Tribune*, Sept. 14, 2001.
8. Allison Romano, "CBS Axes Producer for Arafat Cut-In," *Broadcasting & Cable*, www.broadcastingcable.com, Nov. 12, 2004.
9. Joe Strupp, "Few Newspapers Covering Afghanistan," *Editor & Publisher*, Sept. 29, 2003.
10. Trudy Lieberman: "Imagining Evil," *Columbia Journalism Review*, September/October 2004, p. 24-31.
11. David Folkenflik, "Americans say media less believable: Gallup Poll comes in wake of scandals," *Baltimore Sun*, Sept. 24, 2004.
12. Joseph Carroll, "Trust in News Media Rebounds Somewhat This Year," Gallup Poll News Service, Sept. 27, 2005, http://poll.gallup.com/content/default.aspx?ci=18766, accessed Sept. 27, 2005.
13. Jules Crittenden, Laurel J. Sweet and Laura Raposa, "Blooper Bowl: Janet and Justin show tops for shock value," *Boston Herald*, Feb. 2, 2004, p. 3.
14. Kevin Rothstein, "Payzant submits lean school budget," *Boston Herald*, Feb. 5, 2004, p. 14.
15. City of East Lansing City Council agenda, www.cityofeastlansing.com, accessed July 2003.

CHAPTER 1

1. Fallows, "Breaking the News," p. 240.
2. Brian McGrory, "Dear voters, You're fired," *The Boston Globe*, Jan. 27, 2004.
3. W. Russell Neuman, Marion R. Just, Ann N. Crigler, "Common Knowledge: News and the Construction of Political Meaning." Chicago: The University of Chicago Press, 1992, p. 111. Also cited in Fallows, "Breaking the News," p. 242-243.
4. Merritt and McCombs, "The Two W's of Journalism," p. 69-70.

5. Deborah Potter, "Spectators or Citizens?" Transcript of a Nov. 5, 1995, commentary for NPR's "On the Media" from Poynter Online, http://www.poynter.org/content/content_print.asp?id=5711&custom, accessed Nov. 2, 2004.

6. Dante Chinni, "Campaign premortem postmortem," *The Christian Science Monitor*, Nov. 2, 2004.

7. Kenneth F. Warren, "In Defense of Public Opinion Polling." Boulder: Westview Press, 2001, p. 191.

8. Merritt and McCombs, the "Two W's of Journalism," p. 123-124.

9. Interview with Bob Campbell, Nov. 19, 2004.

10. *Quad-City Times*, Aug. 4, 2004, p. A1.

11. Telephone interview with John Humenik, Dec. 6, 2004.

12. Fallows, "Breaking the News," p. 258.

13. Dwight L. Morris & Associates, "Journalism Interactive: New Attitudes, Tools and Techniques Change Journalism's Landscape," study for Associated Press Managing Editors, Pew Center for Civic Journalism and the National Conference of Editorial Writers, 2002.

14. Ibid.

15. Merritt and McCombs, "The Two W's of Journalism," p. 81-82.

16. Neuman, Just and Crigler, "Common Knowledge," p. 75.

17. Jill Zuckman, "No questions right now; he's gotta run," *Chicago Tribune*, Sept. 10, 2004.

18. Daniel Yankelovich, "The Magic of Dialogue: Transforming Conflict into Cooperation." New York: Simon &Schuster, 1999, p. 166. E.J. Dionne in 1991 also cited this debate as a case of earnest democracy in action in "Why Americans Hate Politics," p. 9-10.

19. Perry Parks, "Rep. Owens goes to Raleigh, and the House gets to work," *The Virginian-Pilot & The Ledger-Star*, Jan. 26, 1995, North Carolina edition, p. B1. Reprinted with permission.

CHAPTER 2

1. Frank Batten Sr., "The Duty of Landmark Newspapers," from *The Virginian-Pilot's* ethics policy, http://welcome.hamptonroads.com/ethics.cfm, accessed Aug. 2, 2005.

2. Davis Merritt, "Public Journalism & Public Life: Why Telling the News is Not Enough," Hillsdale, N.J.: Lawrence Erlbaum Associates, 1995, p. 20.

3. Chris Christoff, "Tax services and spare budget, Michigan coalition urges," *Detroit Free Press*, Jan. 23, 2003.

4. "New groups taking sides in tax debate," Associated Press, Jan. 23, 2003, BC cycle.

5. E-mail from Chris Andrews, Nov. 22, 2004.

6. Stacey Range and Chris Andrews, "100 ways to cut Michigan's 1.7B deficit," *Lansing State Journal*, Feb. 9, 2003, p. 1A.

7. E-mail from Chris Andrews, Nov. 22, 2004.

8. Merritt and McCombs, "Two W's of Journalism," p. 109.

9. Cheryl Gibbs and Tom Wharhover, "Getting the Whole Story: Reporting and Writing the News." New York: The Guilford Press, 2002, p. 164-165.

10. Neuman, Just and Crigler, "Common Knowledge," p. 74.

11. Ibid, p. 112. Also cited in Merritt, "Public Journalism & Public Life," p. 96.

12. Yankelovich, "The Magic of Dialogue," p. 179-180.

13. Liz Cox Barrett, "380 Tons of Explosives? What 380 Tons of Explosives?" *CJR Daily*, Nov. 22, 2004, http://www.cjrdaily.org/archives/001138.asp, accessed May 11, 2005.

14. E-mail from Randolph Brandt, March 22, 2005.

15. Jeff Wilford, "The uninsured driver," *The Journal Times*, June 10, 2003, p. 1A. Reprinted with permission.

16. Laura Meckler of the Associated Press, "Social Security options all involve drawbacks," *Lansing State Journal*, April 10, 2005, p. 16A.

17. Fallows, "Breaking the News," p. 245. Also, the Pew Center for Civic Journalism, "Publications: Tapping Civic Life," http://www.pewcenter.org/doingcj/pubs/tcl/, citing "Meaningful Chaos: How People Form Relationships with Public Concerns," prepared by The Harwood Group of Bethesda, MD, for the Kettering Foundation, Dayton, Ohio, 1993.
18. Telephone interview with Karen Weintraub, Dec. 15, 2004.
19. Liz Bleau, "Ruskin Examines Becoming A City," *The Tampa Tribune*, Sept. 26, 2004, Brandon edition p. 1.
20. Kelly McBride, "Schiavo Case a Chance for Journalists to Lead," Poynter Online, March 23, 2005, http://www.poynter.org/content/content_print.asp?id=80096&custom, accessed March 23, 2005.
21. Scott Shepard, "Questions about political motives surface in Shiavo case," Cox News Service, March 22, 2005.
22. David Goldstein and Steve Kraske, "Area lawmakers defend Schiavo vote," *The Kansas City Star*, March 23, 2005.
23. Ken Thorbourne, "Nun feels Schiavo's family's pain," *Jersey Journal*, March 23, 2005.
24. Lisa Marshall, "Disability-rights challenge: Longmont woman says her daughter, Schiavo have a lot in common," *The Daily Camera*, March 23, 2005.

CHAPTER 3

1. Telephone interview with Karen Weintraub, Dec. 15, 2004.
2. Mike Knepler, "Light rail referendum: The black & white issues," *The Virginian-Pilot*, Oct. 22, 1999, p. A1. Reprinted with permission.
3. Telephone interview with Mike Knepler, Nov. 30, 2004.
4. *Virginian-Pilot* newsroom memo, February 1996.
5. Telephone interview with Tom Warhover, Oct. 25, 2004.
6. Wendy Y. Lawton, "Parents passionate about D-11 tax hike/Many worried about condition of schools," *The Gazette Telegraph*, Oct. 29, 1996, p. 6A.
7. Wendy Y. Lawton and Bill McKeown, "D-11 measures fly through polls/Funds to buy four schools, roofs, repairs," *The Gazette Telegraph*, Nov. 6, 1996, p. 1A.
8. Telephone interview with Kelley L. Carter, Dec. 14, 2004.
9. Roy Peter Clark, "American Leviathan," Poynter Online, Sept. 4, 2005, http://www.poynter.org/content/content_view.asp?id=88295, accessed Sept. 22, 2005.
10. Maynard Institute, www.maynardije.org/programs/faultlines/, accessed Aug. 3, 2005.
11. Haley Harrison, "Students still defying residential living laws," *The University Daily Kansan*, Oct. 12, 2004.
12. Telephone interview with Mike Knepler, Nov. 30, 2004.
13. Dawson Bell, "Gay marriage issue creates two activists," *Detroit Free Press*, Oct. 20, 2004, p. 1A. Reprinted with permission.
14. Telephone interview with Dawson Bell, Dec. 3, 2004.
15. Dawson Bell, "Her stance is not anti-gay, she insists, it's pro-family," *Detroit Free Press*, Oct. 20, 2004, p. 11A. Reprinted with permission.
16. Dawson Bell, "Discrimination is at heart of amendment, opponent says," *Detroit Free Press*, Oct. 20, 2004, p. 11A. Reprinted with permission.
17. Yankelovich, "The Magic of Dialogue," p. 70, 107, 127.

CHAPTER 4

1. E-mail from Lex Alexander, Feb. 17, 2005.
2. CCJ Member Survey, "Journalists Not Satisfied With Their Performance in the Campaign," http://www.journalism.org/resources/research/reports/campaign2004/ccjcamp2004/default2.asp, accessed

Dec. 7, 2004. I participated in the survey.

3. Kovach and Rosenstiel, "The Elements of Journalism," p.17.

4. Telephone interview with Tom Rosenstiel, Dec. 14, 2004.

5. "Hospital facilities subject of ongoing debate," *Indiana Daily Student*, Oct. 7, 2004, p. 1A.

6. Scott Cendrowski, "Some reassembly desired: Representatives look to reform ASMSU's image by remodeling structure," *The State News*, Nov. 29, 2004, p. 1A.

7. E-mail from Scott Cendrowski, May 18, 2005.

8. Report by the Program on International Policy Attitudes, Oct. 28, 2004, www.pipa.org.

9. Dana Milbank, "Bush Disavows Hussein-Sept. 11 Link: Administration Has Been Vague on Issue, but President Says No Evidence Found," *The Washington Post*, Sept. 18, 2003, p. A18.

10. "Newsweek Poll: Republican Convention 2004," Yahoo financial news, Sept. 4, 2004.

11. Dan Froomkin, "Tougher political coverage needed – but does it mean an end to impartiality?" Nieman Watchdog, http://niemanwatchdog.org/index.cfm?fuseaction=background.view&backgroun-did=0037&stoplayout=true&print=true, accessed Nov. 10, 2004.

12. Bryan Keefer, "Tsunami: The Campaign '04 information war is fast, deep, and fraught with lies. The press must rethink its coverage, or drown in a toxic tidal wave," *Columbia Journalism Review*, July/August 2004.

13. Merritt, "Public Journalism & Public Life," p. 94-95.

14. Jay Rosen, "He Said, She Said, We Said," PressThink, http://www.journalism.nyu.edu/pubzone/weblogs/pressthink/2004/06/04/ruten_milbank.html, June 4, 2004, accessed Dec. 9, 2004.

15. Eric Schmitt, "Rumsfeld Sees an Iraq Pullout Within 4 Years," The New York Times, Dec. 7, 2004, cited by Thomas Lang in "Resurrecting the Fact Check," *CJR Daily*, Dec. 8, 2004, www.campaigndesk.org/archives/001168.asp, accessed Dec. 9, 2004.

16. Wendy Y. Lawton, "D-11 fights perception it's top-heavy/8.5 percent of budget goes to central office," *The Gazette Telegraph*, Oct. 31, 1996, p. 2A. Reprinted with permission.

17. "Anderson Cooper 360 Degrees," CNN transcript, Sept. 1, 2005, http://transcripts.cnn.com/TRAN-SCRIPTS/0509/01/acd.01.html, accessed Sept. 24, 2005.

18. "The big disconnect on New Orleans," CNN.com, Sept. 2, 2005.

19. Gardiner Harris, "F.D.A., Responding to a Third Death Linked to Abortion Pill, Strengthens a Warning Label," *The New York Times*, Nov. 16, 2004, p. A24.

20. "Debate continues over RU-486 abortion pill," *The State News*, Nov. 23, 2004, p. 3A.

21. "Beyond the Headlines: Attribution, Verification and the Time Lapse," Poynter Online, Jan. 4, 2006, http://www.poynter.org/content/ content_view.asp?id=94655, accessed May 3, 2006.

22. Thomas Lang, "Resurrecting the Fact Check," *CJR Daily*, Dec. 8, 2004, www.campaigndesk.org/archives/001168.asp, accessed Dec. 9, 2004.

23. Ibid.

24. Shannon Houghton, "2 sexual assaults reported on campus: Police investigate details of Emmons Hall-area incidents," *The State News*, Sept. 10, 2004, p. 1A. Reprinted with permission.

25. Lauren Phillips, "Armed men rob, assault MSU student," *The State News*, Feb. 23, 2005, p. 1A.

26. Scott Shepard, "Questions about political motives surface in Shiavo case," Cox News Service, March 25, 2005.

27. Brian Montopoli, "When Politicians Go Bad, Must the Press Follow?" *CJR Daily*, March 21, 2005, http://www.cjrdaily.org/archives/001390.asp, accessed March 23, 2005.

28. Shepard, "Questions about political motives surface in Shiavo case."

29. David Goldstein and Steve Kraske, "Area lawmakers defend Schiavo vote," *The Kansas City Star*, March 23, 2005.

30. Kovach and Rosenstiel, "The Elements of Journalism," p. 74.

31. Telephone interview with Tom Rosenstiel, Dec. 14, 2004.

32. Memo from Lee Pitts of the *Chattanooga Times Free Press* to fellow staff members, Dec. 8, 2004, posted on Romenesko at Poynter Online, http://poynter.org/forum/view_post.asp?id=8447, accessed Aug. 4, 2005.

33. Tom Griscom, "From the Publisher, an explanation to our readers," *Chattanooga Times Free Press*, Dec. 10, 2004, posted on Romenesko at Poynter Online, http://poynter.org/column.asp?id=45&aid=75479, accessed Aug. 4, 2005.
34. Telephone interview with Tom Rosenstiel, Dec. 14, 2004.

CHAPTER 5

1. Michael X. Delli Carpini and Scott Keeter, "What Americans Know about Politics and Why It Matters." New Haven: Yale University Press, 1996, p. 21.
2. Telephone interview with Tom Warhover, Oct. 25, 2004.
3. "Global goofs: U.S. youth can't find Iraq," Nov. 22, 2002, http://archives.cnn.com/2002/EDUCA-TION/11/20/geography.quiz, accessed Aug. 4, 2005.
4. Ibid.
5. Political knowledge surveys cited in Ilya Somin, "When Ignorance Isn't Bliss: How Political Ignorance Threatens Democracy," Cato Institute report, Sept. 22, 2004, http://www.cato.org/pubs/pas/pa525.pdf, accessed Aug. 4, 2005.
6. Delli Carpini and Keeter, "What Americans Know about Politics and Why it Matters," p. 22.
7. Edith Lederer, "U.N. envoy urges nations to help in Sudan," Associated Press, Dec. 14, 2004.
8. Telephone interview with Tom Rosenstiel, Dec. 14, 2004.
9. Telephone interview with Holly A. Heyser, Jan. 20, 2005.
10. Mary Nesbitt, speaking to the Michigan Press Association in Grand Rapids, Mich., Jan. 29, 2005.
11. Neuman, Just and Crigler, "Common Knowledge," p. 81.
12. Daniel Yankelovich, "Coming to Public Judgment: Making Democracy Work in a Complex World," Syracuse University Press, 1991, p. 63-65.
13. Kovak and Rosenstiel, "The Elements of Journalism," p. 28.
14. Telephone interview with Tom Rosenstiel, Dec. 14, 2004.
15. "Social Security 101," *Lansing State Journal*, Feb. 4, 2005, p. 1A.
16. Chris Andrews, "Why you should care," *Lansing State Journal*, Oct. 6, 2004, p. 3A.
17. Sonia Khaleel, "A defining vote: Prop 2 seeks to amend Mich. Constitution definition of marriage," *The State News*, Oct. 27, 2004, p. 1A. Reprinted with permission.
18. Xochitl Pena, "City gets help in manager hunt," *The Desert Sun*, Jan. 22, 2005, p. B1.
19. E-mail from Carole Leigh Hutton, Oct. 13, 2004.
20. Telephone interview with Dawson Bell, Dec. 3, 2004.
21. Lisa Anderson, "Democracy, Islam share a home in Mali," *Chicago Tribune*, Dec. 15, 2004.
22. *RedEye*, Dec. 22, 2004, p. 10, 12.
23. "Global report," *The Bay City Times*, May 1, 2005, p. 3A.
24. Associated Press and *Lansing State Journal*, "Deaths widespread," map of tsunami damage, *Lansing State Journal*, Dec. 29, 2004, p. 1A.
25. *Wisconsin State Journal*, Dec. 23, 2004, p. A8.
26. Ed Ronco, "Endorsing candidates for office is long-standing newspaper tradition," *The State News*, Oct. 29, 2004, p. 4A. Reprinted with permission.
27. E-mail from Ken Sands, April 25, 2005.
28. Lauren Phillips, "Homelessness a focus for many," *The State News*, Nov. 15, 2004, p. 1A.

CHAPTER 6

1. Michigan State University journalism student Nicole Schilt, during an ethics class discussion on April 26, 2005.
2. Tom Sheehan, "Gas cap? Should state repeal its minimum markup law for gasoline?" *The Journal Times*,

March 15, 2005, p. 1A.

3. E-mail from Randolph Brandt, March 22, 2005.

4. Telephone interview with Tom Warhover, Oct. 25, 2004.

5. From an undated 1996 *Virginian-Pilot* memo.

6. Jonathan Falls, "Paper should offer advice with opinion," letter to *The State News*, Jan. 28, 2005, p. 4A.

7. John Warren, "Aging park is no laughing matter," *The Virginian-Pilot*, July 3, 2005.

8. Marcia Nelesen, "Is cart before the horse for the Janesville City Council?" *The Janesville* (Wis.) *Gazette*, Jan. 9, 2005.

9. Jennifer Ackerman-Haywood, "Book, teacher gain defenders," *The Grand Rapids Press*, Feb. 5, 2005, p. A1.

10. Tom Lambert, "Getting help with heating bills," *Lansing State Journal*, Dec. 16, 2004, p. 1A.

11. Melissa Domsic, "U.S. borders to check passports," *The State News*, April 7, 2005, p. 1A.

12. "How to appeal a reassessed property value," Springfield, Mo., *News-Leader*, March 26, 2005.

13. Andrea Ball, "Helping tsunami victims? Don't give to just anybody," *Austin American-Statesman*, Jan. 9, 2005.

14. "Open-records law: Sample public-records request letter," *Quad-City Times*, March 19, 2005.

15. "Speak out: Students, others must come together to ensure officials know police actions were out of line," *The State News*, April 7, 2005, p. 4A.

16. Tom Sheehan, "Proposal targets contractors' bid process," *Wisconsin State Journal*, Dec. 23, 2004, p. B1.

CHAPTER 7

1. Telephone interview with Roy Peter Clark, Jan. 4, 2005.

2. E-mail from Lex Alexander, Feb. 17, 2005.

3. Dennis Hartig, note to *Virginian-Pilot* staff, June 1998.

4. Kay T. Addis, "What's it Mean to You," memo to *Virginian-Pilot* news staff, Jan. 26, 1998.

5. Interview with Richard Schwarzlose, May 23, 1991.

6. Farnaz Fassihi, "From Baghdad," e-mail to friends, posted by Romenesko at Poynter Online Sept. 29, 2004, http://poynter.org/column.asp?id=45&aid=72140, accessed Oct. 6, 2004.

7. "Whisper of truth: A correspondent in Iraq finds her personal e-mail racing across the Internet, its unofficial nature compelling readers to take notice," *Houston Chronicle*, Oct. 6, 2004, p. B8.

8. Farnaz Fassihi, "Reporters' Notebook: Iraq Breaks From Past," The Wall Street Journal Online, Jan. 31, 2005.

9. "Why Has TV Stopped Covering Politics?" Project for Excellence in Journalism study, Oct. 22, 2002, www.journalism.org/resources/research/reports/tvpolitics/default.asp, accessed March 23, 2005.

10. "'Soulful' night showcases music, dance," *The State News*, Feb. 23, 2004, p. 1A.

11. "Celebracion: Chicano, Latino culture celebrated during 'Latin Xplosion,'" *The State News*, Feb. 23, 2004, p. 1A.

12. Sonia Khaleel, "International students win essay contest," *The State News*, Dec. 8, 2004, p. 6A. Reprinted with permission.

13. KRT News Service, "The price of failure," *Lansing State Journal*, Sept. 11, 2005, p. 3A.

14. Howard Kurtz, "At Last, Reporters' Feelings Rise to the Surface," *The Washington Post*, Sept. 5, 2005, p. C01.

15. E-mail from Carole Leigh Hutton, Oct. 13, 2004.

16. Dawson Bell, "Bush bashing during shows could backfire for Democrats," *Detroit Free Press*, Oct. 4, 2004, p. 1A.

17. Sophia Kazmi, "County court facility gets OK by commission," *Contra Costa Times*, Nov. 11, 2004.

18. TheNewMexicoChannel.com, "Crafters Might Have To Show ID To Buy Glass Etcher," Nov. 11, 2004.

19. Jake Potter, "Police arrest suspect in break-ins," *The Daily Tar Heel*, Nov. 11, 2004.

20. Roy Peter Clark, "Budget review intensifies with some specifics," *St. Petersburg Times*, July 20, 1978.

21. Telephone interview with Roy Peter Clark, Jan. 4, 2005.

22. Nancy Young, "A city in progress: Rapid growth forces Chesapeake to face its future now," *The Virginian-Pilot*, March 8, 1998, p. A1. Reprinted with permission.

23. Telephone interview with John-Henry Doucette, Dec. 30, 2004.

24. John-Henry Doucette, "Suffolk's mayor opens his door to public input," *The Virginian-Pilot*, Dec. 6, 2004. Reprinted with permission.

25. Telephone interview with Tom Warhover, Oct. 25, 2004.

26. E-mail from Mary Nesbitt, May 23, 2005.

CHAPTER 8

1. Gwen Florio and Jim Tankersley, "Caucuses 101," *Rocky Mountain News*, April 9, 2004.

2. E-mail from Nancy Young, May 31, 2005.

3. Telephone interview with Tom Warhover, Oct. 25, 2004.

4. Michael Arrieta-Walden, "Readers thirst for meaningful campaign news," *The Oregonian*, Feb. 15, 2004.

5. Interview with Bob Campbell, Nov. 19, 2004.

6. Kathryn Posch, "Turning the tables: Community members tell journalists what they think the most important issues are for the upcoming election and what they envision in an ideal senator," *Columbia Missourian*, Oct. 12, 2004.

7. Editor's note, *The Virginian-Pilot*, Sept. 1, 1996, p. A1.

8. Scott Thomsen, "Education at the center of election in Colorado," *The Gazette Telegraph*, Nov. 2, 1996, p. 4A. Reprinted with permission.

9. *Missourian*, "Marijuana as medicine?" Oct. 24, 2004, p. 1A.

10. Lon Wagner, "The Real George Allen: Not just a good ol' boy," *The Virginian-Pilot*, Sept. 24, 2000, p. A1. Reprinted with permission.

11. Sarah Frank, "Candidate plays it low key," *The State News*, July 23, 2003. Reprinted with permission.

12. Cindi Deutschman-Ruiz, "Covering the Outsiders," Poynter Online, Feb. 19, 2004, http://www.poynter.org/content/content_view.asp?id=61133, accessed Feb. 19, 2004.

13. E-mail from Ed Ronco, April 12, 2005.

14. Evan Rondeau, "Hitting home: Non-partisan volunteers hit the streets to increase voter participation," *The State News*, Oct. 13, 2004, p. 1A. Reprinted with permission.

15. Interview with Bob Campbell, Nov. 19, 2004.

16. Patricia Montemurri and Alexa Capeloto, "Voting has its enemies – lack of time and interest," *Detroit Free Press*, Oct. 30, 2004. Reprinted with permission.

17. Elizabeth Piet, "Site hopes sex will get ballots cast in election," *The State News*, Sept. 20, 2004, p. 1A.

18. "just VOTE," Lansing State Journal, Oct. 3, 2004, p. 1A.

19. Florio and Tankersley, "Caucuses 101."

20. "Campaign ad watch: Kerry-Edwards campaign - The Truth About Taxes," FactCheck.org analysis published in *The Columbus Dispatch*, Nov. 1, 2004.

21. David Ingram, "Easley easily wins bid for re-election," *Winston-Salem Journal*, Nov. 3, 2004, p. A1.

CHAPTER 9

1. Telephone interview with Roy Peter Clark, Jan. 4, 2005.

2. Bryan Gilmer, "City has $548 million to spend: What do you want?" *St. Petersburg Times*, Aug. 21, 2002, quoted by Roy Peter Clark in "The Greatest Story Never Told," Poynter Online, Nov. 10, 2003, http://www.poynter.org/content/content_view.asp?id=52418, accessed March 8, 2005.

3. Clark, "The Greatest Story Never Told."

4. Telephone interview with Roy Peter Clark, Jan. 4, 2005.

5. Susan Willey, "Focus Groups and Newsroom Style," in Sharon Hartin Iorio (ed.) "Qualitative Research

in Journalism: Taking It to the Streets." Mahwah, N.J.: Lawrence Erlbaum Associates, 2004, p. 75.

6. April M. Washington, "Council backs eateries: Neighborhood restaurants can set up outdoor seating," *Rocky Mountain News*, April 12, 2005. Reprinted with permission.

7. Thomas C. Tobin, "Her lone and potent voice: She's the board's only true believer in Jeb Bush's education policy but doesn't fit a conservative stereotype," *St. Petersburg Times*, Jan. 10, 2005.

8. St. Louis city revised code, chapter 17.20, St. Louis Public Library, http://www.slpl.lib.mo.us/cco/code/data/t1720.htm, accessed Jan. 13, 2005.

9. Tom Lambert, "City Council grills dept. director on sidewalk policies," *Lansing State Journal*, Feb. 4, 2005, p. 1A.

10. E-mail from Mike Feeley, April 11, 2005.

11. E-mail from Randolph Brandt, March 22, 2005.

12. Michael Burke, "Blue Rock news tracker 1-28-05," *The Journal Times*, Jan. 28, 2005.

13. Karen Weintraub, "Virginia Beach's to do list," T*he Virginian-Pilot*, March 5, 1997, p. B3.

14. Telephone interview with Roy Peter Clark, Jan. 4, 2005.

15. John-Henry Doucette, "In Suffolk, sharing city budget plan takes driving force," *The Virginian-Pilot*, April 29, 2004, p. B1. Reprinted with permission.

16. Telephone interview with John-Henry Doucette, Dec. 30, 2004.

CHAPTER 10

1. E-mail from Holly A. Heyser, June 1, 2005.

2. Jim Hinch, "Governor rekindling tax revolt," *The Orange County Register*, Jan. 16, 2005. Reprinted with permission.

3. Telephone interview with Holly A. Heyser, Jan. 20, 2005.

4. Josh Margolin, "Speech to give Codey time in the spotlight," *Newark Star-Ledger*, Jan. 10, 2005.

5. Terrence Dopp, "Codey may tip hand in speech," *Gloucester County Times*, Jan. 10, 2005.

6. Robert A. Rankin, "Translating the messages," *St. Paul Pioneer Press*, Jan. 21, 2005, p. 6A.

7. Kevin Diaz, "Two Minnesota groups go for national exposure," *Minneapolis Star Tribune*, Jan. 21, 2005, p. A12. Reprinted with permission.

8. Melvin Claxton and Ronald J. Hansen, "Job training cuts shut some poor out of work," *The Detroit News*, Sept. 28, 2004, p. 1A.

9. Dennis Cauchon and John Waggoner, "One nation, under debt," *USA Today*, Oct. 4, 2004, p. 1A.

10. "Faces to watch in Inaugural crowd," *The Orange County Register*, Jan. 22, 2005, News p. 2.

11. Adam Entous and Anna Willard of Reuters, "Emergency-spending package in the works," *The Orange County Register*, Jan. 22, 2005, News p. 7.

12. For example: St. Paul *Pioneer Press*, Jan. 21, 2005, p. 11A.

13. Stacey Range and Chris Andrews, "500 state laws pass despite budget woes," Lansing State Journal, Dec. 12, 2004, p. 1A.

14. For example: Hanh Kim Quach, "Moving foreign inmates could save millions," *The Orange County Register*, Oct. 6, 2004.

15. Dave Zweifel, "'People's Legislature' to send a message," *The Capital Times*, Jan. 17, 2005.

CHAPTER 11

1. Pete Hamill: "News is a Verb," New York: The Ballantine Publishing Group, 1998, p. 6.

2. Telephone interview with Raman Narayanan, Jan. 27, 2005.

3. Dennis Ryerson, "Quake, not Manning story, should have been dominant," *The Indianapolis Star*, Jan. 2, 2005. Reprinted with permission.

4. Kim Hart, "Quitting Kabul: The U.S. media presence in Afghanistan continues to dwindle," American

Journalism Review, December/January 2005, http://ajr.org/article_printable.asp?id=3815, accessed Jan. 29, 2005.

5. Howard Kurtz, "Osama Who? When No News Is 'Bad News,'" *The Washington Post*, Jan. 24, 2005, p. C01.

6. Richard C. Paddock and Don Lee, "Militants Jump Into Aceh Aid Efforts," *Los Angeles Times*, Jan. 10, 2005.

7. Dick Rogers, "Looking away as a tragedy unfolds," *The San Francisco Chronicle*, Nov. 21, 2004.

8. Kovach and Rosenstiel, "The Elements of Journalism," p. 164.

9. Telephone interview with Raman Narayanan, Jan. 27, 2005.

10. Moni Basu, "Citizens of two worlds," *The Atlanta Journal-Constitution*, July 3, 2002, p. E1-E2.

11. Mark Bixler, "Green cards of any color a ticket to stay," *The Atlanta Journal-Constitution*, April 10, 2002, p. E1.

12. Yolanda Rodriguez, "American Dream," *The Atlanta Journal-Constitution*, May 15, 2002, p. E1-E3.

13. Doug McGill, "Globalizing Local News," Poynter Online, June 10, 2003, http://www.poynter.org/content/content_print.asp?id=35510&custom accessed Jan. 26, 2005.

14. Janet Majure, "Rich lamb and vegetable mix brings home flavor of Sudan," *The Kansas City Star*, Jan. 26, 2005. Reprinted with permission of The Kansas City Star © Copyright 2005 *The Kansas City Star*. All rights reserved. Format differs from original publication. Not an endorsement.

15. Josh Jarman, "MSU student to cast vote Sunday in Iraqi election," *The State News*, Jan. 27, 2005, p. 1A.

16. Thomas Hargrove and Guido H. Stempel III, "Exploring reader interest in international news," *Newspaper Research Journal*, Fall 2002, Volume 23, Issue 4, p. 46.

17. Scott Peterson, "Amid struggles, an Iraqi family will vote," *The Christian Science Monitor*, Jan. 26, 2005.

18. Telephone interview with David Clark Scott, June 14, 2005.

19. Michael Arrieta-Walden, "Different tack was needed on tsunami coverage," *The Oregonian*, Jan. 9, 2005.

20. Thomas Friedman, "The Lexus and the Olive Tree." New York: Farrar, Straus and Giroux, 2000, p. 15.

21. *Lansing State Journal*, "How to understand the election," Jan. 29, 2005, p. 3A.

22. "Mickey Hirten: India's thirst for energy will affect everyone," *Lansing State Journal*, April 17, 2005.

CHAPTER 12

1. Telephone interview with Jim Russell, Feb. 3, 2005.

2. Thomas Friedman, "The World is Flat: A Brief History of the Twenty-First Century." New York: Farrar, Straus and Giroux, 2005, p. 265.

3. Claire Cummings, "Oodles of Noodles seeks alcohol license approval," *The State News*, Feb. 2, 2005, p. 1A.

4. Sue Pleming, "At least 232 civilians die doing U.S. work in Iraq," Reuters, Jan. 31, 2005.

5. "Marketplace" online edition, Feb. 28, 2005, http://marketplace.publicradio.org/shows/2005/02/28/pm.html, accessed March 2, 2005.

6. Marketplace Morning Report, Feb. 3, 2005, http://marketplace.publicradio.org/shows/2005/02/03/am.html, accessed March 9, 2005.

7. Telephone interview with Jim Russell, Feb. 3, 2005.

8. *Charlotte Business Journal*, "American Community files to merge FNB," Feb. 3, 2005.

9. Edward D. Murphy, "Insurer UnumProvident earns $134.5 million during final 3 months of 2004," *Portland Press Herald*, Feb. 2, 2005.

10. Monica Soto Ouchi, "Street slaps Amazon over higher costs, missed earnings," *The Seattle Times*, Feb. 3, 2005.

11. John J. Oslund, "Diluted earnings," *Star Tribune*, Jan. 21, 2005, p. D8.

12. Vandana Sinha, "A Little Perspective Goes a Long Way in Completing a Story," the Donald W. Reynolds National Center for Business Journalism at the American Press Institute, Nov. 17, 2004, www.businessjournalism.org/content/5726.cfm, accessed Jan. 31, 2005.

13. Chris Serres, "Cash Check," *Star Tribune*, Jan. 21, 2005, p. D8. Reprinted with permission.

14. John Hogan, "More families take out home equity loans for projects," *The Grand Rapids Press*, Feb. 5,

2005, p. B1.

15. Michael Burke, "Sky-high hopes," *The Journal Times*, March 31, 2003. Reprinted with permission.

16. E-mail from Randolph Brandt, March 22, 2005.

17. Carolyn Shapiro, "Drowned out," *The Virginian-Pilot*, Feb. 6, 2005, p. D1.

18. Amy Ellis Nutt and Drew Sheneman, "Action Figure$," *The Star-Ledger*, March 7, 2004, Section 3, Page 1.

19. Telephone interview with Jim Russell, Feb. 3, 2005.

20. Vandana Sinha, "Give a New Twist to the Same Annual Story Dance," the Donald W. Reynolds National Center for Business Journalism at the American Press Institute, Nov. 23, 2004, www.businessjournalism.org/content/5750.cfm, accessed Jan. 31, 2005.

CHAPTER 13

1. Telephone interview with Kay Semion, Feb. 10, 2005.

2. Quoted in Rick Horowitz, "The creative urge: Kids, try this at home," *The Masthead*, Fall, 2002, Volume 54, Issue 3, p. 11.

3. "Put the Opinion Back in Sunday Opinion," letters to the editor, *Los Angeles Times*, Jan. 30, 2005.

4. RJ Smith, "The Kinsley Report," *Los Angeles Magazine*, February 2005.

5. Howard Kurtz, "Michael Kinsley, L.A. Times Part on 'Unfortunate Note,'" *The Washington Post*, Sept. 14, 2005, p. C11.

6. "Editorial: If you write us a letter, use your own words," *The Post-Crescent*, May 8, 2005.

7. Telephone interview with Kay Semion, Feb. 10, 2005.

8. Kay Semion, "Finding local voices for op-ed balance," *The Masthead*, Fall 1999, Volume 51, Issue 3, p. 32.

9. "How U.S. newspapers voted," *Detroit Free Press*, Oct. 31, 2004, p. 3K.

10. "Opinion week in review," *The Orange County Register*, Jan. 22, 2005, Local p.9.

11. "Driven to distraction," *Lansing State Journal*, March 21, 2004, p. 12A.

12. Francis L. Partsch in the preface to "Beyond Argument: A Handbook for Editorial Writers." Maura Casey and Michael Zuzel, eds., National Conference of Editorial Writers, 2001, p. viii.

13. Telephone interview with Kay Semion, Feb. 10, 2005.

14. "Racism bellyachers disregard good news," *The Examiner*, Feb. 25, 2005, p. 15. Reprinted with permission.

15. "Readers to Examiner: You're jerks," *The Examiner*, Feb. 25, 2005, p. 17.

16. "Painful lesson in Newton," *The Star-Ledger*, Feb. 5, 2005.

17. Quoted in Horowitz, "The creative urge: Kids, try this at home!"

18. E-mail from Claire Duquette, June 3, 2005.

19. "28 days left until the presidential election," *The State News*, Oct. 6, 2004, p. 4A.

20. E-mail from Patrick Walters, June 5, 2005.

21. Joe Strupp, "'Sacramento Bee' Editorializes On Same Issue Six Weeks Straight," *Editor & Publisher*, June 25, 2004.

22. E-mail from David Holwerk, June 2, 2005.

CHAPTER 14

1. Lex Alexander, "News-Record.com as public square," News-Record.com, Jan. 4, 2005, http://blog.news-record.com/lexblog/archives/2005/01/newsrecordcom_a_1.html, accessed Feb. 14, 2005.

2. Ibid.

3. John Robinson, "Today's newspaper column," Feb. 13, 2005, http://blog.news-record.com/staff/jrblog/archives/2005/02/todays_newspape.html, accessed Aug. 9, 2005.

4. E-mail from Lex Alexander, Feb. 17, 2005.
5. Howard I. Finberg, "Envisioning the Future of Online Journalism," Poynter Online, Feb. 8, 2005, http://www.poynter.org/column.asp?id=56&aid=78014, accessed Feb. 18, 2005.
6. Julie M. Moos, "Journalism & Blogging: It's About Diversity," Poynter Online, Feb. 14, 2005, http://www.poynter.org/content/content_view.asp?id=78053, accessed Feb. 20, 2005.
7. Janet Weaver, "Journalism, Blogging & Diversity: Janet Weaver Responds," Poynter Online, Feb. 14, 2005, http://www.poynter.org/content/content_print.asp?id=78269&custom accessed Feb. 14, 2005.
8. Gary Farrugia, "Journalism, Blogging & Diversity: Gary Farrugia Responds," Poynter Online, Feb. 10, 2005, http://www.poynter.org/content/content_view.asp?id=78278, accessed Feb. 20, 2005.
9. Dan Gillmor, "We the Media: Grassroots Journalism By the People, For the People." Sebastopol, Calif.: O'Reilly Media, 2004, p. x-xi.
10. Telephone interview with Jan Schaffer, Feb. 23, 2005.
11. Lydia Saad, "Blogs Not Yet in the Media Big Leagues," Gallup News Service, March 11, 2005.
12. Telephone interview with Debbie Galant, April 26, 2005.
13. J-Lab: The Institute for Interactive Journalism, http://j-lab.org/batten.html, accessed Feb. 23, 2005.
14. Sean Polay, speaking at the 2004 James K. Batten Symposium & Awards for Innovations in Journalism at the National Press Club in Washington, D.C., Sept. 10, 2004; http://www.j-lab.org/b04trans_session3.html accessed Feb. 16, 2005.
15. Sean Fagan, speaking at the 2004 James K. Batten Symposium & Awards for Innovations in Journalism at the National Press Club in Washington, D.C., Sept. 10, 2004; http://www.j-lab.org/b04trans_session3.html, accessed Feb. 16, 2005.
16. "Comparing the Candidates," *The Washington Post*, http://www.washingtonpost.com/wp-srv/politics/graphics/issues/bushkerry/issues_pop.html, accessed Feb. 18, 2005.
17. Jane Sutter, "A New Recipe: Tax Game Measures Tax Bills," J-Lab: The Institute for Interactive Journalism, Feb. 3, 2004, http://j-lab.org/rochtaxgame.html accessed Feb. 14, 2005.
18. "Grade the news yourself," Grade the News, http://www.stanford.edu/group/gradethenews/feat/scoring.htm accessed Aug. 27, 2004.
19. Telephone interview with Holly A. Heyser, Jan. 20, 2005.
20. "Comments on hiatus," *Ventura County Star*, May 18, 2005.
21. John Temple, "Temple: YourHub.com will be all about you," *Rocky Mountain News*, April 9, 2005.
22. Jonathan Dube, "California paper undertakes ambitious participatory journalism project," cyberjournalist.net, July 16, 2004.
23. http://www.northwestvoice.com, accessed April 25, 2005.
24. http://mesh.medill.northwestern.edu/goskokie, accessed March 11, 2005.
25. http://www.MyMissourian.com, accessed Feb. 23, 2005.
26. Howard Kurtz, "This Just In, From The Guy Next Door," *The Washington Post*, Dec. 13, 2004, p. C01.
27. Telephone interview with Jan Schaffer, Feb. 23, 2005.

CHAPTER 15

1. Brian Orloff, "How to Reach Young Readers: Avoid Snark Attacks, and Other Tips," *Editor & Publisher*, Jan. 6, 2005.
2. Susan Goldberg, speaking at the National College Newspaper Convention in San Francisco, Feb. 25, 2004; transcript accessed from Romenesko at http://www.poynter.org on Aug. 10, 2005.
3. Nicole Schilt statement during a journalism ethics class discussion at Michigan State University, April 26, 2005.
4. Laura Berman, "Nonreading generation of writers needs 12-step program," *The Detroit News*, Jan. 30, 2005.
5. David T.Z. Mindich, "Tuned Out: Why Americans Under 40 Don't Follow the News." New York: Oxford University Press, 2005, p. 3.
6. Ibid, p. 29.

End Notes

7. Ibid p. 3, 18-33.
8. Ibid, p. 114.
9. YaShekia Smalls, "Speaker targets younger audiences," *The Ball State Daily News*, March 2, 2004.
10. Helen Huntley, "Times offshoot targets younger demographic," *St. Petersburg Times*, Sept. 11, 2004.
11. *Tampa Bay Times*, http://www.tampabay.com/, accessed Feb. 24, 2005.
12. Michael Roberts, "The Message: Hip Hope," *Westword*, Feb. 10, 2005, http://westword.com/issues/2005-02-10/news/message_print.html, accessed Feb. 10, 2005.
13. http://www.biasdotcom.com, accessed June 6, 2005.
14. Mark Fitzgerald, "J-Prof: Chicago 'Red' Papers Succeeding," *Editor & Publisher*, April 13, 2005.
15. "Sun-Times ending youth-oriented Red Streak paper," Associated Press, Dec. 19, 2005.
16. "The State of the News Media 2004," http://www.stateofthenewsmedia.org/printable_ethnicalternative_alternative.asp?media=9.
17. Ann McGlynn, "Calling all teens: Your Mom's off the hinges," *Quad-City Times*, July 24, 2004.
18. Your Mom, "On blackjack boogie, Paris Hilton, and Navy boys," Feb. 24, 2005, http://www.yourmomonline.com/articles/2005/02/24/news_take/doc421df12db9a35627381197.txt, accessed Feb. 24, 2005.
19. Telephone interview with Hillary Rhodes, Feb. 25, 2005.
20. "A year of Your Mom," yourmomonline.com, Dec. 22, 2005.
21. Readership Institute, "Reaching New Readers: Revolution, Not Evolution," July 2004, p. 4-7. Available at www.readership.org.
22. Erik Wemple, "Focus Pocus," *Washington City Paper*, Oct. 1-7, 2004.
23. Readership Institute "Reaching New Readers" report, July 2004, p. 6.
24. Readership Institute, "Reinventing the Newspaper for Young Adults," April 2005, p. 6. Available at www.readership.org.
25. Ibid, p. 7-8.
26. Ibid, p. 11.
27. "Cable and Internet Loom Large in Fragmented Political News Universe," The Pew Research Center for the People and the Press, Jan. 11, 2004, http://people-press.org/reports/display.php3?ReportID=200, accessed Feb. 26, 2005.
28. "Daily Show Viewers Knowledgeable about Presidential Campaign, National Annenberg Election Survey Shows," Annenberg Public Policy Center press release, Sept. 21, 2004.
29. Kevin Collins, "'The Daily Show' approach worth emulating," *The Daily Pennsylvanian*, Sept. 28, 2004.
30. The Center for Information & Research on Civic Learning & Engagement, "Census Data Shows Youth Voter Turnout Surged More Than Any Other Age Group," press release, May 26, 2005. Available at www.civicyouth.org.
31. Jane Eisner, "No Kidding: This May Be the Year For a Youthful Turnout," *The Washington Post*, Oct. 3, 2004, p. B01.
32. Tom Keller, "Survey: MSU voter turnout 'striking,'" *The State News*, Jan. 21, 2005.
33. E-mail from Jane Eisner, June 6, 2005.
34. Telephone interview with Hillary Rhodes, Feb. 25, 2005.
35. "State of the First Amendment," 2005 report of the First Amendment Center, http://www.firstamendmentcenter.org/sofa_reports/index.aspx, accessed Aug. 10, 2005.
36. John S. and James L. Knight Foundation study, "The Future of the First Amendment," p. 4.
37. Nirvi Shah, "Sex article in Wellington High paper censored," *Palm Beach Post*, Feb. 22, 2005.
38. Phil Luciano, "News needs eyes like Thompson's," *Peoria Journal Star*, Feb. 22, 2005.
39. Doug Lederman, "Hitting Too Close to Home," Inside Higher Ed, March 2, 2005, http://www.insidehighered.com/insider/hitting_too_close_to_home, accessed March 2, 2005.
40. Patricia Alex, "Rutgers calls off news censors," NorthJersey.com, March 9, 2005.

RESOURCES

FACT-CHECKING AND MYTH DEBUNKING

- http://www.factcheck.org
- http://www.snopes.com

INDUSTRY ORGANIZATIONS

- Association of Capitol Reporters and Editors: http://www.capitolbeat.org
- National Conference of Editorial Writers: http://www.ncew.org
- Society for News Design: http://www.snd.org

JOURNALISM COMMENT AND CRITICISM

- CJR Daily: http://www.cjrdaily.org
- PressThink: http://www.pressthink.org
- Romenesko: http://www.poynter.org/romenesko

NEW MEDIA

- College Media Advisers' new-media showcase: http://reinventing.collegemedia.org
- J-Lab: The Institute for Interactive Journalism: http://www.j-lab.org

NEWS AND DEMOCRACY

- Jane Eisner, (ITAL)Taking Back the Vote: Getting American Youth Involved in our Democracy(ENDITAL), Beacon Press, 2004.
- David T.Z. Mindich, (ITAL)Tuned Out: Why Americans Under 40 Don't Follow the News"(ENDITAL), Oxford University Press, 2005.
- First Amendment Center: http://www.firstamendmentcenter.org
- The Harwood Institute for Public Innovation: http://www.theharwoodgroup.com
- The McGill Report: http://www.mcgillreport.org
- Pew Center for Civic Journalism: http://www.pewcenter.org
- Public Journalism Network: http://www.pjnet.org

READERSHIP

■ Northwestern University Readership Institute: http://www.readership.org

REPORTING TOOLS AND TRAINING

■ Donald W. Reynolds National Center for Business Journalism: http://www.businessjournalism.org
■ Investigative Reporters and Editors: http://www.ire.org
■ Maynard Institute for Journalism Education: http://www.maynardije.org
■ No Train, No Gain: http://www.notrain-nogain.com
■ Power Reporting: http://www.powerreporting.com
■ The Poynter Institute: http://www.poynter.org
■ Project for Excellence in Journalism: http://www.journalism.org

ACKNOWLEDGEMENTS

I'm indebted to everyone who contributed to this book –- all those mentioned by name and the many others whose efforts have helped shape the way I think about public affairs journalism. My former colleagues at The Virginian-Pilot top this list, most notably Dennis Hartig, who always pushed me to be better, and the wise and innovative Tom Warhover, Cole Campbell, Ronald L. Speer and Mason Peters.

Thanks to the people whose early advice and encouragement helped get this project off the ground, including Steve Lacy, Geneva Overholser, Dante Chinni, Mary Ann Weston and Roy Peter Clark.

I'm grateful to everyone who agreed to be interviewed or answer e-mail questions, including Randy Brandt, Raman Narayanan, Carole Leigh Hutton, Bob Campbell, Dawson Bell, Gene Policinski, Chris Andrews, Mike Knepler, Scott Cendrowski, Patrick Walters, Claire Duquette, Denis Finley, John-Henry Doucette, and John Humenik; and to those who additionally offered feedback on parts of the draft, including Kelley Carter, Karen Weintraub, Ed Ronco, Jim Russell, Holly Heyser, Kay Semion, Vandana Sinha, Hillary Rhodes, Roy Peter Clark, and Tom Rosenstiel. I'm especially grateful to Nancy Young, who read the whole damn thing and provided the kind of careful, thoughtful editing every writer needs; Buzz Merritt, whose authority in the field and insights into the draft helped shape the manuscript; and Jon Ziomek, whose helpful review prompted significant improvements.

This book wouldn't exist without Ron Webb, who introduced me to journalism as adviser to the Dearborn High School Observer; or John Kupetz, whose uniquely entertaining, depressing and inspiring demeanor has prepared thousands of students for the hard knocks of a journalism career. And it wouldn't be as meaningful without my former colleagues at The Daily Northwestern, where I learned how to produce a daily newspaper.

Thanks to Publisher Ed Avis, who gave me the opportunity to write this book. Thanks to College Media Advisers and the Associated Collegiate Press, which sponsored the convention where I met Ed Avis.

Thanks to The State News, one of the best 28,000-circulation newspapers in the country, and to my colleagues on the professional staff, especially General Manager Marty Sturgeon, whose support was instrumental to this book's completion. And a huge thanks to the paper's talented and dedicated student staff, who for more than four years have helped me think deeply about what makes newspapers good and how to make them better.

Finally, thanks to my wife, Amy, who listened to me complain about this book every day for two years and never once got irritated.

Index